SCULPTURE

DALLAS MUSEUM OF ART
NATIONAL GALLERY OF ART

A CENTURY OF MODERN SCULPTURE

The Patsy and Raymond Nasher Collection

EDITED BY Steven A. Nash

RIZZOLI
NEW YORK

PRECEDING PAGES:
Sculpture in the garden of
Patsy and Raymond Nasher, Dallas.
The works of art include:

Voltri VI, 1962, by David Smith (p. 1)
Two Piece Reclining Figure No. 9, 1968, by Henry Moore (pp. 2–3)
La Nuit, c. 1902–09, by Aristide Maillol (pp. 4–5)
Sister Souls, 1961, by Max Ernst (pp. 6–7)
Capricorn, 1948, by Max Ernst (p. 8)

Published in conjunction with the exhibition:

A CENTURY OF MODERN SCULPTURE:
The Patsy and Raymond Nasher Collection

Dallas Museum of Art
April 5–May 31, 1987

National Gallery of Art, Washington, D.C.
June 28, 1987–January 3, 1988

DESIGNED BY Nai Y. Chang

First published in the United States of America
in 1987 by Rizzoli International Publications, Inc.
597 Fifth Avenue, New York, NY 10017

Library of Congress Cataloging-in-Publication Data

A Century of modern sculpture.

    Includes index.
    Contents: Living with art / Elizabeth Frank—
Figures and phantoms : early modern figurative
sculpture / Steven A. Nash—Sculpture in the
Constructivist tradition / Nan Rosenthal — [etc.]
    1. Sculpture, Modern—20th century—Catalogs.
2. Nasher, Raymond—Art collections—Catalogs.
3. Nasher, Patsy—Art collections—Catalogs.
4. Sculpture—Private collections—Texas—Dallas—
Catalogs. I. Frank, Elizabeth, 1945–   . II. Nash,
Steven A., 1944–   . III. Dallas Museum of Art.
NB198.C48   1987   735'.23'00740153   86–43182
ISBN 0–8478–0800–9   ISBN 0–8478–0813–0 (pbk.)

Set in type by Rainsford Type, Ridgefield, Connecticut
Printed and bound in Japan

CONTENTS

FOREWORD

A list of the major private collections of twentieth-century art in America would find that of Patsy and Raymond Nasher among the first entries. Although their art-historical interests range from Guatemalan textiles and Pre-Columbian ceramics to contemporary prints and paintings, modern sculpture is their true love. Their holdings now number more than two hundred objects, ranging from works by Auguste Rodin to those of Scott Burton.

Beginning with the early acquisition of works by Moore, Hepworth, Arp, and Miró, the Nashers have gone on to shape their collection to constitute a cohesive historical continuum. At the same time, they have imparted that rich stamp of personal taste which can distinguish a private collection from its museum or institutional counterpart. Having decided to collect in depth certain modern masters such as Duchamp-Villon, Matisse, Moore, and Giacometti, the Nashers have also elected to be actively involved with new developments on the contemporary scene, acquiring pieces by Borofsky, Segal, and Serra.

The result is a collection that vibrates with the Nashers' sense of excellence and historical importance. Their concept of the stewardship of rare and wonderful objects is highly developed and includes a keen sensitivity to the documentation, provenance, and condition of the works they own. They have eagerly sought to work with members of the academic and curatorial communities. One of the results of that dialogue is the present exhibition and its accompanying catalog. In reality, the project has yielded two exhibitions, one in Dallas and another in Washington. In the Nashers' home city of Dallas, Steven A. Nash, the Dallas Museum of Art's Deputy Director and Chief Curator, has conceived an exhibition that includes not only the full range of the Nashers' sculpture but also some of their significant twentieth-century canvases. Under the direction of Nan Rosenthal, the National Gallery of Art's Curator of Twentieth-Century Art, the Washington showing focuses on sculpture exclusively. In each venue, the exhibition satisfies the Nashers' fundamental wish to share their collection with a wide audience, and their own commitment to the public exhibition of their art has led them to give up these works for almost a year. To Patsy and Raymond Nasher we express our greatest thanks as well as the hope that this endeavor will prove as valuable and rewarding for them as it has been for us.

Our thanks go to Steven Nash and Nan Rosenthal, not only for their work in organizing the exhibition, but also for their essays which appear in this volume. The scholarly catalog entries are the product of Steven Nash's research. Also contributing essays are Elizabeth Frank and Robert Rosenblum, and to them we are particularly grateful. The production of the catalog has been a rewarding undertaking because of Lauren Shakely and Jane Fluegel of Rizzoli, New York. Two teams of dedicated staff members, in Washington and in Dallas, have worked with great conviction and sensitivity to stage this exhibition. Their names appear in the acknowledgments that follow.

It is to Patsy and Raymond Nasher, above all, that we owe our deepest debt of gratitude on behalf of all those visitors in two cities who will be able to share the visual significance of these objects.

J. CARTER BROWN
Director
National Gallery of Art

HARRY S. PARKER III
Director
Dallas Museum of Art

ACKNOWLEDGMENTS

For the Dallas Museum of Art:

Melissa Berry, Associate Museum Educator; Lee Clockman, Photographer; Barney Delabano, Curator of Exhibitions; Anne Gendreau, Assistant Registrar; Sue Graze, Curator of Contemporary Art; JoAnn Griffin, Adjunct Conservator of Objects; Larry Harmon, Technical Designer/Production Manager; Manuel Mauricio, Head Preparator; Anna McFarland, Associate Curator of Exhibitions; Maureen McKenna, Assistant Chief Curator; Janine Orzes, Curatorial Administrative Assistant; Debra Richards, Registrar; Robert Rozelle, Director of Publications and Public Relations; Amy Schaffner, Librarian; Annette Schlagenhauff, McDermott Curatorial Intern; Elizabeth Simon, Curatorial Assistant.

For the National Gallery of Art:

In the Department of Twentieth-Century Art: Jeremy Strick, Assistant Curator, and Debra Easterly; in the Department of Installation and Design: Gaillard F. Ravenel, Chief, Mark A. Leithauser, Assistant Chief, Gordon Anson, Head of Production and Lighting, Bill Schaeffer, Exhibition Specialist. D. Dodge Thompson, Chief, Exhibitions Programs; Ann M. Bigley, Exhibitions Officer, Department of Exhibitions; Mary Suzor, Registrar; Frances P. Smyth, Editor-in-Chief; Donald Hand, Chief Horticulturist; and Dianne Cina, Assistant Horticulturist.

LIVING WITH ART

ELIZABETH
FRANK

Patsy and Raymond Nasher believe that art should be lived with.
The visitor to their Dallas home encounters one of the finest private collections of twentieth-century sculpture in the United
States. Every room abounds with it; and in the terraced garden
and four-and-a-half wooded acres surrounding their single-story
brick-and-glass house, sculptures representing nearly every
modern and contemporary direction stand in dense profusion.

The story of the Nasher collection begins in 1950, when
Raymond Nasher arrived in Dallas from Boston with his wife,
the former Patsy Rabinowitz, herself a Dallas native. Over the
next fifteen years, he developed numerous residential and
industrial real-estate projects in Texas, Oklahoma, and Florida,
earning a name for tough business acumen and visionary ideals
in social planning. During these early years, the Nashers began
to collect art in a modest way, focusing primarily on painting.
They bought work by local artists, among them John Guerin and
Cecil Casebier, and a few pieces of sculpture from local galleries. They bought for pleasure alone, without thinking about
anything as formal and organized as a ''collection.'' But they did
buy Ben Shahn's *Tennis Players*, from Edith Halpert at the Downtown Gallery in New York, and this led to more paintings by
important Americans—Stuart Davis, Charles Sheeler, and John
Marin.

Then, in 1960, they bought, and in 1961 moved into, the
house they have lived in ever since. Built in 1950 by Howard
Meyer, a Dallas architect strongly influenced by Frank Lloyd
Wright, the house looks out upon thick woods at virtually every
point and fulfills the Wrightian ideal of intimate, yet open, shel-
ter situated within an atmosphere of undisturbed natural
harmony. Soon after the Nashers were settled, Patsy Nasher fell
in love with a piece of Pre-Columbian art and began collecting
Pre-Columbian artifacts. Today, examples of Colima, Mochica,
Jalisco, Olmec, Mayan, Nazca, Nayarit, and Veracruz figures
and pottery share space in the Nasher house with twentieth-

BEN SHAHN
Tennis Players, n.d.
Watercolor, 17 x 13"

opposite:
JEAN DUBUFFET
The Gossiper II, 1969–70
Installed in the Nasher garden,
Dallas

Andrea, Raymond, Joanie, Nancy, and Patsy Nasher on site of NorthPark Shopping Center, Dallas, Spring 1963

century sculpture, and the Nashers have made major gifts of Pre-Columbian art to the Dallas Museum of Art.

It may have been this first, happy experience of intensive collecting that awakened a new appetite for art in the Nashers; certainly they realized that their home offered a superb environment for it. Whatever the impetus, they began to spend more time in New York, visiting galleries and museums. In the early sixties, they bought two paintings by Hans Hofmann and Jean Arp's *Torso with Buds* (1961; p. 60). Even then, the idea that they were "collectors" had not taken root. They were raising three young daughters, devoting themselves to important social and

political causes, and pouring themselves into a building project that was more ambitious than any Ray Nasher had ever before attempted.

The result, NorthPark, is a huge urban complex situated on two hundred acres in North Dallas. Its nucleus is a shopping center with over a hundred and fifty stores, NorthPark National Bank, which is chaired and controlled by Nasher, and North-Park East, an expansion developed in the late seventies and early eighties with office buildings, theaters, restaurants, night-clubs, and recreational facilities. NorthPark in its entirety is the brainchild of Raymond Nasher. In the middle sixties, when NorthPark opened, shopping centers were still a relatively new American phenomenon, and Nasher had seen enough of them to know that many were aesthetic disasters. He resolved to cre-ate "not a warehouse, but something that combined aesthetic presence with the democratization of merchandising."

To that end, Nasher assembled a dynamic team of architects and designers, none of whom had ever worked on a shop-ping center before: Kevin Roche, of Eero Saarinen & Asso-ciates, who designed NorthPark's Neiman-Marcus store; E. G. Hamilton, of the Dallas firm Omniplan Architects Harrell & Hamilton; Lawrence Halprin, from the San Francisco landscape architecture firm of Lawrence Halprin Associates; and Herb Rosenthal, Los Angeles graphics consultant. Nasher participated vigorously in all design decisions. He envisioned NorthPark as a unity, similar, he says, "to a piece of sculpture, a single material and form . . . which would strengthen with age rather than depreciate rapidly."

On its opening in August 1965, the inverted-L-shaped cen-ter, with its one million climate-controlled square feet, was hailed as "superbly conceived . . . breathtaking in beauty and size and several leaps ahead of anything like it in the United

page 18:
Raymond and Patsy Nasher, 1965

page 19:
Raymond Nasher and daughter Joanie during installation of *Seated Woman*, 1969–81, by Wil-lem de Kooning, at NorthPark, Dallas, October 1982

NorthPark Shopping Center, Dallas

ELIZABETH FRANK

States." Built in a broadly modernist idiom that reflected affinities with the austere International Style, as well as the low-to-the ground, horizontal Prairie Style, the center featured linked pavilions, avoiding monotony through variations in their exterior and interior heights. Scaled to the pedestrian and his shopping needs, it offered a half-mile vista along a naturally lighted promenade filled with living plants, plazas, and fountains. With J. C. Penney's in one corner and Neiman-Marcus in another, it fulfilled Nasher's goal of democratizing shopping, and it did so within a physical context of complete architectural integrity.

Getting NorthPark built was an all-consuming commitment and left the Nashers little time to collect art. During the center's early years, Ray was called to government service by the Johnson Administration, and he and Patsy traveled frequently to Washington, where Ray spent several years in public life. In 1967–68, he also served as a United States representative and delegate to the General Assembly of the United Nations and as a member of the United States Commission to UNESCO. During this time, he and Patsy lived in New York, where they once again began going to galleries and museums. In London, they bought Barbara Hepworth's *Squares with Two Circles* (1963; p. 82), and they recognized that the time had come to buy a Henry Moore. They visited the artist in 1967 at his studio in the Yorkshire hamlet of Much Hadham, and saw him at work on *Three Piece No. 3: Vertebrae* (p. 68) and *Two Piece Reclining Figure No. 9* (p. 69). Moore, they recall, graciously offered them a choice of one—and they decided they had to have both. The pieces were installed in the Nashers' garden and woods after Moore's exhibition at The Tate Gallery, London, in 1968. That same year the Nashers had their house landscaped by Lawrence Halprin. The idea began to crystallize that their home, both inside and outside, was an ideal site for sculpture. They went on to buy Isamu Noguchi's *Gregory* (1945; p. 88) and to lend pieces from their collection to museums and to Ray Nasher's real-estate developments, a practice they have continued ever since.

After a period of intense government and business activity, the Nashers resumed collecting in the early seventies and bought works by Alexander Calder and Joan Miró. Then, in the mid-seventies, just after they returned to Dallas from Harvard, where Ray had spent three years as a Visiting Fellow at the Graduate School of Education, teaching urban planning and urban economics, Patsy met a young art dealer from Fort Worth named Shaindy Fenton, who in her short life became something of a legend in both the Texas and New York art worlds. She was flamboyant, energetic, adventurous, and she knew the ropes when it came to serious collecting. She and Patsy began flying to New York together, eventually making two trips in the fall and two in the spring, and seeing every museum and gallery show they could possibly squeeze into three or four frenetic days. Through Shaindy Fenton, and through constant study, travel,

opposite:
Raymond Nasher and Henry Moore, Much Hadham, England, September 1967

and discussion, Patsy Nasher learned what she calls "the mechanics" of collecting, by which she means everything from negotiating prices to finding the best possible experts to consult about authenticity, dating, physical condition, and provenance. She learned how to gain access to important dealers, how to find out about the availability of important works, and how to move fast and make quick decisions when necessary.

In the process, the Nasher collection picked up momentum. "The works acquired me. I didn't acquire the works," Patsy says. She and Ray began to make one major purchase after another, among them David Smith's great *Voltri VI* (1962; p. 95), from the estate of Nelson Rockefeller, and three portrait busts by Alberto Giacometti of his brother Diego (1954; p. 64), from the Fondation Maeght. They ventured into contemporary art, buying paintings by Morris Louis and Frank Stella, lead reliefs by Jasper Johns, prints by both Stella and Johns, and sculpture by Anthony Caro, Donald Judd, Sol LeWitt, Roy Lichtenstein, Claes Oldenburg, Richard Serra, and Mark di Suvero.

Despite the increasing level of ambition in their acquisitions, the Nashers say today that for a long time they "never thought about a collection." In fact, Patsy avows, "the first time I thought of this group of objects as a collection was at an exhibition Bill Jordan did at the University Gallery of the Meadows School of Art at Southern Methodist University in 1978. That's the first time I saw a thread running through everything." That thread—the silken thread of quality, of historical breadth and definition—had been recognized by William B. Jordan, at present Deputy Director of Fort Worth's Kimbell Art Museum. He had been keeping a keen eye on the Nashers' acquisitions, and was the first to see that they were building, without the Nashers actually planning it that way, into a collection of growing importance. He pointed out, in the statement accompanying the exhibition, that the collection had a core of works by great masters "born within a decade before or after 1900"—Arp, Calder, Max Ernst, Jacques Lipchitz, Miró, Moore, Noguchi, and David Smith, and a strong, representative group of second-generation artists, "born within the decade after 1923," and including Caro, Johns, Judd, Lichtenstein, Oldenburg, Beverly Pepper, and di Suvero.

Yet it was not until the early eighties that the Nashers finally saw themselves as serious collectors; moreover, they add, it was not until then that dealers saw them in the same light. By 1983, however, the year Shaindy Fenton died from an illness she had been fighting for many years, Patsy Nasher had become a full-time collector, driven by her passion, enthusiasm, and taste to envision major goals for the collection. According to sculptor Beverly Pepper, whom the Nashers commissioned to build a site sculpture, *Dallas Land Canal* (1971; p. 23), at NorthPark, Patsy became "one of the smartest, sharpest bird dogs of art," with a confident eye and the nose to follow important works. The

Nashers' collecting, William Jordan says, "went from something they enjoyed doing to the most important thing in their lives."

Since 1980 the Nasher collection "has really picked up steam," according to Steven A. Nash, Deputy Director and Chief Curator of the Dallas Museum of Art. "They have achieved focus, independence, and feeling. Particularly notable is the drive to represent key artists in special depth, which has led in several cases to complementing sculpture with paintings—by Giacometti and Picasso, for instance." They have fallen in love with major works, pursued them, and acquired them. Early in the decade, after seeing Rodin's *Eve* of 1881 in Switzerland, Ray Nasher suggested to Patsy that they begin to collect "backwards" as well as "forwards." They would make the collection more consciously historical, so that it would include examples from the modernist figurative tradition, beginning with Rodin, and move on to embrace Cubism, Constructivism, Futurism, Surrealism, Abstract Expressionism, Minimalism, and various contemporary tendencies. To that end, they have begun to collect in real depth. They now have not only Rodin's *Eve* (p. 42), but his plaster *Head of Balzac* (1897; p. 43); Matisse's *Madeleine I* (1901; p. 46) in plaster, *Head with*

BEVERLY PEPPER
Dallas Land Canal, 1971
Cor-Ten steel, 60" x 70" x 263'
Installed at NorthPark, Dallas

PABLO PICASSO
Head of a Woman, 1931–32
Acquired by the Nashers in 1986

Necklace (1907; p. 49), *Decorative Figure* (1908; p. 46), *Two Negresses* (1908; p. 46), *Large Seated Nude* (c. 1923–25; p. 48), and *Tiari* (1930; p. 49); Giacometti's *Spoon Woman* (1926–27; p. 61), *Head* (1934; p. 61), *Two Figurines* (c. 1945; p. 62), *The Chariot* (1950; p. 65), *Venice Woman III* (1956; p. 63), and the three portrait busts of the artist's brother. Their Ernst holdings include *The King Playing with the Queen* (1944; p. 59), *Capricorn* (1948; p. 58), and the *Sister Souls* (1961; p. 59). They have collected important works by Raymond Duchamp-Villon, and now have *Torso of a Young Man* (1910; p. 73), *Baudelaire* (1911; p. 76), in plaster, *Maggy* (1912; p. 76), *Large Horse* (1914; p. 72), *Horse and Rider II* (1914; p. 77), and *Portrait of Professor Gosset*

(1918; p. 77). When the Duchamp-Villon heads are juxtaposed with Rodin's *Head of Balzac,* Giacometti's portrait busts and *Head,* Constantin Brancusi's *Portrait of Nancy Cunard* (1925–27; p.51), and Pablo Picasso's Boisgeloup *Head of a Woman* (1931–32; p. 24), an interesting leitmotif can be discerned running through the collection, namely the portrait and what art historian Albert E. Elsen calls "the evocative head." Much of the Nasher collection is figurative, with many works conveying an aura of *luxe, calme, et volupté*: Rodin's *Eve,* Aristide Maillol's *La Nuit* (c. 1902–09; p. 47), Brancusi's *The Kiss* (1907–08; p. 50), Henri Laurens's *Grande Maternité* (1932; pp. 48–49), and Picasso's *Pregnant Woman* (1950–59; p. 55); yet the Nashers are not intimidated by work that evokes more disturbing qualities, that has harshness, even terror in it. In their living room they have hung Picasso's stark 1971 painting *Man and Woman* (p. 109). When Picasso's widow, Jacqueline, visited the Nasher home some years ago, she wept upon seeing the picture again, and told the Nashers' daughters and Harry Parker, Director of the Dallas Museum of Art, who were showing her the collection in the Nashers' absence, that Picasso had recognized in this painting the inevitability and imminence of his own death.

The Nashers are building their Constructivist holdings, having acquired Antoine Pevsner's *Dynamic Projection at Thirty Degrees* (1950–51; p. 83), Naum Gabo's *Linear Construction in*

Patsy Nasher and Jacqueline Picasso, Mougins, July 1985

Space No. 1 (Variation) (1942–43; p. 83), Ivan Puni's *Construction Relief* (c. 1915–16; p. 86), and Alexander Archipenko's Cubist-Constructivist figure *Woman Combing Her Hair* (1914 or 1915; p. 81). They are achieving a fine range in works by David Smith: *House in a Landscape* (1945; p. 91), *The Forest* (1950; pp. 90–91), *9/15/53* (1953; p. 94), *Tower Eight* (1957; p. 94), *Untitled (Voltri)* (1962; p. 94), and *Voltri VI* (1962; p. 95). Among their Calders there is *The Spider* (1940; p. 87); among their Tony Smiths, *The Snake Is Out* (1962; p. 118); among their Anthony Caros, *Carriage* (1966; p. 119). They have painting, sculpture, and prints by a wide variety of contemporary artists, among them Carl Andre, Siah Armajani, Jonathan Borofsky, Scott Burton, John Chamberlain, Richard Deacon, Jim Dine, Barry Flanagan, Anthony Gormley, Anish Kapoor, Alain Kirili, Beverly Pepper, George Segal, Joel Shapiro, and Isaac Witkin. Whereas Ray tends to favor classic modernists, Patsy likes to encourage younger artists. Both Nashers work together, as a team. One may feel more convinced about a piece than the other, but in the end, when they make a decision it is always mutual.

Although the character of the collection has recently become more historical, Patsy Nasher is quick to insist: "It isn't a textbook collection, and it wasn't intended to be. If it's ended up that way, I'm sorry. It's our personal collection, and it doesn't really matter if anyone else likes it," she adds, with characteristic forthrightness.

An interesting fact about the Nasher collection is that its growth roughly parallels the development since 1965 of a strong surge of interest in modern sculpture. Until the early sixties, many collectors regarded sculpture as the stepchild of painting. Unlike painting, sculpture often does not fit in the house; nor does it have the same decorative function; it is *there,* taking up real space. The existence of cast editions seemed to compromise, for many, the romance of the "unique object," and this in turn kept prices relatively low. Modern sculpture has always had its champions and adherents, of course. Chief among these was Curt Valentin, the distinguished German art dealer who came to New York in 1937 and showed many modern masters in his Fifty-seventh Street gallery, among them Rodin, Maillol, Degas, Matisse, Picasso, Arp, Lipchitz, Moore, and Calder. After Valentin died in 1954, Otto Gerson represented many of his artists; but when Gerson died suddenly in 1962, it was feared that the Valentin era was truly at an end. London's Marlborough Fine Art Limited, however, absorbed the Otto Gerson Gallery, becoming the Marlborough-Gerson Gallery in New York. A smaller number of other dealers, among them Sidney Janis, Pierre Matisse, Klaus Perls, and Marian Willard, exhibited European and American sculpture. While Joseph Hirshhorn, Howard and Jean Lipman, Nelson Rockefeller, and a few others amassed important collections of modern sculpture, they were the exception rather than the rule.

From its inception, The Museum of Modern Art, New York, exhibited sculpture, and its very first major acquisition was a bronze by Maillol. Calder and Moore had important shows in the forties. In 1953, a major survey, *Sculpture of the Twentieth Century*, organized by Andrew Carnduff Ritchie, featured works by Rodin, Degas, Maillol, Picasso, Matisse, Arp, Boccioni, Archipenko, Gonzalez, Giacometti, Calder, Lipchitz, Moore, and many others; and major exhibitions and retrospectives devoted to the sculpture of Lipchitz, Gonzalez, David Smith, Picasso, and Matisse have occurred at timely intervals over the past thirty years. Although The Solomon R. Guggenheim Museum, New York, did not exhibit sculpture until 1955, when it held a Brancusi show, it has, since that time, held many sculpture exhibitions, including retrospectives of Arp, Calder, Giacometti, and Gonzalez, and, in 1962, an exhibition featuring selections from the Joseph Hirshhorn collection. Recent attention given to modern sculpture at the National Gallery of Art in Washington, D.C., includes a Lehmbruck exhibition, in 1972, and major exhibitions devoted to Rodin and David Smith, both in 1982.

When the success of Abstract Expressionism and Pop art in the early sixties led to an expanded art market, sculpture was swept up in the general fervor. As prices for paintings went up, so did those for sculpture. The anti-illusionist thrust of Abstract Expressionist, Color Field, Pop, and Minimalist aesthetics gave a new cachet to what had once seemed dubious—the literalness of sculpture and the way it inhabited real space. Collectors suddenly began to find three-dimensional work much more attractive, and to envision sculpture as essential to growing collections in their homes. With the entry of corporate buyers and the proliferation of civic arts projects, both modern and contemporary sculpture, particularly commissioned pieces, have found both the space and the patronage they have needed to flourish. A number of important collectors, among them the Nashers in Dallas and the Harry Andersons in Atherton, California, have, since the late sixties, been building formidable collections. Since the late sixties and seventies, major museum surveys have brought the scope of twentieth-century achievements in sculpture into greater focus—among them, Albert Elsen's *Pioneers of Modern Sculpture*, at the Hayward Gallery, London, in 1973, and more recently, Margit Rowell's *Qu'est-ce que la sculpture moderne?* (to which the Nashers loaned Anthony Caro's *Carriage*), which opened in the summer of 1986 at the Musée National d'Art Moderne, of the Centre Georges Pompidou, Paris. Books such as Jack Burnham's *Beyond Modern Sculpture* and Rosalind E. Krauss's *Passages in Modern Sculpture* have raised the level of critical discourse about modern sculpture to that of the best discourse about modern painting.

While these developments certainly provide a context for the growth of the Nasher collection, they really do not explain it. What makes it special, what defines its "inscape" or internal character, is the way it so actively embodies the Nashers' sense of life. Collecting sculpture, from the beginning, has been an expressive activity for them, a concrete way of surrounding themselves with objects that continually affirm grace, feeling, intelligence, and, above all, the shaping power of the human imagination.

As a youngster growing up in Boston and New York, where his father, the son of Russian immigrants who had fled pogroms in the eighteen-eighties, worked in the garment-manufacturing business, Raymond Nasher and his family made a point of going to concerts and museums as often as possible. When Nasher's father lost everything in the Depression, he moved his family to New York, settling them in Kew Gardens—"when the trolley car went down Queens Boulevard and it was a nickel," Ray remembers—and built his business back up again. Twice a week Ray studied piano at a branch of the Juilliard School of Music in Jamaica, Queens; on Saturdays he had a composition and harmony lesson at Juilliard in Manhattan. As children his parents had been deprived of music and art, and from their point of view, says Ray, "it was a great thing to expose their child to all they had missed."

The Nasher family eventually moved back to Boston, and Ray graduated from the Boston Latin School in 1939. After graduating from Duke University in 1943, he saw duty on both land and sea as Lieutenant Senior Grade in the Navy. When the war ended, he returned to Boston, worked in his father's retail-clothing business by day, and studied law and business at night, receiving an M.A. in economics at Boston University in 1950. In 1948, at an election-night television party, he was impressed when his date, a Smith undergraduate from Dallas named Patsy Rabinowitz, was the only one who predicted Truman's victory over Dewey. They were married the next summer and moved to Dallas the following year.

Today, Ray Nasher is a trim, vigorous man, extremely fit from a lifetime's devotion to tennis. Relaxed in his top-floor office, which looks out over NorthPark, and surrounded by examples of Pre-Columbian and Oceanic art; sculptures by Jim Dine, Alain Kirili, and Beverly Pepper; and a tapestry by Roy Lichtenstein, he nods emphatically when asked whether there is a relation between his work as a developer and his love of sculpture. "Absolutely," he replies. "With sculpture, we touch it, feel it, see it, place it. A piece of sculpture has to stand, face the weather, and be a part of the environment. Painting hangs on a wall; it's illusion. We were drawn to sculpture because the sculptor is really a builder. His work has to be understood in relation to placement and space." Nasher leans forward at his desk and clasps his hands together, his forehead furrowed in concentration. "One of the things we work very hard on is relating a piece of sculpture to a particular location and changing it when it doesn't work. I'm always changing around the works we have in the house, taking them from one room, putting them in another, playing with them. It's like what we do with cities, public places, private spaces. Location, place, light, air, environment —we grow by these and the art grows. It's very hard work."

The Nashers believe that art should be seen in public spaces. In 1978, they loaned David Smith's *Voltri VI* (1962) to the National Gallery of Art for its exhibition *American Art at Mid-Century*, and in 1986 they loaned three David Smith sculptures to *The Drawings of David Smith*, a summer exhibition at the Fort Worth Art Museum. In the same year works by Joan Miró, Ivan Puni, and Frank Stella were on loan to the Dallas Museum of Art. Visitors to NorthPark meet sculpture from the Nasher collection everywhere: in both the interiors and exteriors of office buildings, the NorthPark National Bank, and the shopping center itself. People stop to look at the sculpture, children reach out to touch and explore it. All of this is naturally very gratifying to the Nashers, who in 1986 had George Segal's bronze group, *Rush Hour* (1983; p. 98) installed at the center. "If I'm brave enough to create something in the environment," Ray Nasher asserts, "then I'm obligated to make it affect people in a positive way."

According to Patsy Nasher, Ray does not like to do anything twice. "A new endeavor sparks his mind, lures him," she says. In 1986 he was negotiating with the French government for the right to develop and manage the complex of stores, galleries, restaurants, and other commercial units that will be housed in I. M. Pei's projected Pyramid addition to the Louvre. "This is one of the most exciting projects I've worked on," he says. "Everything about it will relate to the function of bringing art to people, and people to art in one of the greatest single art repositories in the world. It's a commercial quest, but within the framework of culture and humanism." He smiles happily at this prospect; it would be difficult to find an enterprise that better summed up everything that Ray Nasher is about.

Patsy Nasher acknowledges that she is both shy and very forthright. She also acknowledges that she has a good sense of humor "that comes out when I'm under pressure, which is always." Her background has interesting parallels with her husband's. Her father, like Ray's, was the son of Russian immigrants. A Dallas businessman with interests in oil and real estate, he, too, like Ray's father, lost everything in the Depression and made it back again. This bred in Patsy, as in Ray, the conviction that while money could be made and lost and made again, it was the things one could do with it that were the true index of value and achievement. For many years she listed her interests as "educa-

pages 30–31:
Installation view of *Voltri VI*, 1962, by David Smith, in *American Art at Mid-Century: The Subjects of the Artist*, National Gallery of Art, Washington, D.C., 1978

Living room of Patsy and Raymond Nasher in Dallas, 1986. Works of art include sculpture by Joseph Beuys, Alberto Giacometti, and Henri Matisse

tion, art, young people, and world peace,'' and she was committed to a wide range of activities and organizations reflecting all of these, plus all the responsibilities and obligations arising from Ray's years of service in both the Johnson Administration and the United Nations. She is an extremely well-organized woman, who speaks without wasting words, and confronts you with direct, reflective, and curious eyes.

As a child, she remembers, she would accompany her mother on searches for *objets d'art*, which her mother liked to collect. She also recalls spending hours in the Dallas Museum of Fine Arts looking at paintings, especially when her father would be late picking her up from her children's art classes. At Smith College she took courses in the history of American art and majored in American studies; she says today that had she been born into the post-Women's Liberation world, she would most certainly have adopted a profession. As it was, she followed the directives of her generation with professional single-mindedness, devoting herself to her family and taking an active part in her husband's business. Yet, once her children had grown and she began to collect art in earnest, she did so with the ardor of someone whose hitherto suppressed or deferred talents have been released with overwhelming urgency and with the deep pleasure that comes from having earned the right, after years of dedication to others, of doing something that offers supreme rewards to oneself alone. She discovered that she was a born collector—a natural. Alongside her forays into twentieth-century art, she not only amassed her Pre-Columbian collection, but built as well a major collection of Guatemalan textiles, which in 1986 she donated to the Dallas Museum of Art.

"Ray and I," she says, sitting on the long black-and-white tweed sofa in the Nashers' sunken living room (p. 32), "are 'by art possessed.' " In front of her, on the long, oval glass-topped Diego Giacometti table, sits a wonderful array of small bronzes: Archipenko's *Woman Combing Her Hair* (1914 or 1915; p. 81); Matisse's *Tiari* (1930; p. 49), *Two Negresses* (1908; p. 46), and *Head with Necklace* (1907; p. 49); Joseph Beuys's *Animal Woman* (1949; p. 105); Duchamp-Villon's *Horse and Rider II* (1914; p. 77), and Willem de Kooning's maquette for *Seated Woman*. Behind, on the black-veined white-marble banquette, rests a row of larger figures: Duchamp-Villon's terracotta *Torso of a Young Man* (1910; p. 73); Lipchitz's stone *Seated Woman* (1916; p. 80); Matisse's *Decorative Figure* (1908; p. 46) and *Large Seated Nude* (c. 1923–25; p. 48), the two of them flanking Giacometti's three portrait busts. By the white-marble fireplace stand Giacometti's *Venice Woman III* (1956; p. 63) and *The Chariot* (1950; p. 65); between them, over the mantel, one of his paintings. Duchamp-Villon's plaster head of Baudelaire

Installation view of *Guatemalan Textiles from the Collection of Patsy and Raymond D. Nasher,* Dallas Museum of Art, 1980

(1911; p. 76) sits on the piano; on the white carpet, encased in a transparent box, sits Oldenburg's *Pile of Typewriter Erasers* (1970–75; p. 102). This environment, so simple, unpretentious, and frankly comfortable, in the way living rooms were designed and furnished in the fifties and sixties to be comfortable, is deeply hospitable to both art and conversation. Large, monumental pieces are visible in the woods through the full-length glass wall. The dining room has paintings by Morris Louis, Hans Hofmann, and Picasso, as well as Picasso's bronze *Head of a Woman* (1931–32; p. 54) and *Pregnant Woman* (1950–59; p. 55). *The Kiss*, by Brancusi (the 1907–08 version in plaster; p. 50), functions as the centerpiece on the Nashers' long dining table—totem, perhaps, of the Nashers' hospitality, of the fine Southern cooking offered in their home, and even of the venerable Eastern European equation of love and food, which is part of the cultural inheritance they share with visitors and friends.

The Nashers' collecting is a partnership in every sense. Each brings different strengths and predilections. Ray is good at imagining the big picture and keeping the collection's historical design in mind. Patsy, according to Harry Parker, "has sensibility and intensity about the objects. Ray wants to tell the story of modern sculpture so that the whole becomes greater than the sum of its parts. He wants to fill in the gaps. She has independence and adventurousness; she goes for what she likes. Between them there is simplicity and wholeness."

To Patsy, what matters most is quality. This she defines as "an essence your eye detects that has a lasting aesthetic appeal." Her eye continues to develop, she thinks. "I see better and better how pieces work and how they relate to each other." What else does she look for? "Beyond everything else, it is work that renews itself every time you view it, and retains its original sense of excitement," she answers. She sees her collecting as a profession for which she constantly prepares by "doing my homework," as she puts it. This means reading art history monographs and magazine articles and keeping in touch with dealers, curators, scholars, and artists. Learning all she needs to know about a prospective acquisition can take months. She candidly admits that there have been "disappointments, anxiety, and sleepless nights." She recently—and reluctantly—decided against acquiring a sculpture by Picasso, after repeated attempts to verify its date failed to supply her with one she could accept as reliable. "It was impossible to put the story together," she says, her expression at once resolute and resigned. But there have been many wonderful experiences: the thrill of seeing Jacques Lipchitz's *Seated Woman* in New York just after its arrival from Switzerland, saying "I'll take it!" on the spot, and finding out that a major New York dealer saw it shortly afterwards and wanted it, too; and there was Henry Moore's visit to the Nasher home in 1979, when he was so struck by a New Guinea basket mask that he immediately made a drawing of it and gave it to the Nashers. Last year, in the course of negotiating for the acquisition of Brancusi's wood sculpture, *Portrait of Nancy Cunard* (1925–27; p. 51), the Nashers became acquainted with Teeny Duchamp, Marcel Duchamp's American-born widow, to whom Brancusi had given the piece in 1950. During visits to her in Paris and the French countryside, they were charmed by her hospitality, graciousness, and memories of the artists she had known.

Patsy also recalls with a good deal of amusement the first time she and Ray spent what might euphemistically be called "a major sum" on a piece of sculpture. Over the years, she had often seen a cast of Matisse's *Large Seated Nude* in New York, and although she had loved it, the price "had been out of the question." Eventually the piece became available, and though the price was still astronomical, the Nashers put a twenty-four hour reserve on it. As five o'clock approached the next day, they were still undecided. Finally, Ray said to Patsy: "Do whatever you want." She went into another room and made a telephone call. "What did you do?" asked Ray, when she returned. "I bought it," she answered. Despite Ray's momentary reaction—according to Patsy, "He almost dropped"—it was this particular acquisition that served as a kind of initiation for the Nashers, freeing them to think henceforth of their collecting as an unlimited search for the very best.

The Nashers are just as committed to the maintenance and conservation of their collection as they are to building it. Every six months, a freelance conservator, Douglass Kwart, comes to Dallas and spends two weeks carefully examining, cleaning, and polishing every work in the collection. "Any outdoor environment is aggressive—any urban outdoor environment, especially one like Dallas, where the temperature changes are so drastic," he explains. "Intense sunshine can burn out wax coatings; humidity can condense out as acid rain; freezing can delaminate brittle wax and even bring out a change in a work's dimension." Constant maintenance, however, enhances the objects' capacity to withstand the elements they compete with, and visitors to the Nasher home are often struck by the aura of healthiness with which the sculptures reside in the garden and woods, where they seem to be completely at home.

This attention to what one might call nurturing the collection has a further meaning, perhaps the least obvious, for Patsy. Since 1976, she has been beset by a series of illnesses that have caused pain, debilitation, and an enormous waste of time. She speaks frankly about her health, which is now steadily improving, and says: "When you're ill, you let unimportant things go. Things that *were* important become *more* important. Art, for instance. The art saved me." The intellectual challenge of art, "the delicious feeling" of adding a new piece to the collection, the fact that collecting is an activity she can share with her husband wherever they go (they take their "shopping list" of desired acquisitions on airplanes), the pleasures of meeting people in the international art world, have all been crucial aspects of the healing process. Collecting gives her purpose and renews her energy. A Dallas acquaintance, who in the mid-eighties encountered the Nashers in Switzerland, recalls how, in one day, "they looked at several paintings by Léger; saw the plaster of *Madeleine I* for the first time; put a reserve on *The Kiss* [a painting by Picasso]; went to a large exhibition of a private collection at the Basel Kunsthalle; drove to Zürich, visited a private dealer there who had two Max Ernsts they later decided to buy—and instead of retiring to a late dinner, Patsy then went to call on two dealers in Art Deco furniture." Despite illness, or perhaps in defiance of it, she is indefatigable when it comes to collecting, and has no plans to slow down.

Over the past century, from Havemeyer to Hirshhorn, America has produced some great collectors, people who have combined wealth and munificence to endow our museums with great and representative works from the major epochs of both Eastern and Western art. More recently, however, with the disappearance of relatively abundant supplies of old masters and changes in the ways fortunes are made and husbanded, the conditions of major collecting have changed as well. Few of even our wealthiest citizens can collect in the style of those who lived between the post-Civil War Gilded Age and the eve of World War II. Since 1960, a new and disturbing breed of collectors has appeared, one that treats collecting, particularly of contemporary works, as a search for investments and luxury commodities, or as a form of transcendental shopping, in which last year's enthusiasm, trend, neighborhood, gallery, or artist falls to the axe of this year's newest fad.

The Nashers clearly recall the great collectors of an earlier era. They buy art because they love it. They buy art they want to live with, and that is for the keeping. Not surprisingly, they have won the respect and admiration of a good many art professionals. "They are *true* collectors," says Edmund Pillsbury, Director of the Kimbell Art Museum in Fort Worth. "They have this insatiable urge to acquire and build something that is an extension of their own ideals, love, sense of beauty and culture. Their collecting is an expression of something bigger than themselves. And they're able to take tough art. They have an instinct for work that has struggle in it and profundity of expression. When they think about buying a piece, they ask the hardest questions: 'What's its depth of humanism?' 'What's its place in history?' 'Does it knock your socks off?' 'Does it really grab you?' " Ernst Beyeler, of the Galerie Beyeler in Basel, says that "their approach to art is that of the art lover rather than the acquirer. They began to buy, almost with a goal in mind, only what they were convinced by, and their sensitivity has made them known in the art world as collectors of great quality." And J. Carter Brown, Director of the National Gallery of Art, in Washington, D.C., says: "What I admire about the Nashers is their accelerating enthusiasm and their assiduousness in educating themselves. It's endearing the way they really roll their sleeves up and learn about the pieces they want to acquire. They've brought structural thinking and professional standards to their collecting. They also have a gift for outdoor installation, which is a very subtle art. To place sculpture within nature can be an unequal battle; the way they do it, the sculpture triumphs."

As collections go, the Nashers' is, to borrow a phrase more usually applied to artists, in "midcareer." It shows power, range, and matured taste, but the Nashers look forward to years of enrichment. They would like to collect more Cubist, Constructivist, and Futurist work; more sculpture by Americans; and continue their support of younger artists. "A collection should never be finished," Ray Nasher says. "It should always be growing, always getting better." The daily life of the Nashers is deeply rooted in the realities of business and world affairs; yet, they believe that in living with art they are participating in something powerfully mysterious, ancient in its sources, and necessary to human life. "When one deals with art," they say, "one is dealing with animate objects. They aren't decorative; those works are telling you something, becoming part of your life."

The exhibition of their collection at both the Dallas Museum of Art and the National Gallery of Art in Washington gives the Nashers a chance to stand back and measure what they have achieved. They will find a living, growing collection, in which works speak to one another in a language as subtle, deep, and surprising as art in this century can be.

FIGURES AND PHANTOMS

STEVEN A. NASH

Early Modern Figurative Sculpture

Figuration was an embattled tradition in early modern sculpture. Such nineteenth-century artists as Paul Gauguin, Auguste Rodin, and Medardo Rosso had challenged the hegemony of realistic representation, but even for their daring minds, sculpture divorced from nature and the human or animal body was unimaginable. With the dawning of a new century, however, previously undreamable realities became everyday fact, in art as in science. New modes of thought and perception forced new artistic responses. Revolutions that began in painting quickly invaded sculpture; and for many artists exploring new visual forms, any hint of figuration was a debasing link to the past.

Despite these ideological pressures, the human figure not only survived—but also *thrived*—as a source of sculptural inspiration in early modern art. In the hands of artists such as Henri Matisse, Pablo Picasso, Henry Moore, Raymond Duchamp-Villon, and Max Ernst, figural language proved central to the development of modernist sensibilities. Alberto Giacometti, for one, felt that working from nature was, simply put, inevitable, a position requiring considerable personal courage against attacks on naturalism by many friends and colleagues.[1] The bodily image was seen not as discardable baggage from a previous era but rather as a prime vehicle of communication, accessibility, discovery, and shared understanding, open to inexhaustible varieties of personal and formal interpretation. Within the Nasher collection there is found a rich vein of figurative expression. At a moment in contemporary art when many sculptors are returning to the figure as a source of meaning, it seems particularly timely to review and try to reach a closer understanding of this complex tradition.

opposite:
JOAN MIRÓ
Moonbird, 1944–46 (enlarged 1966, cast 1967)
Bronze, 90 × 80½ × 57¾"
No. 54

Rodin, Rosso, Matisse, and Maillol: Tradition Revised

Auguste Rodin straddles the turn of the century like a colossus, one foot in the past, one in the modern present. His artistic ancestry lies in classical sculpture, the work of Michelangelo, and the humanistic tradition of the Renaissance, but his career encompassed events so crucial to new sociopolitical and artistic beginnings as World War I and the birth of Cubism and abstraction. This duality was reflected in his reputation. Immensely productive and honored, Rodin *meant* sculpture for most young artists. The formal and expressive power of his work, his freedom from academic constraint, the psychological acuity of many of his themes, and such innovative devices as the partial figure had long-lasting influence and won the respect of even such determined modernists as Constantin Brancusi and Jacques Lipchitz. For many, however, he epitomized the nineteenth century and a moribund tradition of the *statuaire*—a maker of storytelling sculptures in a heavy and melodramatic figural language.

In early twentieth-century eyes, a critical ambivalence surrounded such works by Rodin as those in the Nasher collection: the *Eve* (1881; p. 42), originally conceived as part of Rodin's great magnum opus, the *Gates of Hell* (1880–1917), and the plaster *Head of Balzac* (1897; p. 43), one of many studies preparatory to his 1898 Balzac monument. Both derive from sculpture with a public purpose of educating, memorializing and communicating on a grand scale certain societal values—a genre that found little favor among the pioneers of modernism. Both, too, are dramatic in feeling and presentation, evidencing what some critics saw in Rodin as "too easy" a manipulation of material and emotion. Conversely, both the *Balzac* and *Gates of Hell* were projects so bold in conception, so full of personal risk, that they seriously challenged the norms of monumental sculpture and compromised contemporary understanding.

At an early stage of work on the *Gates,* Rodin separated the flanking figures of Adam and Eve from the rest of the composition, perhaps for financial as well as sculptural reasons. In constituting *Eve* as an independent work, he set her free from the *Gates*; but he also freed her from the strictures of his biblical and Dantean iconography. Like Michelangelo's Eve in the Sistine Chapel, she represents the fall from grace and the expulsion from paradise, but standing alone in her naked vulnerability, one arm raised in a gesture of self-protection, she also assumes expanded secular meaning as an emblem of torment and spiritual malaise. This extension into modern psychological terrain is reinforced by Rodin's treatment of her anatomy. Instead of presenting a muscled, idealized superwoman, he gives us an image of earthy reality, heavy in midriff and thighs and roughly modeled, especially around the feet and groin. She is capable of feeling, in other words, the pain of life's all too real anxieties and pressures. She speaks of the human condition in a modern lingua franca just as poignant as that in figures by Wilhelm Lehmbruck and Ernst Barlach, and signals in her focus on ''self'' an element of distinctly modernist sensibility.

Two themes of Rodin's work coincide in the *Head of Balzac*: his ability to make a single part carry the meaning of a whole figure, and his concentration on the head as an emblem of the soul or intellect. Even without the monolithic body and robe so physically powerful in the final sculpture, the head conveys Rodin's image of Balzac as a man of visionary genius with a lusty appetite for life. Representing an advanced stage in a long series of studies that evolved from the youthful and naturalistic to the aged and far more symbolic, this head is close to the final version in its wild mane of hair, heavy neck, deeply set eyes, rough modeling, and air of age, experience, and dissipation. Rodin's lack of sentimentality helped bring the sculpture public disfavor when it was finally unveiled. It is an image that projects, however, a largeness of character and creative will, even in the smaller-than-life-size form of the plaster study.

As modern sculpture moved toward hermetic, nonliterary, formal meanings, the sculptor's desire to communicate feeling and observation was not erased. In this light, Rodin's most forthright and personalized themes remained as compelling as ever. But even artists unmoved by his dramaturgy found that his strongly felt surfaces could provide a means of escaping the inertia of sculptural closure. Such was the case with Rosso and Matisse, who redirected the lessons of Rodin toward their own artistic ends.

An interest in the effects of atmosphere, light, distance, and movement on perception led Medardo Rosso to formulate, by means of a Rodinesque modeling, a uniquely impressionistic sculpture. The *Ecce Puer* (1906; p. 43), one of his last works, summarizes what Rosso referred to as ''subjective perception'' and the unification of emotion with environment. The revolutionary aspects of works such as this were honored by the Italian Futurists, among others, who also recognized, however, that they represented ''the same advantages and same faults as impressionist painting.'' What the Futurists termed a ''pictorial and external'' concept of the sculptural object would change dramatically with Matisse.

The sculpture of Henri Matisse is exclusively figurative, almost always feminine in subject, and except for one wood carving, exclusively modeled. A general intimacy of scale and mood led Matisse to keep many of his sculptures around his living and working quarters, and he frequently incorporated them in his paintings as part of a subject matter of everyday reality, relaxation, and delectation. They figure importantly in his projected world of *luxe, calme, et volupté* and in his theories on the

opposite:
AUGUSTE RODIN
Eve, 1881 (cast before 1932)
Bronze, 68 × 17¼ × 25½"
No. 72

left:
AUGUSTE RODIN
Head of Balzac, 1897
Plaster, 7½ × 8 × 6½"
No. 73

below:
MEDARDO ROSSO
Ecce Puer, 1906
Wax over plaster, 16⅜ × 13⅜ × 11¹/₁₆"
No. 74

decorative functions of art, providing personal revelations of aesthetic sensation experienced in the absorbed study of a model. They embody the Elysian side of French classicism, but do so through a liberated handling of surface and anatomy that can mount to a strident, expressive pitch.

Produced concurrently, the Rodinesque *Serf* of 1901–03 and the *Madeleine I* of 1901 (p. 46) announced Matisse's emergence as a major sculptor, one who was able to work in contrasting sculptural modes. Against the solidly planted stance and dramatic modeling of the *Serf, Madeleine*'s serpentine contours seem particularly elegant and graceful, perhaps recalling, as Albert Elsen has suggested, the cool stylizations of nineteenth-century Salon nudes.[2] They also demonstrate Matisse's emphasis, from the time of his earliest works, on synthesizing the figure's overall architecture of form, to which interior detail is subordinated. Even here, however, no surface is left uninflected, as the gentle swells of contour are enlivened throughout by variations of reflection and touch. A comparably restrained facture is seen in such works by Rodin as the *Meditation* (1885), also organized around an exaggerated contrapposto; certainly Matisse's truncation of the limbs in order to clarify the flow of rhythm and silhouette owes much to Rodin's partial figures.

The *Head with Necklace* (1907; p. 49) belongs to a group of very small, sketchy, and seemingly experimental works from about 1905 to 1907. It captures with economy the head of a young girl, and hints, through the somewhat hierarchical treatment of form, at the influence of archaic and tribal art. The latter is far more strongly felt in the ensuing *Two Negresses* (1908; p. 46) and *Decorative Figure* (1908; p. 46), in which Matisse responded to the general primitivizing trends so pervasive in the art of the period.

This invocation of distant artistic sources for invigorating emotional and formal strength, although seen mostly as a manifestation of tribal influences, also subsumes interest in Pre-Columbian art, the art of Egypt, pre-classical Greece, and other archaic traditions. Much less thoroughly absorbed by such sources than Picasso, Matisse nevertheless felt their power, and his move toward a stronger, more "brutal" beauty is seen first in the painting *Blue Nude* and the related sculpture *Reclining Nude* of 1907, followed by the *Two Negresses* and *Decorative Figure* of a year later. For the pose of the two women, he drew upon a photograph of two black girls from a French ethnographical magazine. In transforming the image into sculpture, however, he exaggerated proportions through a pronouncement of the buttocks and breasts, as in Fang or Baule carvings, and through a sometimes harsh paring and reshaping of other features of anatomy. The stony dome of one figure's head, echoed in other globular shapes below, strikes a particularly strong note. The side-by-side pose is full of visual tensions, heightened by a certain sexual ambiguity: one figure seems willfully hermaphroditic, which complicates further the sexual questions raised by the pose itself.

The challenge of contemporaneous works by Georges Braque and Pablo Picasso was helping engender in Matisse's paintings of the time a more analytical distillation of sensual response. A similar mental toughness informs his *Decorative Figure*. Here, the seated nude, an age-old theme of beauty and display, is thoroughly reinterpreted. Voluptuous curves and flowing arabesques, associated with graceful sensuality in works such as the great *Joie de vivre* (1905–06), assume a different spirit through Matisse's abrupt twistings, foreshortenings, and simplifications of form. The hips and buttocks are exaggerated in mass, and the feet are given particularly summary treatment. The head, with masklike features, is positioned in a stiff vertical over the cubic base. Somewhat jarring in her disjointed rhythms and rough surface texture, this figure is not so much a compliant odalisque as a powerful, earthy goddess.

No longer symbolic or narrative in a traditional sense, these works nevertheless "tell a story" of personal observation, response, analysis, and expressive impulse. They contribute to what might be termed the objectification of figural sculpture, in which the Pygmalion dream of duplicating life is abandoned, and life resides instead in the complex messages of the sculpture as an object requiring sensitivity to its own language of communication. For Matisse, there exists no higher expression of these principles, or of his sculptural aims in general, than the *Large Seated Nude* of c. 1923–25 (p. 48). In the slightly later *Tiari* (1930; p. 49), his efforts would relax into an elegant pun on the shape of a flower compared to that of a woman's head. In *Large Seated Nude* they are tense with decision-making and invention. Every form in the base and figure is rethought and integrated into a harsh but dramatic play of slicing, thrusting movement. Every segment holds a wealth of tactile kinesthetic experience. Having submitted in various preliminary versions to a transformation similar to that seen in the earlier Heads of Jeannette (1910–16), Matisse's figure emerges as perhaps the most powerful in his sculptural oeuvre.

Matisse said that he took up sculpture as a means of clarifying his stylistic ideas in a discipline separate from painting. Aristide Maillol also came to sculpture after an early career in other mediums. He too respected the work of Rodin but sought in his own development an art of greater equanimity and balance, one with the solemnity of early Greek and Egyptian sculpture, but also with an ideal of beauty that accepted his personal, fulsome image of womanhood. Equally important, especially for his early sculptures, were his formative years in the orbit of Symbolism under the influence of Maurice Denis and Ker-Xavier Roussel and the spirit of a classical Mediterranean tradition.

La Nuit (p. 47), first executed in small scale around 1902

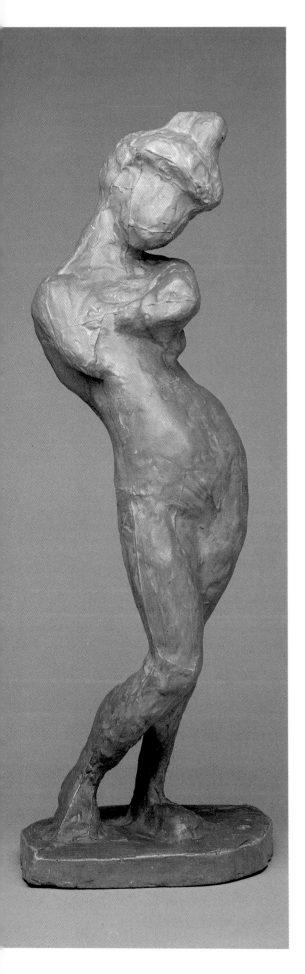

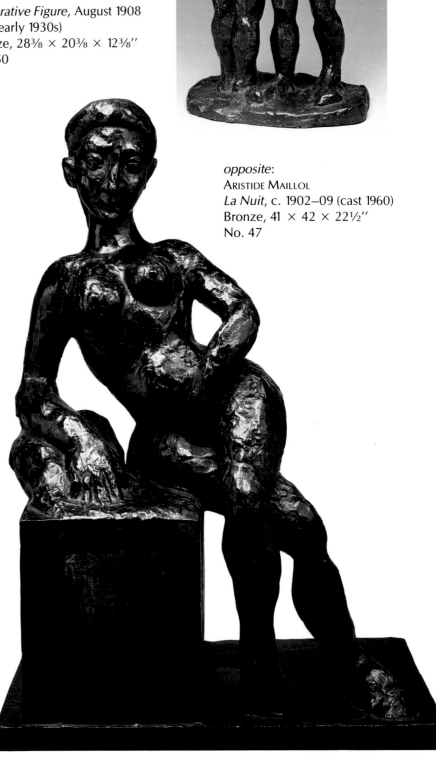

left:
HENRI MATISSE
Madeleine I, 1901 (cast 1903)
Plaster, painted terra-cotta,
23¾ × 9½ × 7½''
No. 48

right:
HENRI MATISSE
Two Negresses, 1908
Bronze, 18⅜ × 10½ × 7½''
No. 51

below:
HENRI MATISSE
Decorative Figure, August 1908
(cast early 1930s)
Bronze, 28⅜ × 20⅜ × 12⅜''
No. 50

opposite:
ARISTIDE MAILLOL
La Nuit, c. 1902–09 (cast 1960)
Bronze, 41 × 42 × 22½''
No. 47

HENRI MATISSE
Large Seated Nude, c. 1923–25
Bronze, 30½ × 31⅝ × 13⅝"
No. 52

and expanded into monumental proportions several years later, was one of Maillol's earliest and most compelling resolutions of these various stylistic strains. Not yet weakened by the stereotypical repetitions that would plague his later work, his classicism here is fresh and alive. It is strengthened by clear references to the volumetric stability of Egyptian art, providing an early example of modern archaizing, and also by an infusion of Symbolist mood. Personifications of night are not uncommon in earlier sculpture, but Maillol's is distinctive for its merging of compact, heavy form with the psychological weight of a profoundly deep state of rest, unconsciousness, and absorption in dreams. His figure connotes the regenerating power of sleep but also the voyage of self-discovery through dreaming. As Matisse had done with the seated nude, Maillol was able to reinvest an old theme with new meanings, conveyed partly through descriptive signals and partly through new formal logic.

Classicism represented for many sculptors of the early twentieth century, including Joseph Bernard, the young Raymond Duchamp-Villon, and to a lesser extent Antoine Bourdelle, a safe compromise with modernist stylization. For Henri Laurens, it was the conservative reversion to classical ideals of stability and order, which emerged so strongly after World War I, that together with the influence of Matisse pulled him out of an early, inventive Cubist idiom. In his *Grande Maternité* (1932; below), there are vestiges of Cubist faceting and

top:
HENRI MATISSE
Tiari, 1930
Bronze, 9⅝ × 7⅞ × 5⅝"
No. 53

above:
HENRI MATISSE
Head with Necklace, 1907
Bronze, 5⅞ × 5⅛ × 3¾"
No. 49

left:
HENRI LAURENS
Grande Maternité, 1932 (cast 1965)
Bronze, 21½ × 55 x 22½"
No. 41

CONSTANTIN BRANCUSI
The Kiss, 1907–08
(cast before 1914)
Plaster, 11 × 10¼ × 8½"
No. 7

simplification but they are absorbed in a far more descriptive figural style notable for its heavy baroque rhythms. This less challenging role was one Laurens would never fully escape.

Brancusi: Nature Stripped Bare

As Matisse and Maillol drew upon culturally and chronologically distant sources in redirecting the figurative tradition of Rodin, Constantin Brancusi followed similar influences to more extreme conclusions, nearly eliminating figural references altogether. For several years after his arrival in Paris in 1904 from Rumania, he was content to work in a vein of Rodinesque naturalism, still relatively new and exciting to him. Beginning with the *Prayer* (1907) and more strongly with *The Kiss* (1907–08; left), however, Brancusi established a radical new course. Crucial to this development was the atavistic ethos referred to above, which saw the Renaissance tradition of illusionism as finally reaching a dead end, and which called for new beginnings based in part on non-Western and nonclassical sources. Common to such models, whether Rumanian folk art or African sculpture, were an apparent simplicity and directness, a concern for underlying structure based on abstract relationships, and an embrace of the physical process of carving.

Despite a deep respect for Rodin, Brancusi felt the need to escape the Frenchman's influence, and *The Kiss* was his answer. He later wrote that in 1907 he started *la taille directe* (direct carving) with *The Kiss* and the *Wisdom of the Earth.* Possible sources for the monolithic, compressed, face-to-face motif of the former are numerous, from Romanesque sculpture to Polynesian fishing weights. And certainly the expressive wooden carvings of Paul Gauguin, seen to full advantage at the Gauguin retrospective in Paris of 1906, and André Derain's *Crouching Man* of 1907, with its squat proportions and minimalized detail, played important roles in the sculpture's conception. Against Rodin's sophisticated naturalism, Brancusi now proposed an elementary anatomy that not so much imitated life as encoded or symbolized it. The grace and beauty of Rodin's famous marble *Kiss* were countered with a calculated crudeness. The traditional, public nature of the theme took a turn toward the arcane and private, involving, as Sidney Geist has revealed, certain personal, biographical facts.[3] And for the effortless—some would have said "degenerate"—facility of nineteenth-century modeling, Brancusi substituted the labor of direct carving, with all its associations of honesty and artisanship.

In its own way, *The Kiss* broke new ground in sculpture as surely as Picasso's *Demoiselles d'Avignon* had a year earlier in painting. By relinquishing outer appearance for an inner essence of form and spirit, it had tremendous long-range ramifications, and shows at least an intuitive alignment with certain contem-

porary changes in scientific and philosophical thought. A shift from the descriptive to the analytic and from the *perceptual* to the *conceptual* characterizes both realms. To delve deeply into nature's structure and processes became Brancusi's lasting objec-

CONSTANTIN BRANCUSI
Portrait of Nancy Cunard, 1925–27
Walnut on marble base,
24¾ × 12½ × 4⅜"
No. 8

tive; yet he felt that science and reason had distinct limitations. As close as his work sometimes came to pure abstraction, he, like Picasso, never abandoned his ties to nature. The extreme distillations in works such as *Beginning of the World* (c. 1920), *Bird in Space* (1922), and the beautiful Nasher collection *Portrait of Nancy Cunard* (1925–27; p. 51) retain natural analogues. In the last of these sculptures, the special problems of representing an actual person are resolved by reducing certain characteristic forms such as the shape of a hairdo or the long narrow silhouette of a face to bare essences that still invoke the original. In this process, to poeticize remained as important as to analyze.

Picasso and Gonzalez: "Fragile Keys to Reality"

No artist demonstrates better than Pablo Picasso the unbounded potential of the figure as a vehicle of communication. Within the constant renewals and transformations of his artistic vision, the figure plays a central role, merging into different stylistic contexts, assuming varying degrees of recognizability, but remaining always present as a partner of invention and revelation. In sculpture as in painting, the figure gave Picasso an entry into empathy as well as a base for stylistic experiment. For an artist whose work was tied so irrevocably to his own biography and the human experience, figuration was unavoidable. Indeed, Picasso could claim: "There is no abstract art. You must always start with something. . . . Everything appears to us in the guise of a 'figure.' "[4]

Picasso enjoyed the physicality of sculpture and responded with a creativity that reached into almost every medium and material. His ability to fuse plastic means with a highly personal, sometimes cathartic symbolism is seen in both the *Head of a Woman* (1931–32; p. 54) and the *Pregnant Woman* (1950–59; p. 55). In the former, he sculpted his passion for the new love in his life, Marie-Thérèse Walter. Like the other five heads in the series, known collectively as the Boisgeloup Heads after their place of origin, Picasso's newly acquired Château de Boisgeloup, this work represents a diametrical shift away from the open-form metallic constructions constituting his immediately preceding sculptures, but intersects with developments in his painting. A new heaviness and fullness of volume, with solid sculptural presence, had begun to fill his paintings from 1931 onward, perhaps in response to the beauty of Marie-Thérèse and his internalized image of soft, voluptuous form. In the Boisgeloup Heads, he gave this new biomorphism full tangible expression.

The series of Heads begins with an image of classical serenity, moves on to an almost violent erotic displacement (as represented by the third Head, in the Nasher collection), and progresses to a simplified, nearly abstract resolution, providing in a sense a mirror to the course of lovemaking. Picasso later credited a characteristic exploitation of chance with the impulse for the series: he said that he put together a complicated construction of wire that looked like nothing until, in a shadow projected by a lamp on the wall, he recognized the features of Marie-Thérèse and went on to add plaster and complete it.[5] The series as a whole, however, rings of purposeful self-analysis.

Reference has often been made to the importance of Picasso's own Nimba mask from the Baga people in Africa for the conception of the Nasher Head. The ritual fertility meanings of this mask, of which Picasso was aware, would have given it added significance under the circumstances. One also wonders about the possible influence of Matisse's Heads of Jeannette, in which similar disfigurements take place, or that of ancient fertility figures. Whatever the mixture of sources, the impassioned coupling of male and female sexual symbols in the eyes, nose, cheeks, and mouth of this figure, embodied with such aggressive tangibility, still remains a startlingly inventive and revealing statement.

The rough, unfinished base of this sculpture, showing the buildup of a crude armature, represents a playful candor on Picasso's part about the process of sculpting, and a similar wit is evident in his *Pregnant Woman*. Françoise Gilot has recounted how Picasso, after he and Gilot settled in the French pottery town of Vallauris in 1948, acquired a small studio and began to make sculpture, often stopping by a nearby scrap heap of discards from local ceramists to look for usable pieces.[6] His knack for utilizing objects in an unforeseen context and thus transforming their definition had been a hallmark since his Cubist days, and in his sculpture of a standing, pregnant woman, Picasso made punning use of both the shapes and symbolism of clay vessels for the figure's distended breasts and stomach. Beyond the humor, however, lies a deeper personal meaning. Picasso wanted to have another child; Françoise Gilot did not. The sculpture thus can be seen as a kind of incantation to fertility, a voodoolike attempt at wish fulfillment. Within such works, removed a step or two from visual fact, are found what poet Paul Eluard referred to in Picasso's art as "the fragile key to the problem of reality."[7]

The variability of Picasso's work in sculpture troubled critics during his lifetime, as he veered closer to and then farther away from his painting and drawing styles. It continually inflected the course of modern sculpture, however, and had particular impact in the case of his fellow Spaniard, Julio Gonzalez. The celebrated collaboration between Picasso and Gonzalez from 1928 to 1931 served both artists well. Through Gonzalez's technical assistance and coaching, Picasso was able to realize some of his more daring ideas regarding metal constructions. And Picasso nurtured in Gonzalez the fruitful concept of a linear articulation of space and also demonstrated the potential of the semiabstract

PABLO PICASSO
Head of a Woman, 1931–32 (cast 1973)
Bronze, 34 × 14⅜ × 19¼"
No. 69

opposite, left:
PABLO PICASSO
Pregnant Woman, 1950–59
Bronze, 42¾ × 11⅜ × 13¼"
No. 70

opposite, right:
JULIO GONZALEZ
Woman with a Mirror, c. 1936–37 (cast c. 1980)
Bronze, 78½ × 21 × 23"
No. 35

figural personage. In work after work, Gonzalez built upon these concepts with his own techniques and gestural sensibility. *Woman with a Mirror* (c. 1936–37; p. 55) is one of his greatest accomplishments (represented in the Nasher collection by one of four bronze casts).

The ancestry of this sculpture lies in works such as Picasso's *Woman in a Garden* (1929–30), which is similar in its upright, jaunty posture, in such details as the spiky projections for hair, and in the constant punning between abstract and representational shapes. Both attack the massiveness of modeled bronzes with open networks of form, replacing the monolith with transparent construction. In the early decades of the century, the new art of Cubism and Constructivism had provided novel ways of imaging the body by eliminating the outside "skin," or surface envelope, by replacing solidity with space and light and joining external and internal form, and by multiplying the old single perspective. No account of modern figurative sculpture could fail to acknowledge contributions by Archipenko, the young Picasso, Gabo, Ivan Puni, and several others, which are highlighted in the accompanying essay by Nan Rosenthal. Constructed figures by these artists exist halfway between nature and biology on the one hand and geometry and technology on the other, while collectively providing for the new age a new symbol of man.

Gonzalez's work grew from this tradition. Distinguishing his figuration, however, is a special elegance of composition—a rhythmic cadence that unifies disjunctive form—and a somewhat playful humanistic element. With the exception of the war-inspired *Montserrat* (1937) and *Cactus Man* (1938–39), his figures are approachable and ingratiating, making the slight ghostliness of their impersonations of nature even more effective. Such works are not just exercises in structure. They reach into internal sources of inspiration to animate the inanimate and propose substitute realities that question observable fact.

Surrealist Surrogates: Miró, Ernst, and Arp

Although Gonzalez stands at the center of the abstraction-figuration spectrum, it was the formal aspect of his art that had greatest impact. The other side—the creation of symbolic, fictive human presences—can be traced, for example, in the development of David Smith but had little meaning for his fellow postwar artists. In the thirties and forties, however, it found a natural liaison in work by the Surrealists, who capitalized fully upon the mythological and metaphorical potentials of the personage device. Duchamp-Villon had characterized the task of modern sculpture as "the creation of unknown beings from elements which are always present but not apparent."[8] He searched in his own work for a human image appropriate to the

new, industrialized world, a metaphor for Machine Age power. The Surrealists, with their many "unknown beings," sought to explore different realities, those at once more timeless and inward. Although the concreteness of sculpture seemed at first to conflict with the very nature of efforts to replicate dreams and fantasy, artists soon found ways to give three-dimensional substance to these images of the mind. "Dream objects" played a particularly key role, but sculpture also was reconciled with the illusionistic side of Surrealist technique. Human and animal anatomy, through syncretism and reinvention and the use of *objets trouvés,* assumed myriad new forms in an open appeal to free association.

The *Moonbird* (1944–46; p. 38) of Joan Miró illustrates the fantastic zoologies that could result. Miró's earlier sculpture had consisted of assemblages of disparate objects, sometimes painted, always poetic and provocative. However, the experience of working with the master ceramist Josep Llorens Artigas led him to modeling. The first version of *Moonbird* was a small clay maquette that was later cast in bronze; twenty years later Miró expanded it to far more imposing proportions. Part humanoid, part bird, and part bull, this intriguing creature seems in turn playful, erotic, and threatening. Lunar symbolism enters in, as do phallic shapes and other references to fertility idols. Such conflations of sign and symbol, purposely denying logic, only enhanced for Miró and his fellow Surrealists an open-endedness of meaning.

In *Caress of a Bird* (1967; p. 57) and *Seated Woman and Child* (1967; p. 57), Miró returned to the assemblage technique, working with found, unrelated objects that he joined together, cast, and painted, all the while continuing his search for provocative equivalents of the figure. In the former, a tall, spindly, basket-headed peasant, a friendly bird perched on his head, is formed out of a long plinth that looks like an ironing board and a discarded bit of woodwork (with a hole that brings to mind Max Ernst's anatomical depressions in *Young Man with Beating Heart*). In the other, the chair itself is equated with a seated figure. Thus humor, reinforced by Miró's bright colors, becomes a part of the Surrealist strategy as much as automatism and mythology.

The same is often the case with Max Ernst, whose sculptures are generally lighter in mood than his frequently troubling and sometimes horrifying canvases. *Capricorn* (1948; p. 58), for example, the greatest and most monumental of his three-dimensional works, dispenses shamanistic and talismanic purposes with considerable wit. Produced as a "guardian" for Ernst's home in Sedona, Arizona, it consists of a stiffly ceremonial king with masklike face (deriving from one of several possible tribal sources) and the goat's horns of the zodiac sign for Capricorn, flanked by a truly comical queen who combines the attributes of a fish (Capricorn is half goat, half fish) with a Cycladic-idol's

body and the face of an Eskimo mask. He holds in his hand and lap an equally humorous child and dog. The king and queen may represent a family portrait of Ernst and his wife Dorothea Tanning, but the royal pair also assumed a magical role of warding off evil spirits. In form they recall certain familiar elements from Ernst's own bestiary of motifs, and show the built-up, syncretic nature of much Surrealist sculpture. In iconography they invoke a world of fetish, totem, and ritual which, more than mere affectation, represents a sincere effort to tap a vein of universal understanding in which myth, folklore, and even humor overlay shared experience.

The King Playing with the Queen (below), dating from 1944, shows Ernst's horned king in a previous incarnation but inhabiting a similar stagelike space, although here he imperiously manipulates the queen, who is just one of many chess pieces. Sexual and authoritarian control share the thematic focus with the game of chess itself, beloved by many Dada and Surrealist artists as a manifestation of strategy, intellect, and chance. Ernst's boardlike, pictorial format, in which symbolic narratives are enacted in a tabletop tableau, had recurring importance in the work of such artists as Alberto Giacometti, Henry Moore, Jean Arp, and David Smith. The construction of another, more minor keyed narrative is seen in Ernst's *Sister Souls* (1961; below), which is fully lighthearted in mood.

opposite:
MAX ERNST
Capricorn, 1948 (cast 1963–64)
Bronze, 89 × 82 × 55¼''
No. 23

below left:
MAX ERNST
The King Playing with the Queen, 1944 (cast 1954)
Bronze, 37⅞ × 33 × 21⅛''
No. 22

below right:
MAX ERNST
Sister Souls, 1961
Bronze, 36⅝ × 12 × 12½''
No. 24

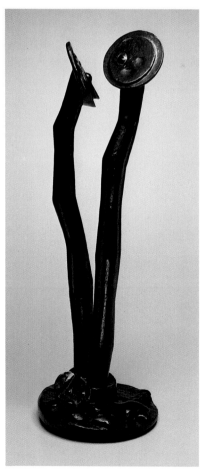

In contrast to the additive technique of much Surrealist sculpture, deriving from collage, that of Jean Arp is conceived as a whole and identifies closely with the organic processes of natural growth. Highly purified in form, its smooth, curving volumes imply an outward expansion from an inner, living nucleus, the opposite of Brancusi's process of subtraction and distillation. Arp had been a key ideologist in the development of both Dada and Surrealism, yet his art consistently rejected the pessimistic, nihilistic side of both movements, stressing instead the poetry and joy of natural creative forces. The biomorphism of a work such as *Torso with Buds* (1961; left) fuses the human and floral into Arp's own species of life and underscores the binding unity of the two. Particularly in its early phase, his sculpture showed a will for abstraction similar to that of Brancusi, but even then, natural references were never long suppressed. Thereafter, his so-called Concretions remained highly consistent in style for over three decades. Although far from polemic, they offered, in the troubled thirties and forties, a message of harmony and humanism with distinct political meaning. In the realm of figuration, they represent yet another way of reimagining anatomy.

Giacometti: Empathetic Perception

The early sculpture of Alberto Giacometti represents a high point in the Surrealist movement. Friend and close colleague of

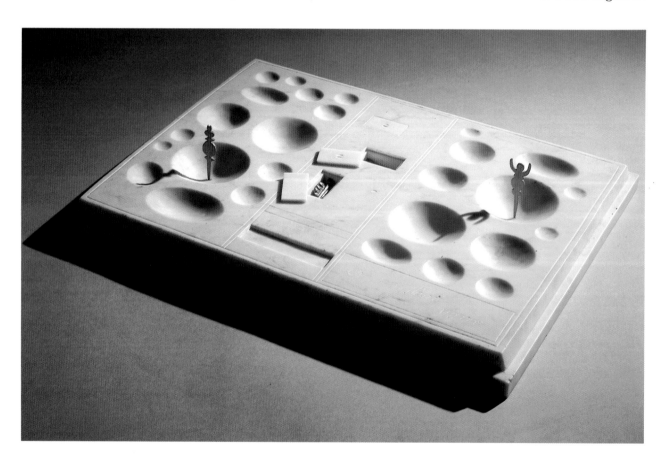

left:
ALBERTO GIACOMETTI
Spoon Woman, 1926–27 (cast 1954)
Bronze, 57¾ × 20 × 7¹⁵/₁₆″
No. 27

above:
ALBERTO GIACOMETTI
Head (Skull), 1934
Marble, 7³/₈ × 7³/₄ × 8¹/₈″
No. 28

opposite:
ALBERTO GIACOMETTI
No More Play, 1931–32
Marble, wood, and bronze,
1⁵/₈ x 22⁷/₈ x 17³/₄″
No. 27A

ALBERTO GIACOMETTI
Two Figurines, c. 1945
Metal with gold leaf, each 1½ ×
⁷⁄₁₆ × ⁷⁄₁₆"
No. 29

many of the founding members of the group, he eschewed a natural facility for representational modeling and draftsmanship in favor of a pictographic mode in which symbolic forms and personages enact with mystery, eroticism, and violence a series of gripping psychodramas. Such works as *Woman with Her Throat Cut* (1932), *Palace at 4 A.M.* (1933), and *Point to the Eye* project an intensity undiminished by time. *Spoon Woman* (1926–27; p. 61) and *Head* (1934; p. 61) are part of this development and embody many of the most important principles of Giacometti's early sculpture.

Spoon Woman was Giacometti's most monumental work to date. Its derivation from African anthropomorphic spoon figures is now well-known, a sign of the artist's enthusiastic participation in the primitivizing trends of the period, and it shares with his *Couple* of 1926 or 1927 and *Woman* of 1928 a sexually diagrammatic language of the female body. The large curving receptacle stands for the torso but also symbolizes genitalia and fecundity. The head and bosom are reduced to faceted blocks. And the face is indicated by only a symbolic crescent. Powerfully monolithic, and thereby opposed to the transparent, skeletal representations of the figure that would soon enter Giacometti's work, she presides as a totem of fertility over his many sexual fantasies of the period.

Head partakes of the necrology that was so strong a concurrent theme. Although the prefix "Cubist" was assigned to the title at some point, suggesting a formal exercise in geometric structure, and although Giacometti did respond in several Surrealist works to Cubist influence, he made the crucial point in his own writings that the sculpture represents not just a head but a skull. The fact that he carved it soon after his father's death in 1933 is undoubtedly relevant. A potent memento mori, its invocation of the blank silence of death is particularly effective in the cool whiteness of the marble as opposed to its bronze versions. It also prefigures the enigmatic masked visage in his *Invisible Object* of 1934–35.

Like Ernst and Miró, Giacometti responded to the urgency of "being modern" with the somewhat paradoxical attempt to link the modern psyche to a timeless continuum. He drew freely from any number of cultural sources, followed the urgings of his own subconscious, and invented a new code of symbolic and figural motifs. Suddenly, however, he came to feel that working from the imagination was empty and futile, and in a dramatic personal reversal, he rejected Surrealist doctrine to return to the human figure as a canon for his art. He wrote:

> I knew . . . I would be obliged someday to sit down on a stool in front of a model and try to copy what I saw. Even if there was no hope of succeeding. I dreaded in a way being obliged to come to that, and I knew that it was inevitable.[9]

Much has been written about the "phenomenology of perception" in Giacometti's later work, weighing his own claim—stated simply, that he wanted to capture as realistically and empirically as possible the figure as he saw it—against seemingly clear signs of emotional and psychological interpretation. The Nasher collection is notably strong in work from his later period, including two of the tiny figurines Giacometti made in the first phases of his return to naturalism, the great *Chariot* of 1950, three outstanding portrait busts of his brother Diego, and one of the classically characteristic standing women. *Three Figures* (1949; below), one of the few paintings in which he deals directly with sculptural motifs, is also part of the collection. As a whole, the group lends insights into Giacometti's struggle, through his sculpture, with questions of perception, vision, and knowledge, and how they interrelate.

The *Two Figurines* (c. 1945; p. 62) are part of the series of works that Giacometti produced in his hotel room in Geneva during World War II. As Jean Paul Sartre jokingly stated, when the artist brought these studies back to Paris, they all fit into a

above:
ALBERTO GIACOMETTI
Venice Woman III, 1956
Bronze, 47½ × 13½ × 6⅞"
No. 34

left:
ALBERTO GIACOMETTI
Three Figures, 1949
Oil on canvas, 18⁵⁄₁₆ × 22¹⁄₁₆"
No. 92

above left:
ALBERTO GIACOMETTI
Bust of Diego, 1954
Painted bronze, 15½ × 13¼ × 8¼″
No. 31

above center:
ALBERTO GIACOMETTI
Diego in a Sweater, 1954
Painted bronze, 19 × 10¾ × 8¼″
No. 33

above right:
ALBERTO GIACOMETTI
Diego in a Cloak, 1954
Painted bronze, 15⅛ × 13½ × 8¾″
No. 32

opposite:
ALBERTO GIACOMETTI
The Chariot, 1950
Painted bronze, 56¼ × 24¼ × 27″
No. 30

couple of matchboxes. Giacometti's working conditions and his attempt to portray silhouettes seen from a distance forced him to think in small scale, and in the strain of his return to the figure, he reworked the images until, as they got smaller and smaller, some fragmented into dust. Even at this early stage of development, his surfaces took on a rough, worked, weathered look, suggesting the transitory effects on vision of changing light, reflection, and atmosphere. Giacometti would occasionally enhance this "impressionism" by hand-painting the surfaces of his plasters and bronzes with mottled, subdued colors, as in the three busts of his brother Diego (1954; above). His pronounced elongation of shape, whether or not influenced by such sources as Etruscan figurines, gives an active role to surrounding, negative space, which seems to mask or bite into the figure's volume.

These combined effects are seen again in the *Venice Woman III* (1956; p. 63), where, in another characteristic adjustment, the feet of the figure are enlarged to counteract the natural tendency to look at first, and to overemphasize, the head. Produced in a furious campaign of preparation for the Venice Biennale of 1956, this figure is one of fifteen made in rapid succession, as Giacometti modeled, destroyed, and remodeled

virtually the same form, stopping only occasionally to preserve, with the help of Diego, a particular stage with a cast.

The same ongoing search for an elusive resolution is seen in his many portraits of his brother such as *Bust of Diego, Diego in a Sweater,* and *Diego in a Cloak* (1954, p. 64). Paintings, drawings, and sculptures of Diego figured in Giacometti's work from its very beginnings. There was no one he knew better, and yet, the sheer extent of this intimacy frustrated the artist as he attempted to transfer with his hands what he saw and what he *knew* into clay. An ultimate, definitive representation, therefore, became impossible, and each sculpture served instead as a frozen moment in the ongoing process of looking and thinking, an attempt to bridge not just a physical but also a psychological gap between individuals. Giacometti occasionally spoke about looking so hard at someone that the image became more and more confused until he could no longer decipher what he really wanted to see. Each sculpture, no matter how small the nuances of difference, was a fresh attempt to overcome these barriers.

None of Giacometti's late works illustrates better the interaction of physiological modes of perception with the subjective and conceptual than *The Chariot* (1950; p. 65). Giacometti himself said the purpose of this sculpture was to elevate the figure into space in order to achieve an all-around, distant perspective. This strictly empirical program, however, conflicts with its clearly poetic implications involving the abrupt discrepancy in scale between figure and wheels, the tenuous balance of the frail figure and the mysterious meaning of the wheels, conjuring up both the antique past and mechanized present. The original intent of the sculpture as a public monument may have prompted Giacometti to think in particularly metaphorical terms. But whatever the specific interpretation, we are assured that Giacometti did not completely abandon in the fifties his sensitivity for mystery and personal meanings.

Henry Moore: Challenging the Old Masters

There is no more widely known, familiar, and distinct figurative sculpture from our century than that of Henry Moore. For well over sixty years, Moore explored the expressive potentials of the human figure, replacing fidelity to nature as a guiding principle with imaginative reconfiguration. Knowledge of a broad range of early traditions, including Pre-Columbian, Egyptian, African, and Renaissance art, nurtured his stylistic development, and brief involvements with nonobjective art and Surrealism left a lasting legacy in his formal language. In contrast to the ideational and fantasy basis of Surrealist sculpture, however, Moore consistently drew inspiration from natural form, even as his work veered in nonfigurative directions. His stimuli were visual rather than theoretical. Landscape, rock formations, bones, flints, and, of course, the configurations of the human and animal anatomy are elements of the physical environment that served repeatedly as sources. Likewise, his sculptural means—carving and modeling versus the additive processes of Surrealist and Constructivist sculpture—helped generate an art of real, solid, tangible mass with tactile and sensuous appeal that triggers an internalized physical response.

Moore's work proclaims that the body is an infinitely complex organism capable of yielding endless provocative interpretations. The strategies in his own approach had been thoroughly rehearsed by the late forties: horizontal segmentation of the figure, introduction of space through tunneling and deep holes, analogizing with other natural forms, and the mixing of internal and external bodily parts. Repeated even further, however, such devices could produce fresh results. The three large works from the Nasher collection—*Three Piece No. 3: Vertebrae, Two Piece Reclining Figure No. 9,* and *Reclining Figure: Angles*—all came relatively late in Moore's career and reflect three different viewpoints in the ongoing dialogue in his late work between abstraction and figuration. *Three Piece No. 3: Vertebrae* (1968; p. 68), the most abstract of the three, seems to speak a language of purified sculptural form not unlike Arp's Concretions of the thirties and forties. It is faithfully based, however, on certain flint stones Moore kept around the studio, their forms, when enlarged and smoothed, resembling individual vertebrae from an animal's backbone. There are distant echoes of Moore's segmented and abstracted "figures" from 1934. Moreover, the compositional dynamics of touching, cradling, and enveloping, all invoke human bodily movement and sensation.

In *Two Piece Reclining Figure No. 9* (1968; p. 69), the figure is a more immediate point of reference but is still largely subsumed into bony, sinewy masses that also suggest rocky outcroppings or heavy pieces of hardened lava. Such open-ended associations were no less important in Moore's work than in that of the Surrealists, but in his case it involves a more strictly visual, physical poetry.

As if the artist felt that occasional returns to realism were necessary in order to balance the abstract side of his work, several naturalistic figures, such as *Reclining Figure: Angles* (1979; p. 69), punctuate his later production. With nobility and grace, the forms of this giant lady spread horizontally in a relaxed but subtly modulated pose. Seen against the landscape, her rhythms complement and add to those of the natural environment. Once again, as throughout Moore's voluminous oeuvre, the temptation arises to interpret such figures, in their organic and geologic universality, as primal earth mothers symbolic of feminine principles of birth, fecundity, and regeneration. Moore himself rejected an overly Freudian or symbolic reading of his work. Like that of Arp, however, it stimulates a larger response beyond an immediate appreciation of the forms themselves. It is capable

top left:
HENRY MOORE
Maquette for Large Torso: Arch,
1962 (cast 1971)
Bronze, 4⅛ × 3⅛ × 2¹³⁄₁₆″
No. 58

top right:
HENRY MOORE
Time-Life Screen: Maquette No. 2, 1952
Bronze, 7⅛ × 12¾ × 1″
No. 57

above:
HENRY MOORE
Three Piece No. 3: Vertebrae, 1968
Polished bronze, 41⅛ × 93 ×
48″, including base
No. 59

opposite, above:
HENRY MOORE
Two Piece Reclining Figure No. 9, 1968
Bronze, 56⅜ × 96 × 52″,
including base
No. 60

opposite, below:
HENRY MOORE
Reclining Figure: Angles, 1979 (cast 1980)
Bronze, 48¼ × 90¼ × 61¾″,
including base
No. 61

of making us feel anew our own bodies and provokes thought about our relationship to a broader natural world.

The figure in early modern sculpture was both a bastion for conservativism and a handmaiden of reform. For the less adventuresome sculptor, fidelity to nature remained a compelling goal, a reliable standard of achievement, and indeed, a buffer against avant-garde extremism. To others, however, the figure provided on the one hand an avenue of emotive identification and on the other, a reference point for artistic license that challenged or reinterpreted nature, yielding alternative realities which, in Picasso's famous formulation, are lies leading to the truth. To the advantages of empathy and access that artists saw in figuration can be added the sense it gave of scale and proportion, of gravity and orientation in space. As Henry Moore put it: "We make the kind of sculpture we make because we are the shape we are, because we have the proportions we have. All those things make us respond to form and shape in certain ways."[10]

Accepting the "given" of natural reference, possibilities of stylistic and iconographic variation have proven inexhaustible. In the hands of Gabo, Archipenko, and Boccioni, for example, the figure accommodated formal breakthroughs regarding space, mass, light, and structure of the highest conceptual order. Figurative works by Belling and Schlemmer project a chillingly technological vision of the future, while those of Barlach, Lehmbruck, and other Germans reflect the disorders of the cultural present. With Brancusi, Moore, and Arp, figuration merged into an advanced abstraction, leaving only a rarefied, but critical, distillate of natural form. For the Surrealist, symbolic body language conveyed the deepest of private mythologies. Matisse always honored the structural order of the body and therefore may appear more conservative, but his analysis and manipulation of that order voices an intense personal expressiveness. For Picasso, the body was the nourishing core of his art, leading to seemingly endless ideas on evocative reconfiguration, while Gonzalez's welded beings gave surprisingly gentle personality to the harsh language of metallic assemblage.

The wealth of formal invention that these and other figurative artists enacted, and the depth of revelation in their work, make their contribution to the modernist enterprise central and vital. Other artists, driven by an ideological commitment to the new and revolutionary, might consider figuration passé (Naum Gabo, for example, when required to include a Constructivist Venus in his set designs for Diaghilev's *La Chatte*, said he could no longer possibly make a figure and gave the task instead to his brother, Antoine Pevsner). And indeed, formalist readings of the history of modern sculpture are contrived against the full humanistic import of the figurative tradition. Led in part by younger artists who have infused new life into figural language, we now look to this tradition with greater attention to its nuances of meaning. Henry Moore's observation voiced twenty-five years ago is more relevant than ever: "If it were only a matter of making a pleasurable relationship between forms, sculpture would lose its fundamental importance."[11]

NOTES

1. James Lord, *Giacometti: A Biography* (New York, 1985), pp. 153–54.

2. Albert Elsen, *The Sculpture of Matisse* (New York, 1972), pp. 50–53.

3. Sidney Geist, *Brancusi/The Kiss* (New York, 1978), pp. 43–44.

4. Conversation recorded by Christian Zervos, 1935; see Dore Ashton, *Picasso on Art: A Selection of Views* (New York, 1980), p. 9.

5. Roland Penrose, *Picasso: His Life and Work* (London, 1958), p. 244.

6. Françoise Gilot and Carleton Lake, *Life with Picasso* (New York, 1964), p. 292.

7. Paul Eluard, *A Pablo Picasso* (Geneva and Paris, 1947), p. 38.

8. Manuscript notes, estate of the artist; see George Heard Hamilton and William Agee, *Raymond Duchamp-Villon* (New York, 1967), p. 112.

9. Lord, 1985, pp. 153–54.

10. Philip James, ed., *Henry Moore on Sculpture* (New York, 1967), p. 115.

11. James, ed., 1967, p. 115.

SCULPTURE IN THE CONSTRUCTIVIST TRADITION

NAN
ROSENTHAL

The Nasher collection is particularly rich in early modern figurative sculpture that extends the tradition of a fictive world separate from the viewer's real one. It contains as well many significant examples that challenge this tradition: representational and abstract sculpture made in the Constructivist mode, from its tentative beginnings in the so-called Cubist sculpture of the teens to its ironic flourishing in the anti-illusionistic Minimal sculpture of the sixties.

What historians of modern sculpture mean by the term "Constructivism" remains confusing and requires explanation. When they speak of the Constructivist movement, the subject under discussion may be—and technically ought to be—the artifacts and ideology of a group of artists working in Russia in the wake of the revolution of 1917.

Beginning in Moscow in 1921, this group, which came to include Rodchenko, Stepanova, Medunetsky, Gan, and the Stenberg brothers, labeled themselves Constructivists. They identified strongly with the goals of the new political order. While they soon began to work in a range of mediums, from textile, furniture, and stage design to photography, photomontage, and architecture, their constructed objects, both those they at first showed as sculpture in exhibitions and those with which they soon afterward taught their students about space, volume, color, and texture, drew heavily on the formal language of the radically innovative abstract three-dimensional art of the pre-revolutionary years, notably Tatlin's counter-reliefs of 1915.

Strongly influenced by Picasso's Cubist collage and relief constructions of 1912 and 1913, Tatlin built his abstract objects from ordinary materials, such as wood, glass, and iron, rather

above:
RAYMOND DUCHAMP-VILLON
Torso of a Young Man, 1910
Terra-cotta, 22⅜ × 12¾ × 16½"
No. 16

opposite:
RAYMOND DUCHAMP-VILLON
Large Horse, 1914 (second enlargement by Marcel Duchamp, 1966)
Bronze, 59½ × 57 × 34"
No. 20

73

than from materials associated with high art, such as marble or bronze. And, in a startling fashion, his objects shared the ambient space of the observer—as, for example, when they stretched across the corners of a room. Unlike most sculpture that preceded them, they were not set off in an imaginary space, that is, a space made conceptually separate from the viewer's own by the convention of the pedestal and the convention that representational, narrative art depicts a world distinct from the viewer's immediate one.

The postrevolutionary Russians who followed Tatlin and labeled themselves Constructivists sought to banish the concept that art is something precious and separate from daily life. They intended their work to be functional, utilitarian, and linked to mass production. As one of their historians put it: "Art as such had no place in the new society. In its stead 'intellectual production' would serve the new communist collective by fusing the formal experience gained from making abstract constructions in three dimensions with the ideology of Marxism and the constraints of industrial production."[1]

However, in the West, almost from the time that a considerable body of East European abstract constructions in three dimensions were exhibited in Berlin in the early twenties, the term "Constructivist" has been and continues to be employed as a kind of stylistic label, referring to characteristic qualities of modern sculpture by a wide group of avant-garde artists of different nationalities. While some of these artists shared aspects of the Utopian vision of the Russians who first called themselves Constructivists, most—including other Russians such as Archipenko, Gabo, and Pevsner—did not see their works as studies of form leading to the manufacture of objects of utilitarian function or political message. Rather, they intended them to be works of art made for aesthetic contemplation. Yet within this continuation of art for art's sake, there was usually a commitment to modernity per se, often in the guise of materials and shapes that suggested machine technology.

Three qualities have come to typify Constructivist sculpture understood as a widely practiced style: a tendency to employ a geometric vocabulary of form; the substitution of volumes of air for volumes of mass; and the employment of additive techniques for making sculptural objects, which, instead of being carved from stone or modeled from clay and cast in bronze, are assembled from a variety of materials.

The tendency to employ a geometric vocabulary of form drew from a number of sources, not least the Euclidean public domain of circles, rectangles, and triangles and their volumetric equivalents. It was affected as well by the work of the first generation of modern architects, such figures as Perret and Garnier in France, Wright in America, and Behrens, Olbrich, and Loos in Central Europe, who were all concerned with an architectonic expression of structure and a rejection of elaborate ornament.

Most important, the tendency to adopt a language of geometry derived from a fascination with successive styles of Cubist painting: the blocky, "cubified" figures of early Cubism, with their link to tribal sculpture; the angled, modeled shards of Analytic Cubism; and the broad, flat planes of later Synthetic Cubism.

There are six works in the Nasher collection by Raymond Duchamp-Villon, and several of them exemplify this trajectory. At Puteaux, to the west of Paris, in the studios of Duchamp-Villon and his older brother, Jacques Villon, the issues of Cubism were analyzed and debated—by them, by their younger brother, Marcel Duchamp, and by Léger, Gleizes, Metzinger, Gris, de la Fresnaye, and Archipenko. Some members of the Puteaux group constituted themselves as rivals to the formal inventors of Cubist painting who lived across Paris, Picasso and Braque, and some used the new style not only to change pictorial space but to express interest in the mathematical and mechanical elements of modern life and to paint their commitment to social change.

Duchamp-Villon's terra-cotta *Torso of a Young Man* (1910; p. 73) absorbs the simplicity and directness of archaic Greek sculpture and the truncated limbs of Rodin's *Walking Man* (1877–78), whose stride it changes to an urgent, forward expression of motion; the *Torso*'s smooth modeling and clear definition of planes suggest the proto-Cubist male figures in Picasso's paintings of 1905–06. With his portrait of the essayist of modern life, the Baudelaire head (1911; p. 76), Duchamp-Villon further reduced his sculptural masses. The following year, with *Maggy* (p. 76), a portrait of the wife of the poet Georges Ribemont-Dessaignes, Duchamp-Villon drew upon the bulky geometric convexities and concavities of Picasso's painting of 1908–09, as well as on his freedom to caricature.

Duchamp-Villon's greatest work before his premature death at the end of World War I, the *Horse* of 1914, is represented in the Nasher collection by a posthumous bronze, the *Large Horse* (p. 72), an enlargement made in 1966 under the supervision of Marcel Duchamp. It was Duchamp-Villon's intention to cast this work in steel, the paradigmatic Machine Age material. One of numerous studies leading to its final plaster, the *Horse and Rider II* (1914; p. 77), is in the Nasher collection, as well, and it enables us to observe part of the process by which the artist engaged planar and curvilinear forms to convert organic equine anatomy into a coiled-to-spring metaphor for mechanical horsepower. *The Large Horse* we see today may be read in two ways: as the most compelling example of Duchamp-Villon's optimism about modern technology, which he expressed in a kind of late-Symbolist, compressed narrative about an animal converting before our very eyes into automobilic energy, and as an example of his artist-brothers' later understanding that his optimism may not have been justified. It speaks to the complexity of the *Horse* that, from the vantage point of the present, we may interpret the

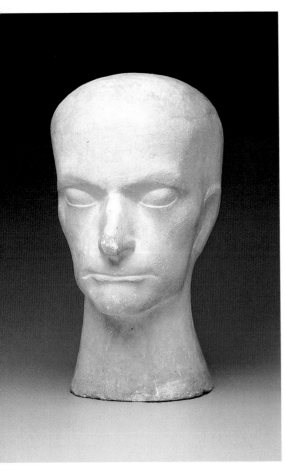

appearance of this 1914 conception as ominous and threatening.[2]

Synthetic Cubist painting emerged in the course of 1913 from the medium of collage into a style of figuration that interlocked flat, brightly colored, geometric planes; these were much larger than the tonally graduated, shifting facets of Analytic Cubism. These larger, opaque planes, with their sharply defined silhouettes, looked as if they had been cut out and pasted to the canvas. It was on this kind of geometricization and on this kind of Cubist painting that Jacques Lipchitz, the Lithuanian sculptor who had come to Paris in 1909, drew for his carved stone figures of the war years. The Nashers' *Seated Woman* (1916; p. 80) has the planar attributes of a Synthetic Cubist personage, one who seems to have stepped from the flatness of the painting style into three solid dimensions. Having thus become a tactile, even portable object, the woman nonetheless appears immobile, made static by her stone material, its unify-

above:
RAYMOND DUCHAMP-VILLON
Baudelaire, 1911
Plaster, 16 × 8⅞ × 10⅛''
No. 17

right:
RAYMOND DUCHAMP-VILLON
Maggy, 1912 (cast 1957)
Bronze, 28 × 13¼ × 15''
No. 18

ing, monochrome coloration, and her restful posture. She sits on a stool with her legs crossed, her left shoulder reading in a clear outline. Her head is indicated by two planes: a tilted wedge that bears a single circle to signify both mouth and eyes and a vertical plinth that functions both as the back of her head and as her backbone.

As Lipchitz captured the "look" of Synthetic Cubist painting in his sculpture between 1914 and 1918, the American John Storrs, in his series of Forms in Space made in the twenties, achieved the geometricized appearance yet not the expression of structure characteristic of the great setback skyscrapers, built or fantasized, of the Machine Age decade. The son of a Chicago architect, Storrs spent much of his adult life in France, where he was trained as a sculptor, at first in the Ecole des Beaux-Arts tradition and then, in the years just before World War I, at Rodin's studio. His figurative work of the late teens blended Synthetic Cubist and Futurist sculpture with the inventive mannerisms of the Vienna Secession, heralding the Art Deco style years in advance of its appearance.

The Nashers' work by Storrs, the *Study in Architectural Forms* (1927; p. 80), is one of the Forms in Space group. First conceived in plaster, it is unusual in being symmetrical, cast from one material, and patinated in one color. In the twenties the artist more typically used mosaiclike arrangements of variously colored metals, stones, mirrors, and plastics. While the *Study in Architectural Forms* bears a strong resemblance to Malevich's architectural models of the same decade, it seems improbable that Storrs was familiar with the Russian painter's plaster studies of the interplay of vertical and horizontal rectangular volumes. More likely, the inspiration for Storrs's essentially mimetic Forms in Space was the *Chicago Tribune* Tower architectural competition of 1922 and his recollection of the remarkable nineteenth-century skyscrapers of his birthplace, to which he often returned. In its careful, straightforward, and elegant detailing of solid volumes and its cultivation of the play of light on an architectural subject, the Nashers' *Study* by Storrs links the artist closely, despite his association with Europe, to American Precisionist painters of his generation, particularly to the work of Charles Sheeler.

Although the tendency to employ geometricized forms has continued for decades to characterize much sculpture in the Constructivist tradition, a number of artists drew on Cubist painting not only for its grid-anchored compositions, angled shards, and flat planes. In a more subtle fashion, they comprehended what the radical new handling of spatial illusion in Analytic Cubist painting implied for three-dimensional art in terms of methods to create volume.

Archipenko and Gabo, for example, invented new ways to build volume in sculpture by substituting for the solid mass of traditional sculpture areas of void or empty space bounded by open planes; this rejection of bulk for air came to be termed "virtual volumes." One of their important sources for this concept were Picasso's and Braque's still lifes, portraits, and landscapes of the years from 1909 to 1911. The building blocks that the painters used to create the illusion of depth or roundness on a two-dimensional surface were nearly monochrome, seemingly transparent, angled tonal shards. These shards, or faceted planes, were as gradually modeled from light to dark as an arm shaded by Raphael to represent cylindrical bulk. However, unlike an arm by Raphael, they were unbounded by outlines at one or two edges. Because they were modeled, the shards constituted pictorial signs of roundness, yet because they were unbounded and lit unnaturalistically, from a number of different directions, they did not depict the full bulk of the subjects they described. It was up to the observer to exploit his memory of a subject's shape in the round and, in his mind's eye, fill in from the edge of one light-filled plane to the edge of another, to imagine a volume.

Alexander Archipenko, who had moved from the Ukraine

to Paris in 1908 and was intimately familiar with theories of Cubism through his friendship with Léger and his participation in the Puteaux discussions, introduced virtual volume to his sculpture in several ways exemplified by the Nashers' *Woman Combing Her Hair* (1914 or 1915; p. 81). The figure is a nude whose right arm is raised up to touch the top of the left side of her head, in just the sort of gesture we might expect from the title of the work. The void or hole that results from this arm-akimbo posture, between her arm and where the substance of her head should be, becomes the illusion of the head itself; as Archipenko often put it: "Sculpture may begin where space is encircled by material." To create still other areas of shaped empty space in the *Woman*, Archipenko exploited the kind of play of convexities against concavities that Picasso had initiated with his Cubist sculpture of 1909, the bronze *Head of a Woman* (Fernande Olivier). For example, the nude's curved right breast is more an empty cup than a solid apple, an effect achieved by merging the breast with the hollow of the figure's armpit. Her thighs, positioned in contrapposto, angle inward to meet one another so steeply that they, too, imply rounded flesh where there is an absence of material. With other versions of this work, Archipenko lightened the mass of his sculpture by using highly reflective surfaces, with the result that the play of light on the object has the effect of dematerializing it. But it was by penetrating solid material to create shaped voids, as with the nude's head, that Archipenko made his most influential contribution. It was an approach to sculptural form that also came to be termed "negative space," and its effects can be seen in later abstract sculpture in the Nasher collection, most vividly in Barbara Hepworth's *Squares with Two Circles* (1963; p. 82).

In the decade of the thirties, Hepworth became one of the leaders of abstract art in Britain. From almost the start of her career, when, early in the decade, she was allied with the Abstraction-Création artists in Paris, she identified herself with the Constructivist movement; in the later thirties, she became one of the founders in Britain of the Constructivist group called Circle. The artists of the group published an important collection of theoretical essays in 1937, titled *Circle* and subtitled *International Survey of Constructive Art.* The volume became a significant disseminator of Constructivist theory in the West; it featured the ideas of Gabo and Mondrian, both of whom had moved to Britain from the Continent by the late thirties because of Nazism. Gabo in particular intermingled with younger British painters and sculptors of like mind, such as Hepworth, Ben Nicholson, and Henry Moore.

The Nashers' *Squares with Two Circles* is one of Hepworth's finest realizations of her common motif: an abstract vertical monolithic form pierced by one or two circular openings. These openings permit sheer space to flow through a work and allow the environment surrounding the object to become

part of the viewer's experiencing of it. Like the slabs of Stonehenge, the Nashers' bronze is monumental in scale without overwhelming the actualities of human height. In the wooded acreage behind the Nashers' Dallas house, an experience of this sculpture may evoke a balanced nature/culture dialogue, between Hepworth's conspicuously cerebral alignments of squares and circles and the vertical reach of the tall trees.

The concept of the virtual volume is one associated even more with Naum Gabo's sculpture than with Archipenko's. From the period of his Constructed Heads and Torsos of 1915 to 1917, in which flat, intersecting planes imply volumes the viewer's eye fills in from the edge of one plane to the edge of another, Gabo was deeply concerned with making sculpture consisting of volumes of space rather than mass. It was an idea he published first in Moscow in his Realistic Manifesto of 1920 and again, with didactic thoroughness, in *Circle* in 1937, where he demonstrated the concept by illustrating two cubes, one representing a solid volume of mass and the other a cubic volume of space formed from two planes bisecting at right angles.

Through most of his career, in the Head and Torso open volumes of the late teens, the opaque and clear-plastic abstract constructions with architectural themes which he made in the twenties, and his work of the forties and fifties, Gabo varied approaches to this basic notion. In the Nashers' *Linear Construction in Space No. 1 (Variation)* (1942–43; p. 83), a late-fifties version of the sculpture which Gabo had designed in England some years earlier, the artist constructed the planes for his virtual volume from two kinds of transparent, light-catching material: colorless plexiglass and clear nylon filament strung in curves over notches in the plastic frame. The interior volume implied by the stringing is elliptical in shape. However, the volumetric effect is ephemeral, for, as the observer moves, ambient light cast on the object shifts, and the viewer's ability to read the curved strings as continuous, volume-shaping planes shifts as well.

Gabo's older brother, Antoine Pevsner, applied Gabo's theoretical principles to his own sculpture. Yet during much of his career he customarily used opaque, impenetrable materials as in the reddish-brown bronze work in the Nasher collection, *Dynamic Projection at Thirty Degrees* (1950–51; p. 83). One of the outstanding examples of Pevsner's Developable Surface series, which the artist began in the late thirties, the work consists of conelike open volumes that seem to twist against each other. Their appearance of torque forms a thrusting diagonal to create a Baroque *illusion* of motion; the effect differs from the diagonals so common to Russian postrevolutionary art, which typically were graphic *signs* of motion, evocative of the intent to move technology and society. The surfaces of the *Dynamic Projection* were formed, in the originating model that preceded casting, by soldering or welding metal rods in alignment so as to

above:
ALEXANDER ARCHIPENKO
Woman Combing Her Hair, 1914 or 1915
Bronze, 14⅛ × 3⅝ × 3³⁄₁₆″
No. 2

opposite, left:
JACQUES LIPCHITZ
Seated Woman, 1916
Stone, 42½ × 11¼ × 12¼″
No. 45

opposite, right:
JOHN STORRS
Study in Architectural Forms, 1927
Steel, 31³⁄₁₆ × 7⅝ × 4⅝″
No. 89

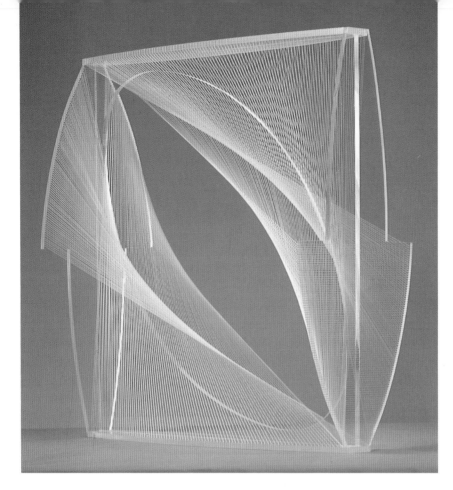

opposite:
BARBARA HEPWORTH
Squares with Two Circles, 1963
(cast 1964)
Bronze, 124 × 65 × 30''
No. 36

left:
NAUM GABO
*Linear Construction in Space No. 1
(Variation)*, 1942–43 (fabricated
c. 1957–58)
Plexiglass with nylon mono-
filament, 24¾ × 24¾ × 9½''
No. 26

below:
ANTOINE PEVSNER
*Dynamic Projection at Thirty
Degrees*, 1950–51 (cast after 1960)
Bronze, 37⅛ × 74¼ × 36''
No. 68

create curved planes. Thus the sculpture began as a constructed assemblage rather than as a shell modeled in clay or plaster.

If the tonal shards of Analytic Cubist painting were the most significant stimulus for the invention of the virtual volume, the creation of such airy, open volumes was no doubt encouraged by the simultaneous appearance of International Style architecture. From its prehistory in such buildings as Walter Gropius's Fagus shoe factory of 1911, the International Style featured buildings whose structure was manifestly visible through transparent glass skins. Such curtain-wall architecture shaped space, de-emphasized mass, and encouraged the onlooker to believe in the lucidity of its techniques of construction. Some of the idealism behind this architecture recurs in nostalgic and perhaps ironic form in an important series of paintings by Fernard Léger from 1950, compositions on the theme of building construction. In the Nashers' gouache *The Construction Workers* (1950; p. 86), one of numerous studies for the great oil of the same title, the painter's feelings about the potential of I-beam scaffolding to improve man's lot seem complex. Painted at a moment when Europe needed to reconstruct its buildings and, in Léger's view, its social structure, the work shows us both the rational three-dimensional grid of modern architecture and the workers whose labor mounts it.

In addition to the adoption of a geometric vocabulary and replacing volumes of mass with volumes of air, the third significant characteristic of sculptors whom historians term Constructivist was their tendency, even among practitioners of highly varying formal styles, to abandon modeling and carving for additive techniques; that is, three-dimensional objects were created by assembling materials and literally engaging in construction. This, too, may be traced to the pictorial source of Cubism, specifically to Picasso's and Braque's invention in 1912 of collage. The rapidity with which such artists as Tatlin learned from Picasso's collage and metal- or wood-relief constructions of 1912 onward, and in turn spread their influence, still astonishes. Tatlin's use of "found" quotidian materials—sometimes, unadorned junk—in his frameless, abstract reliefs of the mid-teens was quickly absorbed by his countryman, Ivan Puni.

The unusually receptive Puni was knowledgeable about Cubism from Russian collections and from visits to Paris just before World War I. He was perhaps as intrigued by the abstract geometry of Malevich's Suprematist painting as by Tatlin's techniques of assembling found materials, and this may account in part for the stylistic elegance of the reliefs Puni made between the years 1914 and 1919. His *Construction Relief* (c. 1915–16; p. 86) represents this crucial development in the history of Constructivism within the Nasher collection. Although Puni did not share Tatlin's or the postrevolutionary Constructivist group's political ideology and although, like Gabo and Pevsner, Puni emigrated to the West several years after the revolution, it is clear from the Nashers' relief that he like Tatlin wished to abandon artistic illusionism and to have his sculpture share the actual space of the observer. Puni's frequent use, as in the Nashers' construction, of common objects such as dinner plates, which still may be read for what they once were, has a double function: the pure geometry of a circle enters the composition, and the viewer's tactile sense is addressed at the literal scale of the real world.

The implications of making sculpture by techniques of assemblage widened throughout the twenties under the spreading influence of Russian and Dutch abstraction and the Dada artists' exploitation of found objects. At the end of the decade, assemblage took a very different turn when, with the technical assistance of Julio Gonzalez, Picasso embarked on a group of figurative constructions made by welding metal rods. These figures of the late twenties and Gonzalez's own welded heads and figures of the next fifteen years were Constructivist not only in technique but in their adherence, for figurative, illusionistic purposes, to the virtual-volume concept. Welded-metal rods and sometimes welded-metal found objects (as in Picasso's use in 1931 of two kitchen colanders to form the cranium of his *Head of a Woman*) became the materials with which the volumes of a human figure were outlined or, as Gonzalez described it, "drawn" around empty space. This process and the expressive gestural ends to which Gonzalez put it are visible in the Nasher collection in a posthumous bronze cast of his originally welded *Woman with a Mirror* (c. 1936–37; p. 55).

When Alexander Calder moved to Paris in 1927, Constructivist techniques, virtual volumes, and the biomorphic vocabulary of Surrealist painting were all in the air. The American used them in a highly personal fashion to invent air-driven kinetic sculpture, which new medium Duchamp dubbed mobiles. The Nashers' *Spider* (1940; p. 87), made of sheet metal and rods painted black and white, is an exceptionally fine example of Calder's slightly later mobile-stabiles. Poised on a tripod of "legs," the catenary link system of the insect's "arms" curves wittily in space, as if to parody both the patterns of motion of the creature it purports to describe and Machine Age earnestness about the significance and complexity of modern technology (Calder, trained as an engineer, knew exactly how simple his technology for setting sculpture in motion actually was). In spite of its low mass, the fundamentally mimetic nature of Calder's sculpture suggests to the imagination of the viewer, if not quite to his perceptual sense, that volumetric images are potentially present. His are almost always inventions for which we are tempted to conjure up fur, flesh, scales, feathers, or the hairiness of limbs. In addition, when the "pods" or flat sail areas of a work by Calder move in response to currents of air, what such planar elements describe as they travel are volumes of air. For all their linearity, Calder's mobiles, then, are also volumetric. Similarly, with the flat black planes that make up the Nashers' *Three Bollards* (1970; p. 88), which is either three linked crea-

right:
FERNAND LÉGER
The Construction Workers, 1950
Gouache on paper, 30 × 21¼″
No. 96

below:
IVAN PUNI
Construction Relief, c. 1915–16
Painted wood and tin on wood
support, 22⅞ × 18⅜ × 3½″
No. 71

opposite:
ALEXANDER CALDER
The Spider, 1940
Painted sheet metal and steel rod,
95 × 99 × 73″
No. 10

tures or one three-headed, three-trunked creature, we are easily tempted to read a virtual volume in precisely the sense illustrated by Gabo's didactic stereometric cubes. The black planes of this mock-monumental stabile are bolted together at right angles, establishing spines for the imaginary animals they cartoon and encouraging the eye to fill in a quarter turn from the edge of one jutting plane to the next.

Isamu Noguchi's *Gregory* (1945; left), a 1969 bronze cast of a work first made from smooth slabs of carved slate, appears to draw on nearly the same sources: the biomorphism of Surrealist painting and the crossing at right angles of flat planes, used here to establish the implied volume of a solemn standing figure. And while its parts were carved (and later cast), the Noguchi work is very much a constructed object in the most elemental sense, for its parts slot together, and it achieves stability through its existence as a structure.

One of the intriguing aspects of the Nasher collection is that it contains such a range of examples by certain of the most important sculptors of the century that we may study them in depth. The Nashers' six works by David Smith, from the highly personal *House in a Landscape (Rural Landscape with Manless House)* of 1945 (p. 91) to the imposing *Voltri VI* of 1962 (p. 95), allow us to look closely at aspects of the way that America's greatest modern sculptor absorbed yet radically changed tenets of the Constructivist and Surrealist modes of Europe.

Smith's appreciation of Picasso's and Gonzalez's welded sculpture of the late twenties is well-known, and indeed he once said, I "make definite outright thanks to Cubism and Constructivism." His fascination with the Surrealists' concern for soliciting the unconscious to prompt artistic creation and, more specifically, with Giacometti's inventive Surrealist tableaux and structures of the late twenties and early thirties, is also well-documented. And of course *House in a Landscape* aligns Smith with the Constructivist tradition in that it is assembled—welded together from parts that in this case were not found scrap but pieces of steel shaped by the artist to describe the mysteriously inhabited house of the title.

Not unlike one of Giacometti's Surrealist tabletop objects, such as the Nashers' *No More Play* of 1931–32 (p. 60), the *House* is a tableau that sits on a horizontal plane parallel to the ground and hints at a story. The house itself is indicated by a slender vertical plane rising from the middle of this ground; on either side of the flat vertical house and perpendicular to it, two equally flat treelike shapes constitute the landscape. On one face of the vertical house plane there is a relief of a woman looking out the window; halfway up the other face, a platform juts out, and in this second-story "room," also framed by a window, a female figure reaches out to a phallic shape. The intersecting vertical and horizontal planes of this scene appear to be employed to describe the cubic volume of a house, as if to exemplify Gabo's stereometric cube of air. Yet Smith also seems here to be questioning the Constructivist notion of a virtual volume formed by planes.

As Rosalind Krauss has shown, one of Smith's discoveries in the landscape sculptures of the forties was that by exploiting the fact that freestanding objects have successive faces—different sides that we cannot know until we actually see them—Smith could undermine the viewer's sense of an internally coherent volume, that is, either a volume in fact transparent to vision (as in a plexiglass work by Gabo, a welded-iron linear figure by Gonzalez, and an open bronze cage by Giacometti) or a volume transparent conceptually. He could thwart a viewer's expectations about the appearance of the far side of a solid observed from the front.[3] There is great tension in *House in a Landscape* between our sense of an implied box—the house—and our realization that we cannot see through this object to grasp its

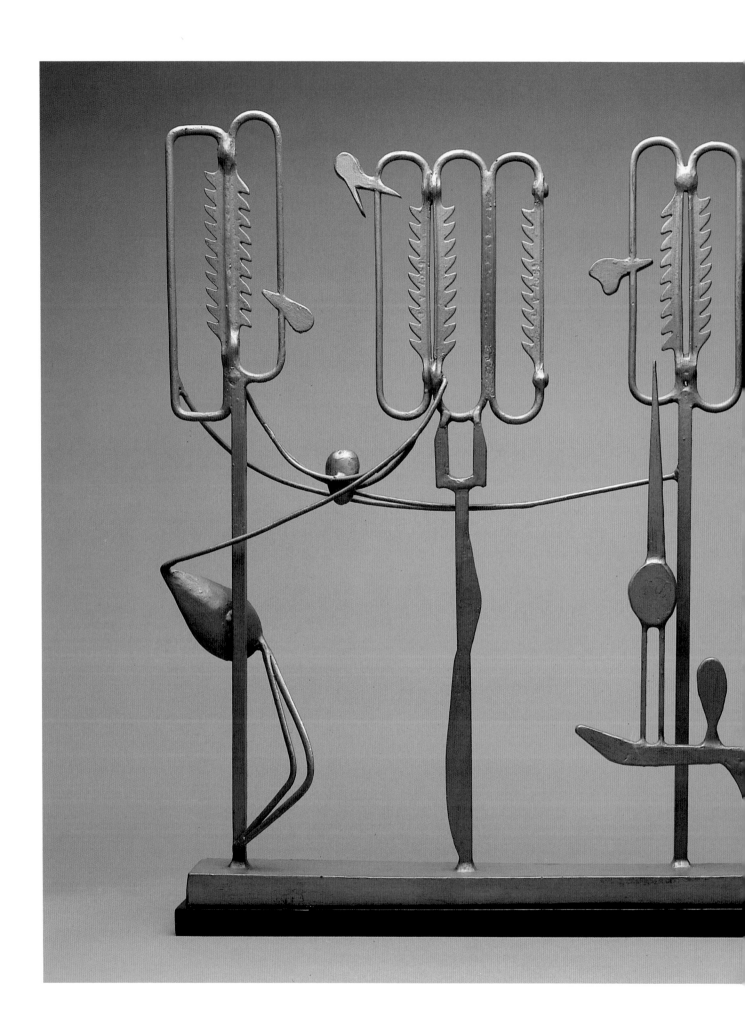

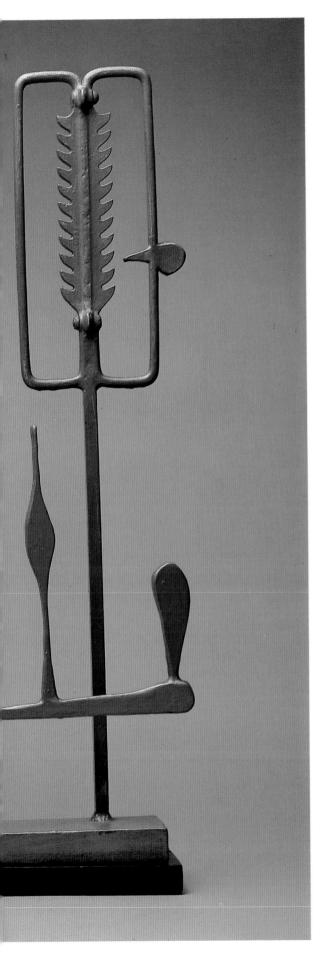

above:
DAVID SMITH
House in a Landscape, 1945
Steel, 18⅛ × 24½ × 6¾"
No. 78

left:
DAVID SMITH
The Forest, 1950
Polychromed steel,
36⅝ × 36¾ × 4½"
No. 79

contents from any single position. And there is irony in the fact that the very planes which position the boxy house in the landscape—the silhouettes of trees—and the planes which suggest its cubic form—the thin vertical and horizontal rectangles—are themselves so conspicuously flat that they undercut our sense of volume at the same time that they propose it.

The full meaning of the complex imagery in this sculpture is as elusive as our perception of its volume. Steven Nash has suggested (cat. no. 78) that the "manless house" of the subtitle refers to American households which had lost men to World War II. Like related sculptures of 1945, such as *Home of the Welder*, the work surely draws upon Smith's personal life of that year, when he was building his own house in the Adirondack mountains and his wife left their home for a time.

In *The Forest* (1950; pp. 90–91) Smith returned to the subject of landscape, welding saw-toothed found objects into the foliage of four starkly frontal trees, on which perch the silhouettes of four birds. To the left a figure with a tear-shaped head and torso and bent knees appears ready to climb the trees. Painted in shades of soft green and silvery pink and so rectangular in format that it signifies the medium of painting, this work is predicated on the eschewal of virtual volume. Drawn graphically in space, the linear elements of the sculpture remain within a very shallow, flat plane; they suggest volume only by descriptive allusion to natural forms, rather than by graphic demarcation in depth in the manner of Gonzalez.

Smith tends in much of his sculpture to arrest our attention and confound our expectations by introducing boldly executed quirks. This characteristic, while rarely discussed, influenced the following generation of American and British sculptors enormously. Often it took the form of eccentric alignments and unpredictable juxtapositions of the welded parts that compose his objects. In *The Forest* the quirk is conceptual: an organic material, the foliage of trees, has been depicted with the teeth of an industrially produced tool. The odd amalgam results in an image that is lyrical yet resolutely unsentimental.

When Smith first exhibited works such as *The Forest*, they were criticized for their two-dimensionality. One of his responses was to confront this criticism directly, and in 1953 he made a series of small sculptures which he called Drawings and which he titled individually with the day, month, and year of their completion, as he might have titled a page in a sketchbook. Like the Agricola series of the previous year, the Drawings were assembled from disused farm machinery and other found objects Smith manipulated, and several of the Drawings, including the Nashers' *9/15/53* (p. 94), resemble certain Agricolas in composition as well. The *9/15/53* consists of linear elements rising vertically from a long horizontal member raised on a short, eccentrically positioned, steel post. Observing this work from the front, so to speak, as if the horizontal beam were a kind of horizon line or indicator of a picture plane, the viewer cannot easily determine to what extent the series of vertical linear elements tilt backward or forward in space from the beam on which they are welded. Smith wrote about this issue in 1953:

> If a sculpture could be a line drawing, then speculate that a line drawing removed from its paper bond and viewed from the side would be a beautiful thing. . . . The end-view or profile of an interesting person or object arouses the mind to completion of the imagined personality and physiognomy, since a work of art or an object of interest is always completed by the viewer and is never seen the same by any two persons.[4]

One point Smith wanted to make clear with this statement was that his sculpture could not be read from one position but demanded to be seen from successive positions—not only a hypothetical front but also an "end-view." Smith's quirky positioning of the steel parts in relation to one another seems designed to force the viewer into undertaking a series of different stances in order to attempt to grasp a work. In this Smith is again countering the logical transparency of the virtual volume.

While Smith's *Tower Eight* (1957; p. 94) at first glance appears to rely upon the drawn-in-space volumes of Gonzalez's standing figures of the thirties, such as *Woman with a Mirror* or still-more linear figures, in fact it, too, extends Smith's concern to move the observer into successive positions around a sculpture. For unlike constructed figures by Gonzalez and Picasso of the twenties and thirties, *Tower Eight* has such a radically reduced set of mimetic clues to its figural imagery that we cannot determine the back of this body from its front. And when we do encircle the work, seeking to make its lines cohere into a volume, the "drawing" we see at each quarter turn is very different from the previous and subsequent ones. The tension between a clearly implied volume and a volume whose shape appears to change dramatically as we walk around it is heightened by Smith's use of silver as the material for this work, for the reflectivity of the precious metal makes the linear structure of the sculpture seem fugitive at times.

Smith's legendary Voltri series consists of twenty-seven sculptures made in the month of June 1962 at several abandoned government-owned steel factories in Voltri, Italy, near Genoa, for organizers of a sculpture exhibition that was part of the 1962 Spoleto Festival of Two Worlds. The series is represented in the Nasher collection by two works: *Untitled (Voltri)* (p. 94), a gift from Smith to Gian Carlo Menotti, the composer and impresario of the Spoleto Festival, and *Voltri VI* (p. 95), sometimes known as *Wagon*. Like all of the works in the series, *Voltri VI* was welded from the abundance of scrap metal and old machinery that Smith found in the former metal factories he elected to make his studio in Italy.

Particularly when seen in the context of the earlier nonanthropomorphic works by Smith in the Nasher collection—*House*

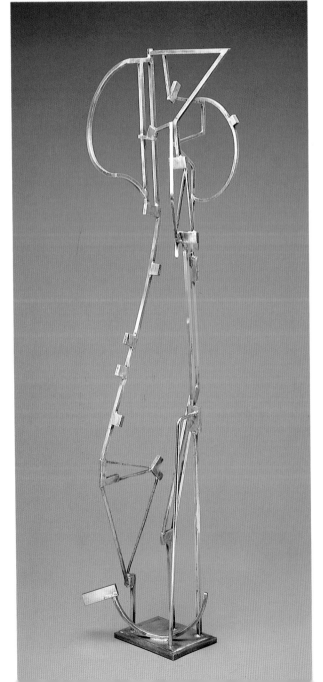

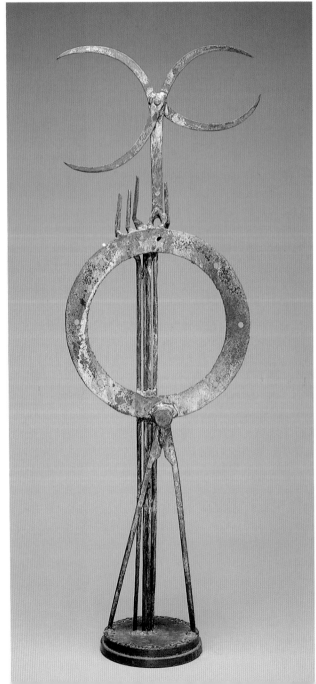

in a Landscape, The Forest, and *9/15/53—Voltri VI* proclaims the artist's extraordinary gift for juxtaposing horizontal and vertical elements in a manner that is at once tense and resolved. On one underside of the horizontal spine of *Voltri VI* there are two wheels; although they appear stationary, they have the capacity to move. On the opposite underside of the horizontal member, a single leg announces a resolute stop, of the sort that follows the jerk of a railroad car as it comes to a halt at the station. The contradictory qualities here, of "let's roll" and abrupt pause, are paralleled by the contradictory morphology of the work's main vertical members, which juxtapose straight lines and bold circular elements. For the material of these vertical planes, which Smith termed "chopped clouds," the artist employed discarded pieces of unfinished rolled steel. These were trimmed to nearly straight edges on their inner perimeters and left in softly jagged curves, produced by the rolling process, on their outer perimeters. The empty space between the two "clouds," like a space between two railroad cars, establishes another emphatic vertical to counter the course of the horizontal base.

Smith scholars have compared this vertical gap of negative space in *Voltri VI,* with its barely jagged edges, to the slightly smeared vertical stripes, or Zips, in the paintings of Smith's contemporary, Barnett Newman. In the Nashers' garden, this comparison is given dynamic reinforcement by the presence, nearby and on axis with *Voltri VI,* of one of Newman's Zips in sculptural form, *Here III* (1965–66; left). This sculpture consists of a tall stainless-steel shaft welded to a low, mastabalike base made of Cor-Ten steel. In contrast with the sleekly finished, reflective stainless shaft, the Cor-Ten mound is finished roughly at the bottom. Within it, an invisible recessed base permits the mound to appear to hover above the ground, so that for all the apparent simplicity and straightforwardness of the object, it proposes for itself a metaphorical potential to ascend skyward.

Sculpture of the sixties extended two aspects of the Constructivist tradition—its geometric vocabulary and its replacement of modeling and carving with assembling—and it rejected another: Constructivist sculpture's illusionism, that is, its concern to create idealized volumes of air comprehensible from one point of view. It did this in terms that were partly engendered by Smith's will to move the viewer around his objects. One effect was to focus attention, once again, on the real space in which the viewer stands and through which he walks as he observes. With the geometricized three-dimensional constructions of the sixties and beyond, such as Carl Andre's *Aluminum and Magnesium Plain* (1969; p. 97) and Richard Serra's *Inverted House of Cards* (1969–70; p. 97), actively sharing the ambient ground space of the observer becomes one of sculpture's main reasons for being. In this respect such sculpture renews the Constructivist tradition as it was briefly practiced in the Russian revolutionary years, by Tatlin and his immediate followers.

opposite:
BARNETT NEWMAN
Here III, 1965–66
Stainless and Cor-Ten steel,
125 × 23½ × 18⅝''
No. 62

above:
CARL ANDRE
Aluminum and Magnesium Plain, 1969
Aluminum and magnesium, 36
pieces; overall ⅜ × 72 × 72''
No. 1

left:
RICHARD SERRA
Inverted House of Cards, 1969–70
Cor-Ten steel, assembled:
55¼ x 101¾ x 101½''; each sheet:
55¼ × 55¼ × 1''
No. 76

NOTES

1. Christina Lodder, *Russian Constructivism* (New Haven and London, 1983), p. 3.

2. Duchamp-Villon's *Horse* of 1914 has been meticulously analyzed by Angelica Rudenstine in *The Peggy Guggenheim Collection, Venice* (New York, 1985), pp. 270–81.

3. Rosalind E. Krauss, *Terminal Iron Works: The Sculpture of David Smith* (Cambridge and London, 1971), passim.

4. Rosalind E. Krauss, *The Sculpture of David Smith: A Catalogue Raisonné* (New York and London, 1977), p. 59.

BETWEEN APOCALYPSES

ROBERT
ROSENBLUM

Art After 1945

Living after 1945, in an era ushered in by one apocalypse and haunted by the expectation of another, it is all too easy to imagine a scenario in which some future traveler in space and time will stumble upon the ruins of our destroyed civilization in the way that mid-eighteenth-century antiquarians uncovered the buried ghosts of art and life in Pompeii and Herculaneum. It is less easy, however, to imagine how these relics might be pieced together to decode our civilization, a thought prompted here by my task of introducing an anthology of first-rate art created in Europe and America after 1945 and now residing, both indoors and outdoors, at the Nasher home and other locations in and around Dallas. Looking at this cross section of painting, of sculpture, and of works that refuse to comply with either of these two traditional categories, one may well wonder what some twenty-first-century Gulliver would be able to recognize about life in our own long-lost world.

As for the people who lived in it, the most immediate record would probably be the one provided by George Segal in *Rush Hour* (1983; p. 98), a dour sextet of figures who, like the agonized human beings and dogs incinerated and fossilized in 79 A.D. by the ashes of Vesuvius, have been preserved for us to see. Stopped dead in their tracks and embalmed for eternity in the clothing they wore at that moment, they are caught in a split second of prosaic reality during a humdrum daily cycle of mass transport from home to job and back. But the group, viewed from a post-1945 time capsule, also reflects a grim image of our communal lives, in which anonymous individuals, like herds,

opposite:
GEORGE SEGAL
Rush Hour, 1983 (cast 1985–86)
Bronze, 73 × 74 × 67"
No. 75

turn into collective forces ignorant and unquestioning of their own destinies. It is a point made all the more poignant by the inevitable contrast of Segal's earthbound walkers with Auguste Rodin's *Burghers of Calais* (1884–95), another tragic sextet who, unlike these benumbed urbanites of the nineteen-eighties, exalt the drama of history with a heroism both private and shared. Literal, then, as Segal's document may at first appear, it quickly becomes a sociological allegory of the mindless and joyless flow of urban masses caught in midstream.

These robot ghosts, so ubiquitous in our late-twentieth-century populations, can be pushed to far more fantastic, hallucinatory extremes: witness Jonathan Borofsky's *Hammering Man* (1984–85), the silhouette of a 20-foot-tall steel giant whose motorized arm moves a hammer up and down with relentness monotony. Again, a nineteenth-century past is evoked, but such early echoes of heroic images of labor are now transformed into a crazily displaced creature, a monstrous and weary titan who still performs grueling manual labor in a world of computers and machines. And should our space-time traveler look about for some of the artifacts of this expiring civilization, the clues would be no less disquieting. What strange surf would wash up Claes Oldenburg's *Mannikin Torso: Two-Piece Bathing Suit* (1960; p. 102), and what odd creature would have frolicked in it? What fearful giant of a secretary would have used his Brobdingnagian *Typewriter Eraser* (1976; p. 102), and what thirsty robot would have drunk from Roy Lichtenstein's *Double Glass* (1979–80; p. 103)? Perhaps the answer to this archaeological riddle could be found in the vicinity of Lichtenstein's *Head with Blue Shadow* (1965; p. 103), a minor clone from a major goddess whose emotions, if any, could only be registered on a computer graph.

But wait. Here and there pulsations of a different breed of creature can be felt, throwbacks, perhaps, to a precomputer culture. A post-1945 Alice in Wonderland tour through the Nasher sculpture garden might turn up, for instance, some strange deities, both human and animal. As for the latter, Barry Flanagan's *Large Leaping Hare* (1982; p. 104), suspended weightlessly above a pyramidal base, could offer archaeologists a strange hieroglyph whose decoding might unlock the mysteries of some ancient religion akin to Egypt's; and a further clue might be found in Mimmo Paladino's *A Surrounded Figure* (1983; p. 105), a survivor of a mysterious animal cult in which an eerily quiet oracle seems at one with three fawns, an enormous ritual urn, and a string of ceremonial masks. Elsewhere, too, one falls upon what must once have been a sacred object belonging to another stratum of prehistory, such as a hybrid *Animal Woman* (1949; p. 105) by Joseph Beuys, a bronze fertility idol who suggests a still more remote archaeological site, a relic perhaps from some paleolithic excavation in Northern Europe.

But in this pantheon of lonely deities whose worshipers have vanished from our planet, there are also more familiar

opposite:
JONATHAN BOROFSKY
Hammering Man, 1984–85
Painted steel plate and Cor-Ten steel, 240 × 108 × 18½"
No. 6

opposite, top left:
CLAES OLDENBURG
*Mannikin Torso: Two-Piece
Bathing Suit*, 1960
Cloth soaked in plaster over wire
frame and painted, 32½ × 14¾ × 4½"
No. 64

opposite, top right:
CLAES OLDENBURG
Pile of Typewriter Erasers, 1970–75
Canvas filled with kapok, painted
in acrylic, 7 × 28 × 22", variable
No. 65

opposite, below:
CLAES OLDENBURG
Typewriter Eraser, 1976
Ferro cement, stainless steel, and
aluminum, 89 × 90 × 63"
No. 66

left:
ROY LICHTENSTEIN
Double Glass, 1979–80
Painted bronze, 56¼ × 41 1/16 × 17¼"
No. 44

below:
ROY LICHTENSTEIN
Head with Blue Shadow, 1965
Glazed ceramic, 15 × 8¼ × 8"
No. 43

opposite:
BARRY FLANAGAN
Large Leaping Hare, 1982
Gilded bronze with painted
tubular-steel base, 110 × 111 × 44″
No. 25

below left:
MIMMO PALADINO
A Surrounded Figure, 1983
Bronze, 55⅜ × 47¼ × 50⅜″
No. 67

below right:
JOSEPH BEUYS
Animal Woman, 1949 (cast 1984)
Bronze, 18 × 5⁷⁄₁₆ × 3⅞″
No. 5

human types, such as Jean Dubuffet's 10-foot-high *The Gossiper II* (1969–70; p. 106). Enthroned in an ancestral chair stitched together from the same jigsaw-puzzle components found in such Dubuffet collages as *Conjugaison* (1975; above), this grotesquely animated near-mortal prattles and gestures endlessly like a demented ruler. Could he be of the same race as Willem de Kooning's even more agitated *Hostess* (1973; below)? Inspired perhaps by some busty barmaid, this frenetic goddess also looks both comical and demonic, the lava of her bronze effigy erupting convulsively to create a mirage of three or four flailing arms, a shrill laugh, and ripples of zaftig flesh so mobile that they spill down and over her feet.

  Should we wish to find after 1945 more familiar glimmers of old-fashioned human behavior, we had best turn to the oldest artist in this group, a survivor from another age, Pablo Picasso. His trio of late paintings tell us about the once-abiding verities of life, love, and art in terms alien to our computer age. In *The Studio* (1961–62; p. 108), the mysteries of the artist at his easel are evoked yet again in a tradition-bound meditation upon the magic of transforming living models into painting, a metamorphosis that, in Picasso's case, alludes, as usual, to the history of art (with specters here from the harems of J.-A.-D. Ingres and Eugène Delacroix) and to his own love life. And in his very last years, as he approached his ninetieth birthday, these private revelations reach a poignant intensity in *The Kiss* (October 1969; p. 108), with its Remembrance of Erotic Things Past, or most potently, in his *Man and Woman* (August 1971; p. 109), a frighteningly bold confrontation with his literally naked and aged self, his painter's fist clenched in an urgent symbol of defiant vitality as both man and artist and his naked female companion still serving as lover, muse, and, in the incomplete suggestion of a child's body in her lap, mother of his living progeny as well.

opposite:
JEAN DUBUFFET
The Gossiper II, 1969–70
(fabricated 1984)
Painted polyester resin,
120 × 81¾ × 85¼"
No. 15

above:
JEAN DUBUFFET
Conjugaison, November 1975
Acrylic on paper mounted on
cloth, 52⅜ × 119¾"
No. 91

below:
WILLEM DE KOONING
Hostess, 1973
Bronze, 48¾ × 38 × 25¾"
No. 40

right:
PABLO PICASSO
The Studio, 1961–62
Oil on canvas, 29 × 36''
No. 99

below:
PABLO PICASSO
The Kiss, October 1969
Oil on canvas, 38⅛ × 51³⁄₁₆''
No. 100

opposite:
PABLO PICASSO
Man and Woman, August 1971
Oil on canvas, 76⅝ × 51⅛''
No. 101

ALAIN KIRILI
Generations, 1985
Forged and painted iron, 85 ×
58 × 33½"
No. 39

These bold assertions of human will and energy, a vertical thrust against the passive horizontality of the earth, reach an abstract extreme in Barnett Newman's *Here III* (1965–66; p. 96), a gleaming, stainless-steel shaft over 10 feet high that springs in proud majesty from a grounded plinth. Like an ancient obelisk, this absolute image conveys a heroic human presence that will conquer and endure. Whether evoking the first or the last man on earth, Newman's lonely and mighty metal beam of luminous vitality conveys, on this planet after 1945, an all-too-appropriate metaphor of courageous survival and regeneration against all odds. It is a faith that also radiates from Alain Kirili's *Generations* (1985; above). Here a dense biological metaphor of the growth of a community of beings, at once human and botanical, recalls again the familiar experience of an alien explorer falling upon the remains of an ancient civilization or the beginnings of a new one in the aftermath of a near-total annihilation. Kirili's alphabet of forms and primary colors, both freshly invented and venerable, spells out a ritual language consonant with that quest for myth or religion which animates so many of these would-be ceremonial objects from lost cultures created in the last decades of our expiring century.

These quests may lead us deep into mountains and forests, too, as when Richard Long in *Slate Line* (1979; p. 112) marks out the archetypal human trail in a linear path some 25 feet long, composed of five rough-hewn fragments of Welsh slate. As in Newman's *Here III*, we sense again some urgent, primitive impulse to record the existence of a lone human presence in the undifferentiated face of nature. Other excursions into the wilderness may take us to a more elaborate, Jungian poetic landscape, as in the case of Anish Kapoor's *In Search of the Mountain I* (1984; p. 112), in which a primal, organic force, strongly phallic in connotation, invades the image of mountain as earth mother. And our adventure in these primeval forests explored by modern mythmakers may even lead to the cavernous dwelling places of unseen deities who might well reside on the settee and two chairs of Scott Burton's *Schist Furniture Group* (1983–84; p. 113). Cut from rocks in a Maryland quarry, Burton's primeval conversation piece suggests, in its rudimentary contrast of rough stone and cleanly incised planes, a mythic environment suitable perhaps for a meeting of Wotan and his family in Valhalla.

After scrutinizing what might seem poetic vestiges of ancient religions and myths, our imaginary space-time traveler, coming upon other artifacts from our century's later decades, might also reconstruct this civilization from the investigations of some rigorous geometers and architects who would explicate, like resurrected Euclids, the first principles of cerebral law and order. Works such as Carl Andre's *Aluminum and Magnesium Plain* (1969; p. 97) and Sol LeWitt's *Modular Cube/Base* (1968; p. 114) amply testify to the potency of the *tabula rasa* of constructive forms as an image of elementary force and hope for a new world in the shadow of the destruction of an old one. Andre's checkerboard, 6-foot-square pattern of six-times-six alternating aluminum and magnesium squares provides, on the ground we would stand on, both a literal and metaphorical basis for examining the most rudimentary, unpolluted statement of shapes and materials. It presents the Platonic ideal, so to speak, of a pavement upon which an uncorrupted language of pure forms could be erected. And LeWitt's even more insistently modular flat base actually does provide the two-dimensional foundation for a three-dimensional modular structure, instantly transforming a square into a cube, and thereby establishing a time-capsule

page 112, top:
RICHARD LONG
Slate Line, 1979
Five pieces of Welsh slate, approx. 336" long
No. 46

page 112, bottom:
ANISH KAPOOR
In Search of the Mountain I, 1984
Wood, gesso, and pigment, 44⅞ × 44⅞ × 100"
No. 38

page 113:
SCOTT BURTON
Schist Furniture Group, 1983–84
Schist, chairs: 43 × 28 × 32" and 39 × 27½ × 35"; settee: 39 × 71 × 47½"
No. 9

ROBERT ROSENBLUM

nugget of architectonic order to inspire, in its pristine, symbolic perfection, thoughts of Utopias to come. Underlining this impulse to reassert the distilled principles of construction and mensuration, there is also Don Judd's untitled realization of a geometric progression (1976; below), in which lean, sharp-edged shapes and the spatial intervals between them at once increase and diminish with a linear, mathematical beat that seems infinitely extendable. Despite its material presence (the sculpture is made of rectilinear aluminum tubes that may be peered through from either end), Judd's sculpture hovers like an unusable shelf upon the wall, conveying, in the weightless, disembodied way of LeWitt's modular cubes, the image of cerebration, floating far above an earthly world dominated by weight-bound matter and the laws of gravity.

Works like these resemble abstract blueprints for a modular system of architecture that exists more in the mind than on the ground; but there are other sculptures here that put more bone and muscle into these mental constructions. Richard Serra's *Inverted House of Cards* (1969–70; p. 97) provides an elementary exercise in the laws of load and support that are so often repealed in modern sculpture. It insists instead upon a simple statement of leaning and propped-up forms which, like some variant of a Neolithic dolmen, might have survived through the millennia. Yet typical for our own time, this cluster of stability is precarious, and we sense that given only one

opposite:
SOL LEWITT
Modular Cube/Base, 1968
Painted steel, cube: 19⅛ × 19⅛ × 19⅛"; base: 1 × 58½ × 58½"
No. 42

below:
DONALD JUDD
Untitled, June 1976
Aluminum and anodized aluminum, 8¼ × 161 × 8"
No. 37

pages 116–117:
TONY SMITH
Ten Elements, 1975–79 (fabricated 1980)
Painted aluminum, tallest element 50" high; shortest element 42" high
No. 86

unfortunate man-made or natural tremor, this metaphorical house of cards would fall apart before our eyes with a tremendous thud. The same unstable image that would seesaw between collapse and construction is found, too, in *The Snake Is Out* (1962; below) by Tony Smith, who was in fact a practicing architect and had worked in his youth on buildings by Frank Lloyd Wright. To a visitor from another planet, his *Ten Elements* (1975–79; pp. 116–17) might well resemble playthings hurled from Olympus by some titanic god of architecture and strewn about on our earth, ruins of an immaculately wrought and fitted monument that wait to be pieced together again. And in Smith's *For Dolores* (c. 1973–75; p. 119), we feel some giant microscope has disclosed the scientific core of a molecular structure that we may choose to build or to destroy.

In other sculpture, a far more explicit sense of the language and dynamics of modern architecture can be felt. In Anthony Caro's *Carriage* (1966; p. 119), a lucid network of fragmentary steel beams asserts, as in a painting by Piet Mondrian, the elementary forces of horizontal and vertical

TONY SMITH
The Snake Is Out, 1962
(fabricated 1981)
Painted steel, 180 × 278 × 226″
No. 84

TONY SMITH
For Dolores, c. 1973–75
Carrara marble, 44¼ × 44¾ ×
45¼"
No. 85

ANTHONY CARO
Carriage, 1966
Painted steel, 77 × 80 × 156"
No. 12

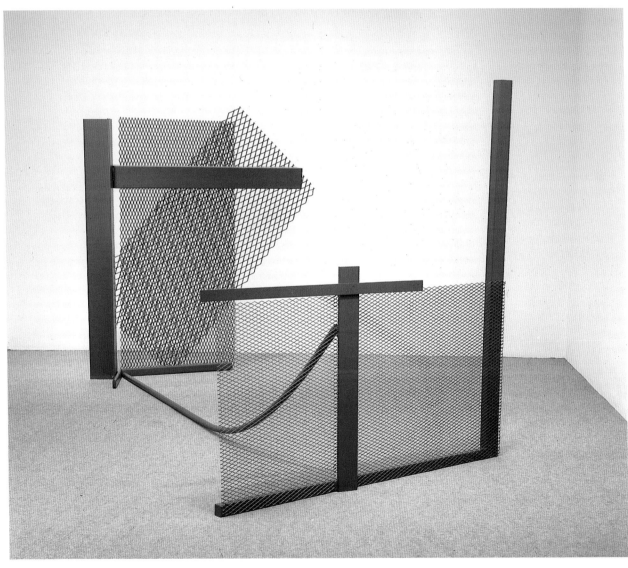

thrust, But this opaque metal skeleton is further complicated by an interior dialogue of fine mesh screens that, like windows in a skyscraper, lend a Machine Age translucence to an open frame. And these points become still more explicit in the work of Siah Armajani, who intentionally blurs the line between sculpture and architecture, offering, for instance, a series of first principles entitled, as in a primer to reconstruct the world, "Dictionary for Building." In a typical construction from this new alphabet of forms, *Door in Window #2* (1982–83; left), fundamental dualities of oval versus rectangle, frame versus aperture, translucent versus opaque are juggled in a theoretical object both abstract and potentially utilitarian, both free-floating and obedient to the pull of wall and floor. Reflections of modern engineering are clear, too, in Mark di Suvero's *In the Bushes* (1970–75; p. 121), where an upheaval of I beams and girders collide at sharp and crazy angles, echoing the earsplitting mechanical energies that clash at any urban construction site. But characteristically in the sculpture of Caro, di Suvero, and Armajani, not to mention Tony Smith, we have the sense of a fragment from a much larger whole that hovers between the sense of ruin and the sense of a future Utopia, to be reconstructed, perhaps, only in the mind's eye.

As for such speculations, our future archaeologist might

Siah Armajani
Dictionary for Building: Door in Window #2, 1982–83
Painted wood, plexiglass, and screen, 88 × 48 × 20½"
No. 3

right:
John Chamberlain
Zaar, 1959
Welded steel, painted,
51¼ × 68⅜ × 19⅝"
No. 13

opposite:
Mark di Suvero
In the Bushes, 1970–75
Painted steel, 142 × 126 × 81"
No. 90

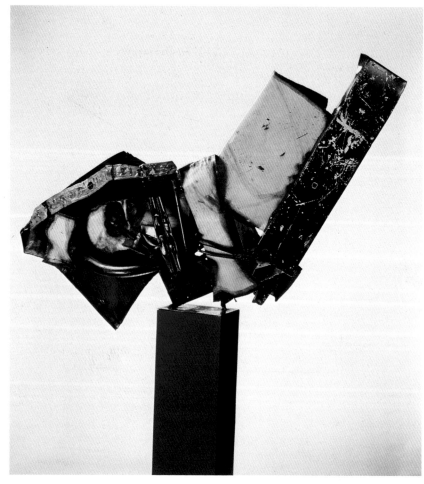

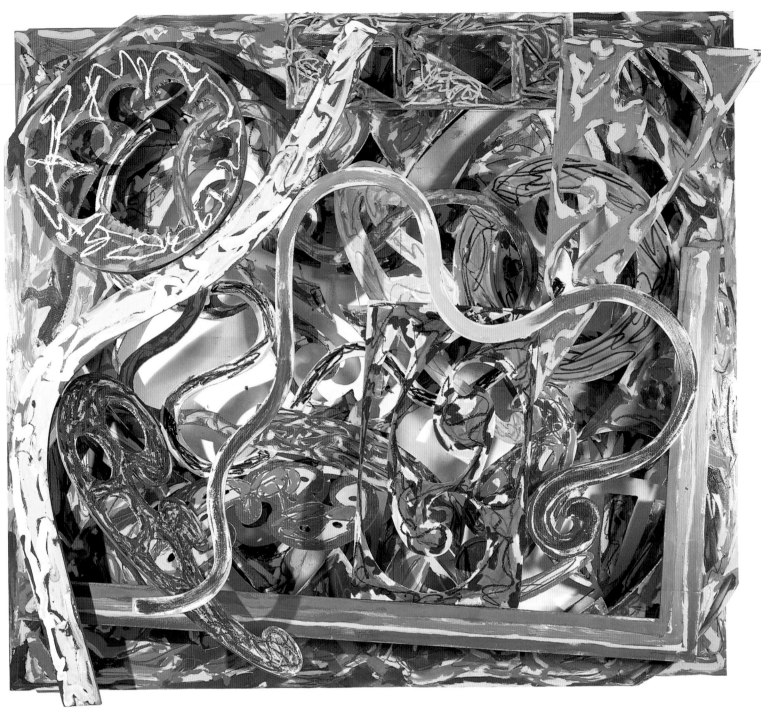

FRANK STELLA
Diepholz II, 1982
Mixed media on aluminum and
fiberglass, 106½ × 120 × 24″
No. 88

also be able to gather from this sculpture anthology some idea of the ubiquitous presence of the automobile in our century, as evidenced in works by John Chamberlain and Frank Stella. In the former's *Zaar* (1959; p. 120), a jagged crunch of welded and painted steel might become, like a dinosaur bone, the fragmentary clue to the reconstruction of an ordinary species of car or truck that, after collision, had been buried in a scrap heap. And in Stella's *Diepholz II* (1982; above), named after a racetrack in Germany, such a study would move to a more aristocratic stratum of automobile culture; for this labyrinthine *perpetuum mobile* of painted-aluminum ribbons could be shown to mirror the streamlined velocities and serpentine circuits of the racing cars and grand-prix courses that form so consistent a motif throughout Stella's art and life.

In such a mechanized landscape, what kind of creatures might have existed? As for animals, there is a clue in Richard Deacon's *Like a Bird* (1984; below), for the species that might be found in the nearby woods is metamorphosed into three linear round-trip paths of laminated wood that trace, as on a computer screen, the fluid motion of a lithe, airborne spirit, camouflaged by the surrounding trees and foliage. As for the human species, a suggestion is offered in Joel Shapiro's unti-

RICHARD DEACON
Like a Bird, 1984
Laminated wood, 121 × 208 × 205''
No. 14

JOEL SHAPIRO
Untitled, 1983
Bronze, 85¾ × 15 × 36″
No. 77

tled bronze (1983; above), a mutation of our race clearly more adaptable to the computerized movements of the late twentieth century than Borofsky's nightmarish *Hammering Man.* Here we sense the hard-edged ghost of some anthropomorphic being whose robotlike force, now striding and flexing, seems controlled by a brain that resembles a floating cube, suitable perhaps even for extraterrestrial calculations.

And what kind of pleasurable two-dimensional sensations, our space-time traveler might ask, were accessible to the eyes of those creatures who inhabited our planet after World War II? Here, some answers might be found in a group of post-1945 paintings in the Nasher collection that still cling to the conventional, time-honored format of a rectangular field, but invade that familiar shape with an uncommon intensity of color and surface. Among them, there are even some, our visitor might note, that adhere to the equally traditional sense of the artist's own hand and brush at work, a relic, it would seem, from an older culture that valued handicraft. Not surprisingly, such works are by the oldest painters of the group, Hans Hofmann and Willem de Kooning. As for the latter's untitled painting of 1976 (p. 126), it appears, like the very late Picassos here, to be almost an anachronism in its vigorous avowal of a world of handmade, viscerally felt impulses, an eruption of both muscular and emotional sensations that parallel the intimacies of a diary entry. And here, too, despite the effacement of any legible image by the molten lava of de Kooning's paint, we sense, as in the aging Picasso, the turbulent glimmer of erotic memories, so that the pink of flesh and the gold of hair register with the potency of a subliminal hurricane. As for Hans Hofmann's *String Quartet* (1959–60; p. 127), its attack, too, is directed to the realm of the senses, but in a domain of aesthetic purity. Its very title conjures up the analogies between abstract painting and music that, from Whistler to Kandinsky, were used to defend the possibilities of a visual art that could communicate without images; and the abstract character of architecture is also evoked here in the visual affinities to a towering constructive order, composed of modular square and rectangular units of blazing color. But within this calculated order, we sense throughout the willed presence of the artist's personal and vibrant touch, which makes straight lines quiver and opaque surfaces ripple with unexpected shimmers of light.

The sheer chromatic impact of Hofmann's painting, with its hot and glowing hues, is matched in a more voluptuous and veiled way by Morris Louis's *Aleph Series VI* (1960; p. 128), which counters the troweled opacity of Hofmann's bricks of color with an engulfing liquidity of paint. Earth has turned into air and water, and the material stuff of conventional pigment has been dissolved into rainbow floods that would immerse the spectator in a hothouse of vaporous hues. And here, too, our space-time traveler might note the familiar post-1945 impulse to regress to an extreme of primitive, natural experience as an antidote to the overwhelming presence of a technological society. Here, the colors of an organic spectrum seem resurrected in all their freshness, and the pulse and shape of landscape, flowing and burgeoning before our eyes, are evoked in a hymn to a long-lost organic world.

The tonic pleasure of pure color and the restorative power of nature are also suggested in Ellsworth Kelly's *Block Island II* (1960; p. 129). Here, the chromatic complexities of Hofmann and Louis are filtered out and replaced by a bold and emblematic trio of green, blue, and black, echoing the natural topographical facts of the North Atlantic island referred to in Kelly's title. But this organic source in landscape, sky, and water now enters a dialogue with a pictorial language that echoes, in turn, a more mechanized world. The brushless surfaces, the immaculate clarity of hue, the razor's-edge precision of contour translate these memories of nature into our own

WILLEM DE KOONING
Untitled VIII, 1976
Oil on canvas, 59¼ × 55"
No. 95

Hans Hofmann
String Quartet, 1959–60
Oil on canvas, 50⅛ × 40¼″
No. 93

MORRIS LOUIS
Aleph Series VI, Spring 1960
Acrylic on canvas, 78⁹⁄₁₆ × 104¾″
No. 98

ELLSWORTH KELLY
Block Island II, 1960
Acrylic on canvas, 88 × 66''
No. 94

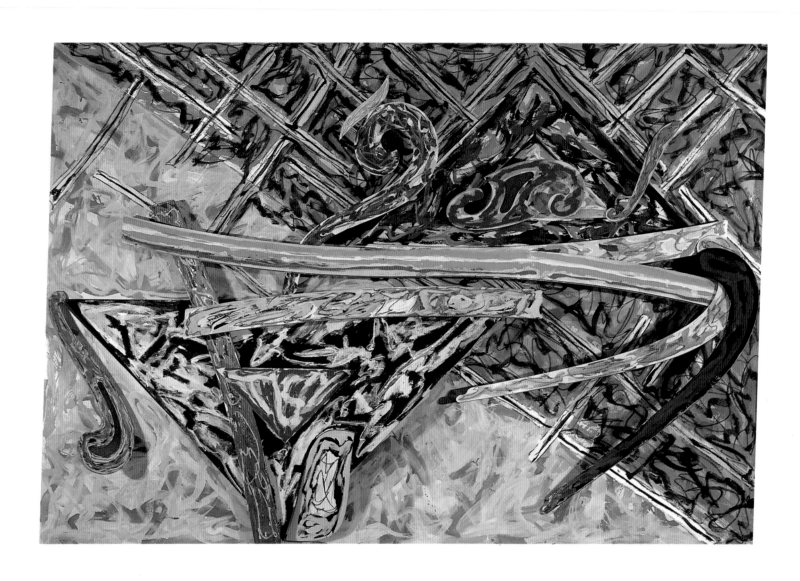

Frank Stella
Washington Island Gadwall,
1980–81
Mixed media on aluminum, 154 × 225 × 26''
No. 87

ROY LICHTENSTEIN
Reclining Bather, 1977
Oil and acrylic on canvas, 60 × 90"
No. 97

late-twentieth-century language, and establish a delicate equipoise between these two colliding modes of experience, the machine-made and the organic.

It is a balance made visually far more intricate in Frank Stella's *Washington Island Gadwall* (1980–81; p. 130), one of the Exotic Birds series that is inspired by this or that gorgeously plumed species. In this case, the spectacular colors and feathered arabesques of these rare winged creatures are metamorphosed into a hard-edged vocabulary of standardized, curvilinear drafting instruments that flutter about a rectangular field of brilliant honeycomb patterns like birds confined in a geometric cage, an image of nature's most sensuous wonders translated for our own times.

And for our future voyager seeking to reconstruct art and life in the late twentieth century, it is Roy Lichtenstein's *Reclining Bather* (1977; p. 131) that may have the final word; for the landscape and the figure it depicts are at so many removes from nature that we would never be able to decipher what cloud and flesh, sun and sky might have looked like on our planet. Here, the edge of the sea is illuminated and reflected by an overhead lamp and mirror borrowed from Lichtenstein's own earlier work, which in turn had translated the phenomena of natural light into the language of the TV screen and computer graphics. But within this regimented vocabulary of stripes and dots, suitable for Machine Age image-making, lie buried memories not only of nature, but of art as it was practiced in an earlier twentieth-century culture obliterated by World War II. For on this remote beach, marked by the remains of snail and starfish, the pulsating domain of Surrealism, which would push our human race back to its most primitive roots in sexuality, in myth, in the ebb and flow of nature, is fossilized and parodied. One of Miró's ladders leads up to the sky of dreams, and one of Picasso's tentacular sex traps is transformed in turn into a blonde goddess from an archaic Hollywood fantasy. History, art, nature, so our visitor might guess, have become strange relics from the past, alternately poignant and comical.

CATALOG

Sculpture

CARL ANDRE (American, born 1935)

*1. *Aluminum and Magnesium Plain*, 1969
Aluminum and magnesium, 36 plates; overall ⅜ x 72 x 72 (.95 x 182.9 x 182.9)

MARKINGS: None

PROVENANCE: John Weber Gallery, New York
To Sam Green
To Mr. and Mrs. Burton Tremaine, New York and Connecticut, 1974
To Nasher collection, 1985

LITERATURE: Cf. David Bourdon, *Carl Andre: Sculpture 1959–1977*, New York, 1978, pp. 32, 56 (ill. p. 33, as part of ensemble)

EXHIBITIONS: *Carl Andre*, The Solomon R. Guggenheim Museum, New York, 1970, cat. no. 32 (ill. p. 56, as part of ensemble)

The Tremaine Collection: 20th Century Masters, the Spirit of Modernism, Wadsworth Atheneum, Hartford, 1984, p. 132 (ill. of a similar work)

Carl Andre's ground-hugging metal sculptures made of thin, square, unattached plates are the *reductio ad extremum* of the principles of modular structure he had begun to examine in his first brick floor pieces of 1966. The intuitions behind this development have been described by David Bourdon:

> During the summer of 1965, Andre experienced a revelation while canoeing on a New Hampshire lake. He had long wanted to break away from the vertical in his sculpture, and it now suddenly occurred to him that his work should be as level as water. He wondered how he could go about putting the equivalent of Brancusi's *Endless Column* on the ground instead of in the air [Bourdon, 1978, p 26].

The brick sculptures of 1966–67 were followed, in turn, by Andre's first metal floor piece in 1967, which was made of a steel plate, already cut into squares, purchased from a salvage yard. The relatively thick plate in this work gave way in subsequent sculptures to thinner, standardized, industrial-grade metal squares. Although highly conceptual in approach, these works retain a definite physical presence in their spatial breadth and slight height, density of material, texture (which results from combining two or more metals), and variations in wear (as the different plates are walked upon). This physical, even geographical quality is reinforced in Andre's substitution of the word "plain" for "plane" in many of his titles.

Documentation supplied by the artist indicates that this sculpture was exhibited in the Andre survey at The Solomon R. Guggenheim Museum, New York, in 1970, presumably as one of the thirty-six Plains joined together to form the monumental *37 Pieces of Work* combining 1,296 individual plates and six different metals. Each metal was used alone to form one of the thirty-six Plains, then combined with each of the other metals in every possible permutation, creating a syncopated visual design based, however, on an underlying mathematical order.

NOTES

Title: The most common or preferred title is cited first, followed by the alternate titles in brackets.
Date: The date following the title is that of the object's conception. If the date of casting or fabrication is different and is known, it appears in parentheses.
Dimensions: The dimensions are cited first in inches, followed by centimeters in parentheses. Height precedes width precedes depth.
Literature: The listing of bibliographical references is highly selective, including only the most authoritative or commonly used sources. If a particular source refers to a different cast or version of the object, it is preceded by "cf."
Exhibitions: Cited are only those exhibitions in which the particular object in the Nasher collection was included, that is, exclusive of different casts or versions.
Abbreviations:
* Work in exhibition at the Dallas Museum of Art only
** Work in exhibition at the National Gallery of Art only
ex-cat. outside of catalog
n.n. not numbered
ill. illustrated
n.p. no page numbers

ALEXANDER ARCHIPENKO (American, born Russia, 1887–1964)

*2. *Woman Combing Her Hair* [*Femme debout*], 1914 or 1915
Bronze, 14⅛ x 3⅝ x 3³⁄₁₆ (36 x 9.3 x 8.1)

MARKINGS: Upper edge of base at left: "Archipenko 1915"

PROVENANCE: Far Gallery, New York
To Nasher collection, 1984

LITERATURE: Cf. Alexander Archipenko et al., *Archipenko: Fifty Creative Years, 1908–1958*, New York, 1960, p. 52, pls. 145–46

Cf. Katherine Janszky Michaelsen, *Archipenko: A Study of the Early Works, 1908–1920*, New York and London, 1977, pp. 70–71, cat. no. S 59

Cf. Ronald Alley, *Catalogue of the Tate Gallery's Collection of Modern Art Other Than Works by British Artists*, London, 1981, pp. 17–18, no. T335 (ill.)

Cf. Donald Karshan, *Archipenko: Sculpture, Drawings, and Prints, 1908–1963*, Centre College of Kentucky, Danville, Kentucky, 1985, cat. no. 28, fig. 28

EXHIBITIONS: None

Archipenko's *Woman Combing Her Hair*, generally thought to date from 1915 but possibly made in 1914, was the first in a series of standing figures by the artist, including the *Statuette* of 1915, *Standing Figure* of 1916, and *Egyptian Motif* of 1917, all based on formal inventions initially seen in his work in the well-known *Walking Woman* of 1912. In the Cubist-inspired syntax of that figure, Archipenko rejected solidity and continuity of form, substituting voids for masses, reversing concavities and convexities, and replacing anatomical with geometrical logic. In the statuettes of 1915–17, although more classically proportioned, he canceled the solidity of the head with penetrating holes, and articulated breasts, abdomen, and legs by alternating positive and negative volumes. The introduction of space into interior forms in these works, linking front and back, inside and outside, constitutes one of Archipenko's major contributions to twentieth-century sculpture and parallels contemporaneous inventions in the art of Umberto Boccioni and Naum Gabo.

The dating and history of casting of the *Woman Combing Her Hair* remain problematic. Most of the dated casts are marked 1915 but some are inscribed 1914. Donald Karshan has conjectured that the latter date is correct and that Archipenko inadvertently misdated later castings 1915 (Karshan, 1985, no. 28). An undetermined number of bronze casts, without casting numbers, were made of the original so-called "13¾-inch version" and exhibited before 1920. In the fifties, an edition reportedly of twelve casts was published, each bearing a number. The existence of numbered casts that are differently dated (1914 rather than 1915) and marked in different locations, and of casts that are unnumbered (e.g., the Nasher bronze) indicates that more than one generation of late castings occurred, the number and dates of which are unknown.

Additionally, there are casts in polished and gilded bronze. As with several other of his early works, Archipenko enlarged this figure late in life, producing a version 63.5 centimeters high (edition of eight casts) and another 180.5 centimeters high (edition of seven casts).

SIAH ARMAJANI (American, born Iran 1939)

*3. *Dictionary for Building: Door in Window #2*, 1982–83
Painted wood, plexiglass, and screen, 88 x 48 x 20½ (224 x 122 x 52)

MARKINGS: None

PROVENANCE: From artist to Max Protetch Gallery, New York
To Nasher collection, 1985

LITERATURE: None

EXHIBITIONS: *Dictionary for Building II*, Max Protetch Gallery, New York, 1983

American Sculpture, Margo Leavin's Hilldale Gallery, Los Angeles, 1984

Max Protetch Gallery, Dallas Trade Mart, Dallas, 1984

Siah Armajani, Institute of Contemporary Art, University of Pennsylvania, Philadelphia, 1985, cat. p. 94 (ill. p. 54)

The Dictionary for Building is a subtheme in the "archisculpture" that Armajani began in 1979, invoking historical lexicons of architecture and positing a vocabulary of mixed architectural details in an abstract sculptural language. These works reexamine architectural fragments for their formal value, take up structural themes such as physical entry and the expression of the overall construction in individual elements, and also conjure images of a highly personal and innovative architectural style. Their roots lie in the functionalist sculpture of Russian Constructivists such as El Lissitzky and Gustav Klutsis and in the work of a number of young American sculptors who attempt to bridge personal and social values using architectural metaphors.

Janet Kardon has noted that the slightly earlier *Door in Window #1* (1979–82, Stedelijk Museum, Amsterdam) introduced

> . . . a cluster of works investigating the idea of container and contained, since the doors or windows

contain other windows. At this point, the materials became more decorative. Black, painted wood frames bronze screening; slender wood circles or ovals surmount doors, quoting the circular fanlights of eighteenth century doors. *Door in Window #1* is Armajani's version of a window that also functions as a door in Jefferson's "Honeymoon Cottage" at the University of Virginia [*Armajani*, Institute of Contemporary Art, 1985,p. 50].

Door in Window #2 (1982–83) concentrates on the elegant play of oval within oval and bronze against black while also exploiting spatial complexities of open and transparent forms.

JEAN ARP (Swiss, 1887–1966)

4. *Torso with Buds* [*Nu aux bourgeons*], 1961
   Bronze, 73⅞ x 15½ x 15 (187.7 x 39.4 x 38.1)

MARKINGS: None

PROVENANCE: From artist to Sidney Janis Gallery, New
             York
             To Nasher collection, 1967

LITERATURE: Cf. Eduard Trier, Marguerite Arp-Hagenbach, François Arp, *Jean Arp: Sculpture, His Last Ten Years*, New York, 1968, cat. no. 256 (ill. p. 52)

25 *Years of Janis*, Sidney Janis Gallery, New York, 1973, cat. no. 8 (ill.)

Ionel Jianou, *Jean Arp*, Paris, 1973, cat. no. 257, pl. 54

EXHIBITIONS: *Exhibition of Sculpture of Jean Arp in Marble, Bronze, and Wood Relief*, Sidney Janis Gallery, New York, 1963, cat. no. 27 (ill.)

20th Century Sculpture: Mr. and Mrs. Raymond D. Nasher Collection, University Gallery, Southern Methodist University, Dallas, 1978, cat. no. 1 (ill.)

Torso with Buds is one of a long series of works by Arp synthesizing the human and botanical to produce an imaginative new species of anatomy. Precedents are found as early as the *Torso* of 1931 and *Growth* of 1938 (C. Giedion-Welcker, *Jean Arp*, New York, 1957, pp. 63 and 86) and continue into the *Dancing Flower* and *Flower Nude* of 1957, *Torso Sheaf* of 1958, and *Bud Figure* of 1959 (Trier et al., 1968, pls. 3, 5, 6, and 22). Deriving ultimately from Art Nouveau and Symbolist art, Arp's biomorphic language infused Surrealism with images alluding to growth, fecundity, and the natural world in general, helping give universality to private interior images. Free of Surrealist psychology, however, Arp's sculpture is marked by a poetry of wonder and joy celebrating life itself, as is felt strongly in the light, upward rhythms and jaunty posture of *Torso with Buds*.

There are three plasters of this sculpture, two in the Fondation Arp and Sophie Täuber-Arp in Rolandseck, West Germany, and one in the Von der Heydt Museum, in Wuppertal, West Germany, the gift of Marguerite Arp-Hagenbach. According to a certificate in the Nasher archives written and signed by Arp in March 1963, this cast was number one from an edition of three. A photograph published in 1968 (Trier et al., 1968, p. 52) shows one of these casts installed in Arp's own garden at Meudon in France. According to the Fondation Arp, the 0/3 cast has not yet been made but is still planned (correspondence with the author, 1986).

JOSEPH BEUYS (German, 1921–1986)

*5. *Animal Woman* [*Tierfrau*], 1949 (cast 1984)
   Bronze, 18 x 5⁷⁄₁₆ x 3⁷⁄₈ (45.7 x 13.8 x 9.8)

MARKINGS: In red paint on underside of solid cast: "Joseph Beuys 1949"

PROVENANCE: From artist to Galerie Beyeler, Basel
To Nasher collection, 1985

LITERATURE: Cf. Diane Waldman, *Transformations in Sculpture: Four Decades of American and European Art*, The Solomon R. Guggenheim Museum, New York, 1985, cat. no. 97 (ill.)

EXHIBITIONS: None

The original version of *Animal Woman* (Collection Eva Beuys) is made of metal and rubber tubing and dates from 1949 when Beuys was still a student at the Academy in Düsseldorf. A concern for themes of mythology, folklore, and universality had already arisen in his work. Soon after enrolling at the Academy in 1947, he showed a group of drawings and sculptures of animals and the human figure to Ewald Mataré, a strongly independent professor of sculpture who himself was interested in the fetishistic and folkloric and the expressive potential of ordinary materials. Mataré told Beuys that he should be a painter, not a sculptor, but agreed nevertheless in 1949 to accept him as a student (G. Adriani et al., *Joseph Beuys: Life and Works*, New York, 1979, pp. 25, 28). Mataré's example and instruction further encouraged Beuys's primitivizing tendencies, and there followed a group of sculptures, including *Animal Woman*, that seem to find their main source of inspiration in prehistoric fertility figures (see also *Joseph Beuys: Arbeiten aus münchner Sammlungen*, 1981, pl. 221).

Perched atop a tall narrow base like a votive object, *Animal Woman* has the heavy thighs, abdomen, and breasts typical of figures such as the Willendorf Venus. The general outlines of her anatomy closely follow a watercolor-and-pencil drawing by Beuys dating from 1947 (*Joseph Beuys Zeichnungen*, Nationalgalerie, Berlin, 1979, cat. no. 5) and may also relate to idols carved by Mataré in the twenties and thirties. Even as Beuys's later work moved in the direction of sociopolitical discourse and antiformalist structure and materials, he frequently made drawings of similar isolated, totemic figures.

An edition of seven bronze casts plus one artist's proof of *Animal Woman* was published in 1984 by Editions Schellmann and Klüser in Munich. Beuys's interest in the technical possibilities of all media is evident in his experimentation in this work with different patinas and his decision to allow the bronze to remain crude along the mold seams, leaving an irregular flange that varies with each cast. The Nasher cast does not have the protruding "ear" at the very top that is found in a number of other examples.

JONATHAN BOROFSKY (American, born 1942)

6. *Hammering Man*, 1984–85
   Painted steel plate and Cor-Ten steel, 240 x 108 x 18½ (610 x 274 x 47)

MARKINGS: Back foot: "2947538"

PROVENANCE: From artist to Paula Cooper Gallery, New York
To Nasher collection, 1985

LITERATURE: Cf. Mark Rosenthal and Richard Marshall, *Jonathan Borofsky*, Philadelphia Museum of Art and Whitney Museum of American Art, New York, 1984, pp. 18, 97–98, 101–03, 169–71 (ill.)

EXHIBITIONS: None

True to the dream and fantasy imagery that populates Borofsky's work, *Hammering Man*, in its different sizes and contextual placements, evokes a wide range of associations.

Its history is complex. Its first manifestation was in a wall drawing of a Tunisian shoemaker cutting a wooden sabot, executed at the Paula Cooper Gallery, New York, in 1976 and based on an illustration in the *Book of Knowledge* (see Rosenthal and Marshall, 1984, pl. 17). Transformed into the dark silhouette of an anonymous modern worker, the image reappears in different guises in numerous drawings, prints, and sketchbook pages (e.g., Rosenthal and Marshall, 1984, figs. 18, 19, 20, pl. 170). Based on the photocopy of one of these drawings, distributed at the Venice Biennale of 1980, Borofsky was inspired to make a three-dimensional *Hammering Man* whose arm would actually move (Rosenthal and Marshall, 1984, p. 171). The first version, about 11½ feet tall, painted black, appeared at Paula Cooper Gallery in 1980. A slightly larger version, painted red and stenciled with the word "strike," was shown in 1981 at the Los Angeles County Museum of Art, and a third man, now enlarged to 24 feet, was part of a group of installation works at the Kunsthalle, Basel, in 1981. In 1982, Borofsky created *Hammering Men*, a group of five figures for an installation at the Boymans–van Beuningen Museum, Rotterdam, and this work was later acquired by the Nashers and placed with *Hammering Man* at NorthPark.

Huge in scale, with head bent and motorized arm continuously moving up and down, the *Hammering Man* signifies both the drudgery and heroism of labor. The artist himself has stressed that the figure has an overlay of personal, political, and social meaning:

> The Hammering Man is a giant, and it goes back to my childhood. I liked to sit on my father's lap and have him tell me giant stories— especially about friendly giants. The Hammering Man is also a worker, and I idolize the worker in myself. . . . At the same time, it seems that the boring, monotonous repetition of the moving arm implies the fate of the mechanistic world. . . . it could lead to some associations with Marxist ideology. . . . And finally, this figure symbolizes the underpaid worker in this new, computerized revolution.
>
> The Hammering Man could be me, but I tried to make it both male and female. . . . Although anything I make is "me" and since I am not that different from anyone else on this planet, I hope the images are universal or archetypal [Rosenthal and Marshall, 1984, p. 171].

This 20-foot version was commissioned by the Nashers and executed at Lippincott, Inc., in North Haven, Connecticut. It is the only version in this scale. In addition to two five-figure groups, a total of six larger-than-life-size Hammering Men exist. They are signed with sequential numbers rather than a signature, a practice Borofsky adopted early in his career.

CONSTANTIN BRANCUSI (French, born Rumania, 1876–1957)

7. *The Kiss*, 1907–08 (cast before 1914)
   Plaster, 11 x 10¼ x 8½ (28 x 26 x 21.5)

MARKINGS: None

PROVENANCE: From artist to Alexandre Mercereau, Paris
             To Harold Diamond, New York
             To private collection, New York and Delaware

To Elkon Gallery, New York
To Nasher collection, 1986

LITERATURE: Cf. Barbu Brezianu, *Brancusi in Rumania*, Bucharest, 1976, cat. no. 21 (ill.) and no. 22 (ill.)

              Cf. Sidney Geist, *Brancusi: The Kiss*, New York, 1978, *passim* (ill.)

              Cf. Idem., *Brancusi: A Study of the Sculpture*, New York, 1968, pp. 28, 231, cat. no. 39 (ill.); rev. ed., 1983, cat. no. 55, p. 279 (ill.)

              Art in America 73, no. 11, November 1985, p. 7 (ill.)

EXHIBITIONS: *Moderní Umení XXXXV, Vystrava*, Manes Fine Art Society, Prague, 1914, cat. no. 124

This is one of six known plaster casts that Brancusi made at an early date from the first of several versions of *The Kiss* (1907–08), his first true masterpiece. The original stone carving is in the Muzeul de Artă at Craiova, Rumania. Brancusi recalled beginning work on this sculpture in 1907 but also sometimes gave its date as 1908 (see Geist, 1983, cat. no. 55). The chronology of ensuing versions of *The Kiss* is problematic but has been worked out most authoritatively by Sidney Geist: he dates the slightly larger and more primitivized stone version in the Diamond collection about 1908 (Geist, 1983, cat. no. 57), the still larger stone monument in Montparnasse Cemetery, Paris, 1909 (Geist, cat no. 68), and the stone version in the Philadelphia Museum of Art 1912 (Geist, cat. no. 81). Other, still later variations on the same theme provide evidence of its consuming hold on Brancusi's creative imagination. In conversations with the author (June 1985), Geist confirmed that Brancusi made the plasters himself soon after the carving of the original stone, most likely as a sign of affection for the original and as a means of extending his involvement with the project. They also made more works available for public exhibition. Brancusi frequently gave his plasters away as gifts but regarded them as self-sufficient art works, sometimes putting a price on them in exhibitions. He included a plaster of this version of *The Kiss* in the Armory Show of 1913 (probably the Rockefeller-Latner cast), and showed the present plaster in an exhibition of modern art at the Manes Society in Prague in 1914, subsequently giving it to the exhibition's organizer, Alexandre Mercereau. The following list updates the census of plaster casts of this work published by Geist in 1983, and is based in part on new information from him: Kunsthalle, Hamburg; Latner Family Collection, Toronto (ex-Gordon Farquhar and Nelson Rockefeller); Storck collection, Bu-

charest; The Edward R. Broida Trust, Los Angeles (purchased at Sotheby's, New York, November 4, 1982); Hakone Open-Air Museum, Japan; and the Nasher collection. Erosion along the top surfaces and certain driplike stains on the Nasher cast indicate that at some point it was placed outdoors.

The Kiss responds in a primitive mode to Auguste Rodin's famous marble *Kiss* of 1888, but its rough surface, squat proportions, and blunt expressiveness counter the sweet, fluid grace of the Rodin. Numerous sources have been proposed as possible influences, to which could be added the double tikis and net weights with two joined figures from the Hiva Islands in Polynesia. Almost certainly inspired in part by André Derain's carved *Crouching Man* of 1907, *The Kiss* breaks irrevocably with the tradition of Rodin, locking in its compact form a tender idyll on the unity of love, and announcing Brancusi's penchant for the simplified and primitive, for direct carving, and for poetic symbolism, traits that would mark his work for the rest of his life.

---

8. *Portrait of Nancy Cunard* [*Sophisticated Young Lady*], 1925–27
Walnut on marble base, 24¾ x 12½ x 4⅜ (62.8 x 31.7 x 11.1)

MARKINGS: None

PROVENANCE: From artist to Mme Marcel Duchamp, Villiers-sous-Grez, France, and New York, 1950 To Nasher collection, 1986

LITERATURE: Rene Huyghe, *Dialogue avec le visible*, Paris, 1955, p. 114 (dated 1928; ill.)

Ionel Jianou, *Constantin Brancusi*, Paris, 1963, p. 110 (dated 1928); rev. ed., Paris,

1982, p. 113 (dated 1927)

Sidney Geist, *Brancusi: A Study of the Sculpture*, New York, 1968, pp. 93–94, 111, cat. no. 160, fig. 160; rev. ed., New York, 1983, cat. no. 184, fig. 160 (dated 1925–27)

Idem, Brancusi: The Sculpture and Drawings, New York, 1975, cat. no. 184, ill. p. 131 (dated 1925–27)

EXHIBITIONS: *Brancusi*, Brummer Gallery, New York, 1933–34, cat. no. 36

Brancusi, Staempfli Gallery, New York, 1960, cat. no. 8 (ill.)

Constantin Brancusi 1876–1957: A Retrospective Exhibition, The Solomon R. Guggenheim Museum, New York, 1969, cat. pp. 116–17 (dated 1925; ill.)

There are several versions of Brancusi's *Portrait of Nancy Cunard*: this original carving in wood; a slightly larger plaster (a preparatory study for the bronze) in the Musée National d'Art Moderne, Paris (Geist, 1983, under cat. no. 184); a polished bronze, collection of Mr. and Mrs. Frederick Stafford, New York (Geist, 1983, cat. no. 205); and a posthumous bronze made in 1973 (see *Constantin Brancusi*, Galerie Tokoro, Tokyo, 1985). Sidney Geist has dated this original wooden version 1925–27 on the basis of two pieces of evidence. The plaster is inscribed "1925–28," which he interprets as marking, first, the beginning of the project, and secondly, the date of the plaster; and a photograph published of this work in 1935 is captioned "1927" (E. M. Benson, "Forms of Art: III," *American Magazine of Art*, May 1935, p. 299). The bronze made in the artist's lifetime is marked with two dates, 1928 and 1932, which Geist believes refer respectively to the plaster and the casting of the bronze.

Nancy Cunard was a poet, a patron of poets, and an attractive luminary in avant-garde artistic circles in Paris during the twenties. Brancusi had met her by 1923, when he and George Moore were her guests at a Christmas Eve dinner at La Rotonde. He seems not to have seen much of her after this occasion, and Geist reports that she was not aware until much later that Brancusi had made a portrait head of her, perhaps partly because it bore an alternate title, *Sophisticated Young Lady* (*Brancusi*, The Solomon R. Guggenheim Museum, 1969, p. 116). In his depiction, Brancusi employed a language of form involving extreme simplification of the head and neck and smooth, ovoid protrusions away from a vertical backline, similar to that in his *Portrait of Mrs. Meyer*, begun in 1916, and *The Chief* of 1925 (Geist,

1975, nos. 196 and 169), but with different expressive effect in each case. Here the impression is that of elegance but also airiness and charming humor due largely to the plump curve of the face and the corkscrew chignon perched so lightly and jauntily at the top. In transferring his composition from wood to metal, Brancusi was able to turn this juncture so that the chignon is more nearly vertical; he also pinched in the upper circumference of the neck, making the work taller and its lines slightly more springy.

SCOTT BURTON (American, born 1939)

9. *Schist Furniture Group* [*Settee with Two Chairs*], 1983–84
   Schist, chairs: 43 x 28 x 32 and 39 x 27½ x 35 (109 x 71 x 81 and 99 x 70 x 89); settee: 39 x 71 x 47½ (99 x 180 x 120.5)

MARKINGS: None

PROVENANCE: From artist to Max Protetch Gallery, New York
              To Nasher collection, 1985

LITERATURE: Cf. *Scott Burton*, The Tate Gallery, London, 1985, *passim*

              Cf. *Scott Burton Chairs*, Contemporary Arts Center, Cincinnati, and Fort Worth Art Museum, 1983, pp. 32–35

EXHIBITIONS: *Hidden Desires: Six American Sculptors, Acquisition Priorities for a Second Decade*, Neuberger Museum, Purchase, New York, 1984 (chairs only)

              Max Protetch Gallery, Dallas Trade Mart, 1984 (chairs only)

An effort to place art in a broader context and to counteract the division between fine art and usable object has led to Burton's ongoing production of sculptural furniture since 1972. He has explored a variety of formal approaches in this genre, whether creatively usurping an earlier furniture style, applying familiar stylistic principles in functional expressions, or creating his own new design formulas. His stone furniture, cut with minimal incisions from boulders and outcroppings, falls into the latter category, and is distinctive for its weight, solidity, and rustic, natural character. In a sophisticated but ironic art dialogue, it harks back to and perhaps parodies the rock installations familiar from seventies Minimalism, but it also evokes the populist historical tradition of outdoor rustic chairs and benches. The particular forms of the *Schist Furniture Group*, large chunks of stone sawed off at the bottom to create flat surfaces and notched-out to form seats, follow designs of earlier stone chairs by Burton dating back to 1979–80. He first conceived the format in 1979 and the next year included it in an unexecuted proposal for seating in a city park in Rockville, Maryland (see *Scott Burton Chairs*, 1983, p. 33). The first examples of the chair forms were made from gneiss boulders in 1980–81 and exhibited in the 1981 Biennial at the Whitney Museum of American Art, New York. Although numerous other examples in different stones have since been made, the wider, settee form is less common. The schist for the Nasher group was found at the Stoneyhurst Quarries in Maryland, a site Mrs. Nasher visited with Burton's dealer, Max Protetch, to examine the settee after it was cut.

ALEXANDER CALDER (American, 1898–1976)

10. *The Spider*, 1940
    Painted sheet metal and steel rod, 95 x 99 x 73 (241 x 251 x 185)

MARKINGS: The five hanging elements are numbered 1–5

PROVENANCE: From artist to Pierre Matisse Gallery, New York
              To Herbert Matter, Connecticut, 1941
              To Marlborough Gallery, New York

To Nasher collection, 1984

LITERATURE: P. G. Bruguière, "L'Objet-mobile de Calder," *Cahiers d'Art*, no. 2, 1954, p. 224 (ill.)

EXHIBITIONS: Pierre Matisse Gallery, New York, 1941

Calder's Universe, Whitney Museum of American Art, New York, 1976–77, cat. p. 284 (ill.)

Masters of 19th and 20th Centuries, Marlborough Gallery, New York, 1983, cat. no. 7 (ill.)

Masters of Modern and Contemporary Sculpture, Marlborough Gallery, New York, 1984, cat. no. 11 (ill.)

Calder pioneered the form of the standing mobile around 1930 and developed it in such major works as the *Calderberry Bush* (1932) and *The Praying Mantis* (1936). *Spider* of 1940, following in the same path, was one of Calder's largest indoor works in the genre to that date. A 1939 version (*Spider*, 78¾ inches high, in *Alexander Calder*, The Solomon R. Guggenheim Museum, New York, 1964, p. 72) has an archlike stand and a more horizontal disposition of elements. The Nasher version, resting on a tripod stand, evolved from a small maquette, c. 1939, called *Baby Spider* and a midsize version, c. 1940, titled *Little Spider* (*Calder's Universe*, 1976–77, cat. p. 273). The latter, which has a slightly different rhythm of parts and selectively colored "petals," has more strands than the final sculpture. Despite the stark black-and-white coloration of the final version, its primary effect is one of lightness and delicacy, of graceful movement combining leaflike appendages with long spidery legs or branches. Each element, cut or shaped by Calder, preserves a quality of handworked liveliness. With its compound suspensions and balances, *The Spider* responds readily to the slightest air current and offers one of the finest examples of the resolution in such works between opposing states: stability and mobility, suspension and support, the geometric and organic. Calder would again vary the theme with his *Hanging Spider* mobile, c. 1940, and, much later, with two large stabiles called *Spider* and *Big Spider* (see *Calder: An Autobiography with Pictures*, New York, 1966, pp. 228–29).

Herbert Matter, longtime owner of this work, was a filmmaker and photographer and a personal friend of Calder's. He saw *The Spider* in an exhibition in 1941 and purchased it from the show (documentation courtesy Marlborough Gallery). A film he made on Calder includes footage of this work.

---

11. *Three Bollards* [*Trois Bollards*], 1970
    Painted steel, 137 x 114 x 137 (350 x 290 x 350)

MARKINGS: Front of left front "leg": "CA 70"

PROVENANCE: Galerie Maeght, Paris
Studio Marconi, Milan, through Gimpel Fils, London
To Nasher collection, 1972

LITERATURE: Carlos Franqui, "Calder," *Derrière le miroir* 190, no. 2, February 1971, p. 26 (ill. pp. 7, 8, 10, 12–13, 17, 22–23, 26)

EXHIBITIONS: *Calder*, Studio Marconi, Milan, 1971, cat. no. 3 (ill.)

Calder, Musée Toulouse-Lautrec, Albi, France, 1971, cat. no. 1 (ill.)

Calder's first stabiles, dating from the thirties, translated into three-dimensional form the lyrical, biomorphic colored planes that had impressed him so deeply in the art of Joan Miró and Jean Arp. Cut from sheet metal, assembled with rivets or bolts, and frequently painted flat black, these works reflect Calder's training as an engineer and his interest in modern processes of construction. They join technology, however, with a witty vocabulary of semibiological shapes and configurations, as seen in the *Whale* (1937) and *Spherical Triangle* (1939). Calder adopted the techniques of planar composition developed by Russian Constructivist and Cubist artists, refracting them through Surrealism and his own punning, gestural sensibility. In the fifties, as the artist attracted more commissions and the number and scale of his stabiles grew, he turned for assistance in fabrication to the Segre Iron Works in Waterbury, Connecticut, and the Etablissements Biémont in Tours, near his home in France, limiting his direct involvement in construction of the large pieces to production of the maquette and supervision of the work.

Three Bollards follows within this genealogy. Typifying the play between abstraction and nature in Calder's work, its composition of flat, black, abstract planes also suggests a many headed, multilegged insect with a wide, arching stance. It hints further, through its title and the three posts at its top, at a functional structure for docking boats or tying up ropes. The maquette for *Three Bollards* is made from thin sheets of cardboard or sheet metal stapled together and marked "No. 87" on the side, the meaning of which is unknown (Franqui, 1971, pp. 5, 7, ill.; present location unknown).

ANTHONY CARO (British, born 1924)

12. *Carriage*, 1966
    Painted steel, 77 x 80 x 156 (196 x 203 x 396)

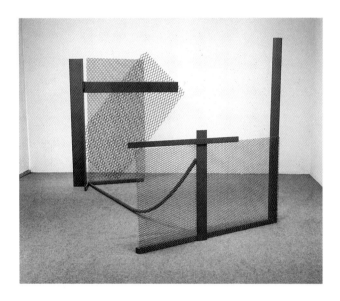

MARKINGS: None

PROVENANCE: From artist to André Emmerich Gallery, New York
To Mr. and Mrs. Henry Feiwel, Woodstock, New York
To André Emmerich Gallery, New York
To Nasher collection, 1986

LITERATURE: Rosalind Krauss, "On Anthony Caro's Latest Work," *Art International* 11, no. 1, January 20, 1967, pp. 26–28 (ill.)

William Rubin, *Anthony Caro*, New York, 1975, pp. 7, 136, 138 (ill. p. 81)

Richard Whelan, *Anthony Caro*, New York, 1975, pp. 61–62, fig. 25

Dieter Blume, *Anthony Caro: Catalogue Raisonné Vol. III, Steel Sculptures 1960–1980*, Cologne, 1981, no. 894, p. 197 (ill.)

Diane Waldman, *Anthony Caro*, New York, 1982, pp. 59–61, pl. 50

EXHIBITIONS: *Anthony Caro*, André Emmerich Gallery, New York, 1966

X Bienal de São Paulo, British Pavilion, São Paulo, Brazil, 1969, "Anthony Caro," cat. no. 4 (ill.)

Anthony Caro, The Arts Council of Great Britain, Hayward Gallery, London, 1969, cat. no. 28 (ill. pp. 10 and 50)

The Great Decade of American Abstraction: Modernist Art 1960 to 1970, Museum of Fine Arts, Houston, 1974, cat. no. 8 (ill. p. 49)

Large-Scale Master Paintings and Sculpture, André Emmerich Gallery, New York, 1984

Qu'est-ce que la sculpture moderne?, Musée National d'Art Moderne, Centre Georges Pompidou, Paris, 1986, cat. no. 143, p. 125 (ill.)

Carriage belongs to a series of works from 1966–67 in which Anthony Caro introduced into his low-lying, horizontal, segmented compositions the use of mesh planes. Open, transparent grids replaced solidity with spatial penetration and lightened even further the graceful cadences characteristic of his work of the period. As William Rubin has observed:

> In the sculptures of 1966 Caro solved the "problem" of the opacity of vertical panels—such as that of *Early One Morning*—by introducing rectangular grids made of street gratings or expanded-metal mesh of the type used for reinforcing walls. These made possible compositions based on semitransparent upright planes dispersed through lateral space with an autonomy that Caro emphasized by making their linkages extremely tenuous.... The relative transparency of the grids permits them to function almost as surrounding walls [Rubin, 1975, p. 136].

According to the artist's records, the sequence of major works incorporating mesh grids consists of *Aroma* (1966), *Red Splash* (1966), *Carriage* (1966), *Span* (1966), *The Window* (1966–67), and *Source* (1967) (Rubin, 1975, p. 7). It is a stylistic device, however, that almost completely disappeared from Caro's work after 1967.

In *Carriage*, two discrete upright segments are joined by a gently curved tubular bar that spans an open space of almost twelve feet, raising the possibility that the title derives from a vague suggestion of a horse linked by drooping reins to a carriage. Viewed from the side, the sculpture is read primarily as a two-walled delimiter of open space. From the ends, it merges several complex pictorial themes: the rectilinear interaction of the solid vertical and horizontal elements, the foreshortened collapse of space between the two vertical planes, and the changing patterns of one mesh grid seen against the two superimposed grids. Caro's choice of a blue-green color tends also to emphasize a pictorial rather than tactile or literal quality. When *Carriage* was first exhibited in New York in 1966, it immediately drew con-siderable critical attention as one of Caro's most important sculptures to date (see Krauss, 1967; Michael Fried, *Artforum* 5, no. 6, February 1967, pp. 46–47; and Cindy Nemser, *Arts Magazine* 41, no. 3, December 1966–January 1967, p. 63).

JOHN CHAMBERLAIN (American, born 1927)

13. *Zaar*, 1959
  Welded steel, painted, 51¼ x 68⅜ x 19⅝ (130.2 x 173.7 x 49.8), without base

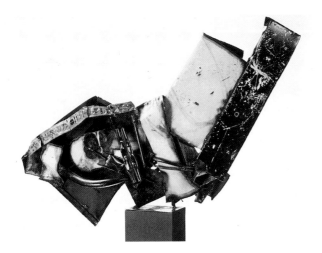

MARKINGS: None

PROVENANCE: Leo Castelli Gallery, New York
  Robert and Ethel Scull, New York
  Sold at Sotheby Parke Bernet, New York, October 18, 1973
  Dayton's Gallery 12, Minneapolis, and James Corcoran Gallery, Los Angeles
  Joyce and Ted Ashley, New York
  Larry Gagosian Gallery, New York and Los Angeles
  To Nasher collection, 1984

LITERATURE: "From Exhibitions Here and There," *Art International* 4, no. 1, 1960 (ill. p. 67)

  Grégoire Müller, "Points of View: A Taped Conversation with Robert C. Scull," *Arts Magazine* 45, no. 2, November 1970, p. 39 (ill.)

  A Selection of Fifty Works from the Collection of Robert C. Scull, Sotheby Parke Bernet, New York, October 18, 1973, cat. no. 2 (ill.)

  Julie Sylvester, *John Chamberlain: A Catalogue Raisonné of the Sculpture 1954–85*, New York, 1986, cat. no. 37 (ill.)

EXHIBITIONS: *The Art of Assemblage*, The Museum of Modern Art, New York, 1961–62, cat. no. 32

  Poets of the Cities: New York and San Francisco 1950–1965, Dallas Museum of Fine Arts and Southern Methodist University, Dallas, 1974, cat. no. 6 (ill. p. 105)

  John Chamberlain Retrospective, Museum of Contemporary Art, Los Angeles, 1986, cat. no. 37 (ill.)

Compared to the massive and dense compressions of brightly painted metal that characterize John Chamberlain's mature style, relatively consistent from the early sixties onward, his early work dating from 1954 to 1961 tends to be more open in form and diverse in color and texture. Linear elements made from bent rods and bars interweave with the dynamic syntax of assembled metal planes and curves. Surfaces are rough and coloration is part of the "found" nature of the materials. The general effect is one of gestural energy relating closely to American abstract painting of the fifties and combining the strength and roughness associated with forging and welding with an almost delicate command of line, mass, and color. Chamberlain's distinctive contribution to the assemblage ethos added a new dimension to techniques absorbed from such artists as Julio Gonzalez, David Smith, and Richard Stankiewicz, and has now outlived its early associations with the Pop art and American automobile cultures.
  Zaar is a strong example of the early phases of Chamberlain's development. It has been well-known since entering the Robert and Ethel Scull collection, New York.

RICHARD DEACON (Welsh, born 1949)

*14. *Like a Bird*, 1984
  Laminated wood, 121 x 208 x 205 (307 x 528 x 521)

MARKINGS: None

PROVENANCE: From artist to Lisson Gallery, London
  To Nasher collection, 1985

LITERATURE: None

EXHIBITIONS: International Garden Festival, Liverpool, England, 1984

  Richard Deacon: Sculpture 1980–1984, The Fruitmarket Gallery, Edinburgh; Le Nouveau Musée, Lyon, 1984–85, cat. pp. 26–27 (ill.)

  Nouvelle Biennale de Paris, Paris, 1985

Deacon's evocative objects cross-reference the natural and the fabricated, the organic and the man-made. The lobed shapes in *Like a Bird*, seen in different configurations in earlier drawings and sculptures such as an untitled work of 1981 and *For Those Who Have Ears No. 2* (1983) (*Deacon*, The Fruitmarket Gallery, 1984–85, pp. 10, 21, 37), combine with the title to suggest the looping paths and delicate movement of birds in flight. The structure consists of a closed line in a single plane that has been rotated into three positions, carving out a large three-dimensional volume. Thin sheets of metal and laminated strips of wood are Deacon's two favored materials. Both stress a personal ethic of the handmade (so different from the impersonality of much Minimalist technique), while the latter imparts a particular delicacy to his structures. The novel shapes, the straightforward materials and technique (unencumbered by art-historical associations), and the physical presence of the object give *Like a Bird* a fresh eloquence that is characteristic of Deacon's work in general.

JEAN DUBUFFET (French, 1901–1985)

15. *The Gossiper II* [*Le Deviseur II*], 1969–70 (fabricated 1984)
   Painted polyester resin, 120 x 81¾ x 85¼ (304.8 x 207.7 x 216.5)

MARKINGS: None

PROVENANCE: From artist to The Pace Gallery, New York
             To Nasher collection, 1985

LITERATURE: Cf. Max Loreau, *Catalogue des travaux de Jean Dubuffet*, fasc. XXIV, "Tour aux figures, amoncellements, cabinet logologique," Lausanne, 1973, no. 133 (ill.)

             Cf. Andreas Franzke, *Dubuffet*, New York, 1981, p. 188 (ill. p. 187)

EXHIBITIONS: *Jean Dubuffet Rétrospective*, Fondation Maeght, Saint-Paul-de-Vence, France, 1985, cat. no. 85 (ill.)

Dubuffet's protean sculptural output of the late sixties evolved stylistically from his earlier Hourloupe paintings, as he projected their undulating patterns of brightly colored, puzzlelike shapes into exuberant, sometimes quite monumental three-dimensionality. The writhing "script," which in the paintings helps reduce forms to flatness, in the sculpture reinforces the irregular movement of surface and contour. Dubuffet himself saw the work as "painting monumentalized." His wide-ranging iconography includes not just whimsical figures and objects such as tables and chairs but also towers, giant trees, architectural fantasies, and even elaborate public environments. Shaped from styrofoam and sometimes cast in resin in techniques that Dubuffet first developed in 1966, these objects constitute a bizarre "monde Dubuffet" experienced in full intensity in such large-scale installations as the famous Coucou Bazar.

Among the many productions of the period are several seated figures with such titles as *Le Siégéant*, *L'Auditeur*, and *Le Délibérant* (*Catalogue des travaux*, fasc. XXIII, 1972, nos. 52 and 71; fasc. XXIV, 1973, nos. 134–35). The latter is contemporaneous with *The Gossiper* and closely related in design, but while *The Gossiper* holds his hands outward in an exclamatory gesture, *Le Délibérant* sits with his arms crossed, quietly listening.

This version of *The Gossiper* is a unique enlargement of two much smaller versions (each 114 x 85 x 85 cm); one, dating from March–September 1969, is painted black and white, and a second, dating from March 1969–May 1970, is colored (*Catalogue des travaux*, fasc. XXIV, nos. 132–33). The former appeared in a Dubuffet exhibition at the Montreal Museum of Fine Arts in December 1969. For enlargements such as this, the original model, carved from styrofoam by the artist, generally was "pointed up" under his supervision into a full-scale styrofoam model, which then was used to make a mold for a polyester-resin cast. The polyurethane paint that is used bonds chemically with the surface of the cast. In this case, the chair and the figure were made separately and doweled together.

RAYMOND DUCHAMP-VILLON (French, 1876–1918)

16. *Torso of a Young Man* [*The Athlete*], 1910
Terra-cotta, 22⅜ x 12¾ x 16½ (57 x 32.5 x 42)

MARKINGS: None

PROVENANCE: From artist to Jacques Villon
To Marcel Duchamp
To Mme Marcel Duchamp, Villiers-sous-Grez, France
To Arnold Herstand and Co., New York
To Nasher collection, 1986

LITERATURE: Cf. Walter Pach, *Raymond Duchamp-Villon: Sculpteur*, Paris, 1924, p. 16 (ill. p. 47)

Cf. George Heard Hamilton and William Agee, *Raymond Duchamp-Villon*, New York, 1967, pp. 14, 16, 47–51, figs. 26, 27

Cf. Albert Elsen, *The Partial Figure in Modern Sculpture from Rodin to 1969*, 1969, pp. 42–44, cat. no. 19 (ill.)

EXHIBITIONS: *Moderní Umení XXXXV, Vystrava*, Manes Fine Art Society, Prague, 1914, cat. no. 127 (this torso? this terra-cotta?)

Galerie André Groult, Paris, 1914, no. 7 (this terra-cotta?)

Exposition Rétrospective, Salon des Indépendants, Paris, 1926, no. 2929 (this terra-cotta?)

Memorial Exhibition of the Works of Raymond Duchamp-Villon, Brummer Gallery, New York, 1929, no. 28 (this terra-cotta?)

Sculptures de Duchamp-Villon, Galerie Pierre, Paris, 1931, cat. no. 7 (this terra-cotta?)

Les 3 Duchamps, Galerie Tokoro, Tokyo, 1984, cat. no. 14 (ill.)

The Brothers Duchamp, Arnold Herstand and Co., New York, 1986, cat. p. 27 (ill.)

Torso of a Young Man, Duchamp-Villon's first fully mature sculpture, is a revision of the male figure in his *Pastorale* (1910), a classicized pairing of male and female, Adam and Eve. Walter Pach wrote that the *Torso*, with its simplified planar modeling, was partly inspired by the poses and archaic style of figures on the pediment of the temple of Aphaia at Aegina (see *Raymond Duchamp-Villon*, 1924, p. 16). This connection can be seen more clearly by considering the full figure in *Pastorale*. Its correspondence with certain of the striding warriors on the pediment helps explain the otherwise ambiguous gesture of Duchamp-Villon's figure, his arms raised to hold a shield and sword. In the *Torso*, truncation of the limbs eliminates gesture in favor of a less narrative figure, a clearer reading of the strained, striding pose, and a far more terse formal statement. The primary impression is that of strong forward movement. The power and dynamism that Duchamp-Villon saw as so characteristic of his age are thus expressed without recourse to mechanical references in a style that continues but energizes the French classical tradition.

Duchamp-Villon exhibited the plaster version of the *Torso*, now in the Hirshhorn Museum and Sculpture Garden, Washington, D.C., at the New York Armory Show of 1913, dating it 1911 on his entry registration form (Walt Kuhn Papers, Archives of American Art; information courtesy of Judith Zilczer). In catalogs of subsequent exhibitions from 1914, 1926, and 1931 (see Exhibitions above), however, the date is invariably listed as 1910. In each of these instances, a terra-cotta version was shown, probably the one now in the Nasher collection. Considerable confusion still exists as to the number and dating of the various casts in different materials. In the Hirshhorn plaster, probably the earliest extant version, the legs are cut off above the knees, the surface modeling is relatively smooth, and a block is inserted under the left leg to level the figure on its attached base. In the Nasher terra-cotta, the legs are extended below the knees and the surface, composed of pellets of clay pressed together and only partially smoothed, has more texture. In the bronzes (three lifetime casts and a posthumous edition by Galerie Louis Carré numbered through 8/8), the composition of the legs and the surface detail of the terra-cotta are preserved, but the base is eliminated. A photograph published by Walter Pach (1924, p. 47) records yet another plaster or terra-cotta, a version similar to the Nasher terra-cotta but without the base.

A drawing in the Musée National d'Art Moderne, Paris, has been associated with this sculpture but may well be later in date (see Hamilton and Agee, 1967, fig. 28). The *Torso* appears more frequently than any other sculpture by Duchamp-Villon as a motif in the many drawings, paintings, and prints of Jacques Villon based upon his brother's work (Daniel Robbins, *Jacques Villon*, Fogg Art Museum, Cambridge, Massachusetts, 1976, p. 101).

17. *Baudelaire*, 1911
   Plaster, 16 x 8⅞ x 10⅛ (40.6 x 22.5 x 25.7)

MARKINGS: Lower right side: "Duchamp-Villon / 1911"

PROVENANCE: From artist to Jacques Villon
   To André Salmon, 1931
   To Galerie Louis Carré, Paris
   To Arnold Herstand and Co., New York, 1984
   To Nasher collection, 1984

LITERATURE: Cf. Marie-Noëlle Pradel, "Dessins de
   Duchamp-Villon," *Revue des Arts: Musées
   de France* 10, nos. 4–5, 1960, pp. 222, 224

   Cf. Albert Elsen, "The Sculpture of
   Duchamp-Villon," *Artforum* 6, no. 2,
   October 1967, esp. p. 21 (ill. p. 24)

   Cf. George Heard Hamilton and William
   Agee, *Raymond Duchamp-Villon*, New
   York, 1967, pp. 16, 56–60, fig. 35

   Cf. Judith Zilczer, "Raymond Duchamp-
   Villon: Pioneer of Modern Sculpture,"
   Philadelphia Museum of Art Bulletin 76,
   no. 330, Fall 1980, esp. pp. 6–7 (ill.)

EXHIBITIONS: None

This austerely reductive and contemplative head of Baudelaire, dating from a year after the *Torso of a Young Man*,
deepened the rupture between Duchamp-Villon's mature
work and his earlier, Maillol-inspired style. Pride of accom-
plishment is reflected in his exhibition of casts of the *Bau-*

delaire (not yet individually identified) at the 1911 Salon
d'Automne (a plaster), the Galerie de l'Art Ancien et de l'Art
Contemporain in November and December 1911, possibly
the Salon de la Section d'Or of 1912, and the Armory Show
of 1913 (a terra-cotta). In 1912, Duchamp-Villon donated a
plaster to the museum in Rouen, his native city. In a letter
written in 1955, Jacques Villon attested that his brother had
made five or six plaster casts and three or four terra-cottas
of the *Baudelaire*, as well as three lifetime bronze casts
(correspondence in the Wellesley College archives; quoted
by Zilczer, 1980, p. 23 n. 12). To date, five plasters have
been identified (Nasher collection; Philadelphia Museum
of Art, gift of the artist's family; Musée des Beaux-Arts de
Rouen; private collection in Germany; and Musée de Saint-
Denis, from the collection of Paul Eluard). Four terra-cottas
are known (Wellesley College, Art Gallery of Ontario, New
York art market, Ny Carlsberg Glyptothek, Copenhagen),
and a full edition of bronzes numbered through 8/8 plus
one artist's proof was completed posthumously. The Nasher
cast belonged to Jacques Villon, who gave it to André
Salmon in return for the preface Salmon contributed to the
catalog of the Duchamp-Villon exhibition at the Galerie
Pierre in 1931 (information from the archives of Galerie Louis
Carré).

   A compelling precedent for this head was Rodin's famous *Portrait of Baudelaire* (1892), certainly known to Duchamp-Villon. His friend the critic Jacques Crepet is also
known to have supplied the artist with photographs of Baudelaire by Nadar and Carjat. Rodin's sensuous surfaces and
the historical accuracy of the photographs were displaced,
however, by Duchamp-Villon's search for a timeless, distilled essence of form. A small study in wax (present location
unknown) that was later cast in an edition of bronzes (see
Hamilton and Agee, 1967, p. 59) is relatively close to the
Rodin in form and feeling. A drawing now in the Musée
National d'Art Moderne in Paris (Hamilton and Agee, 1967,
p. 59) shows a further stage of development; the head is
more rigid and surfaces trued and flattened, clearly under
the influence of Cubism. Various authors have noted Duchamp-Villon's historical consciousness and interest in
French Gothic art and the affinities of the *Baudelaire* with
certain heads on the Portail Royal at Chartres. However,
Louis Hautecoeur's invocation of its Egyptianness seems
more apt; the stony hard volumes, blank eyes, and firmly
set features indeed recall black basalt and diorite heads of
the Late Period.

   The *Baudelaire* was the subject of much discussion
within the Puteaux group, which focused primarily on an
analysis of its planar structure and its potential decompo-
sition in space. Villon based a long series of works on the
piece starting in 1919 (see Daniel Robbins, *Jacques Villon*,
Fogg Art Museum, Cambridge, Massachusetts, 1976, pp.
92f).

---

18. *Maggy*, 1912 (cast 1957)
   Bronze, 28 x 13¼ x 15 (71 x 33.5 x 38)

MARKINGS: Left side, lower left: "Duchamp-Villon"
   Back, lower left: "Louis Carré editeur 1957"
   Back, lower right: "Georges Rudier /
   Fondeur Paris"

PROVENANCE: Galerie Louis Carré, Paris
   To Richard K. Weil Collection, St. Louis
   To Galerie Beyeler, Basel, 1985
   To Nasher collection, 1986

LITERATURE: Cf. *Sculptures de Duchamp-Villon*, Galerie
   Louis Carré, Paris, 1963, cat. no. 4 (ill.)

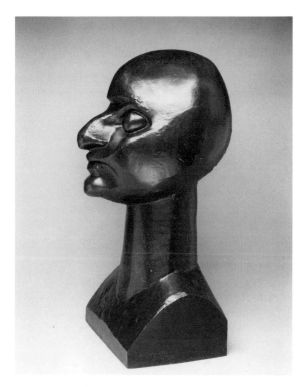

Cf. George Heard Hamilton and William Agee, *Raymond Duchamp-Villon*, New York, 1967, pp. 16–19, 61–63, fig. 39

Cf. Albert Elsen, *The Sculpture of Henri Matisse*, New York, 1972, p. 136, fig. 181

Cf. *Raymond Duchamp-Villon*, Musée des Beaux-Arts, Rouen, 1976, cat. no. 12 (ill.)

EXHIBITIONS: *Aus privaten Sammlungen*, Galerie Beyeler, Basel, 1986, cat. no. 16 (ill.)

This daring "portrait" depicts Maggy Ribemont-Dessaignes, wife of the poet and painter Georges Ribemont-Dessaignes, both of whom were friends of Duchamp-Villon and frequent visitors of the Puteaux group. A first, smaller study (see Hamilton and Agee, 1967, p. 62), apparently from the same year as the ultimate version, is far more Rodinesque and naturalistic in treatment, manifesting certain highly individualistic facial features that are still detectable beneath the bold exaggerations of the final head: the large sloping nose, pointed chin, tight lips, sharp cheek bones, and blunt curve of the skull. In the progression from study to final version, the influence both of Matisse's Jeannette series and of African reliquary heads and headdresses is felt, the latter particularly in the long shaftlike neck, bulging eyes, and general sense of a carved totemic idol. Hardly flattering, *Maggy's* abstractions nevertheless retain an essence of the sitter while projecting like a clenched fist an image of latent power.

Although this sculpture is sometimes dated 1911 (see Hamilton and Agee, 1967, p. 61), early exhibition listings identifiable with it indicate instead a date of 1912. In April-May 1914, the Galerie André Groult in Paris exhibited a terra-cotta *Visage de femme* dated 1912 belonging to "G.R.D." The Exposition de la Section d'Or at the Galerie Vavin-Raspail in January 1925 included both a *Portrait de Madame G.R.-D.* of 1912 and a *Maquette pour le Portrait de Madame G.R.-D.*, also of 1912. In addition to the terracotta version mentioned above, an unknown number of plasters and a wax exist (both a plaster and a wax were exhibited at the Brummer Gallery, New York, 1929; the catalog entry for the Duchamp-Villon exhibition at Rouen, 1976, refers to four plasters but no locations are given). A small group of bronzes were cast during the artist's lifetime (number unknown), and Galerie Louis Carré issued a posthumous edition of eight bronzes plus proofs, cast by Georges Rudier. This cast is not numbered but is recorded by Galerie Louis Carré as number four of eight.

---

*19. *Horse and Rider II* [*Cheval et chevalier II*], 1914
Bronze, 10¾ x 7½ x 4 (27.3 x 19 x 10.2)

MARKINGS: Top of base at back: "Duchamp-Villon" Side of base at left: "Alexis Rudier / Fondeur Paris"

PROVENANCE: Mme Jean Crotti
To Arnold Herstand and Co., New York
To Nasher collection, 1986

LITERATURE: Cf. Albert Elsen, "The Sculpture of Duchamp-Villon," *Artforum* 6, no. 2, October 1967, pp. 22–25 (ill. p. 23)

Cf. George Heard Hamilton and William Agee, *Raymond Duchamp-Villon*, New York, 1967, pp. 86–103, fig. 61

EXHIBITIONS: *The Brothers Duchamp*, Arnold Herstand and Co., New York, 1986, ex-cat.

The Horse is Duchamp-Villon's most famous sculpture and a definitive statement of his ideas on merging natural and mechanized forms as a metaphor of modern Machine Age power. Theories as to when Duchamp-Villon began work on the project differ considerably, but Judith Zilczer has shown that the germ of the idea exists in a sketch for the Cubist House, c. 1912 ("Raymond Duchamp-Villon: Pioneer of Modern Sculpture," *Philadelphia Museum of Art Bulletin*, Fall 1980, pp. 15–16). The conception then progressed through numerous drawings (most still in the estate of the artist; e.g., Zilczer, 1980, p. 16; and Angelica Rudenstine, *Peggy Guggenheim Collection, Venice*, New York, 1985, pp. 277–78) and several three-dimensional studies beginning with *Horse and Rider I* and moving on to *Horse and Rider II, Small Horse*, several tiny models, and plaster maquettes for the final version (Hamilton and Agee, 1967, figs. 60, 61, 62, 64; Rudenstine, 1985, pp. 274, 279). Concentrated work began in the spring of 1914, and most of these studies can be dated to that year, although their exact sequence remains uncertain. The early phase represented by *Horse and Rider I* and *Horse and Rider II*, however, is relatively naturalistic compared to later stages, Duchamp-Villon perhaps basing his roughly modeled studies of the Horse and Rider theme on observations of polo matches and other equestrian events. In the first version, the horse seems to

be pulling to an abrupt stop, the rear legs bending sharply forward under the strain and the rider pulling back hard on the reins. In the more vertical *Horse and Rider II*, the legs are drawn together at the bottom, almost as if the animal were balancing circuslike on a small platform. The treatment of anatomy in the latter is already considerably more regularized and mechanized; the horse's shoulders, legs, and haunches are particularly suggestive of gears, flywheels, and piston rods. In subsequent studies, this machine imagery gradually becomes more pronounced.

Although it was Duchamp-Villon's practice to cast his clay models first in plaster and/or terra-cotta and then in bronze, no surviving plasters or terra-cottas of *Horse and Rider II* are known to this author. The date of casting of the Nasher bronze is also uncertain, although its provenance and publication by Alexis Rudier are signs of relatively early origin (bronze casts had been made by the time of the Duchamp-Villon exhibition at Galerie Pierre in 1931). A later edition of eight numbered bronzes was issued by Louis Carré and marked with his name.

---

*20. *Large Horse* [*Le Cheval majeur*], 1914 (second enlargement by Marcel Duchamp, 1966)
Bronze, 59½ x 57 x 34 (151 x 144.8 x 86.3)

MARKINGS: At front, lower right: "R. Duchamp-Villon 1914 7/9 Louis Carré, Editeur Susse Fondeur, Paris"

PROVENANCE: Mme Marcel Duchamp, Villiers-sous-Grez, France
To Artemis Fine Arts, Ltd., London, 1974
To Xavier Fourcade, Inc., New York
To Nasher collection, 1980

LITERATURE: Cf. *Duchamp-Villon: Le Cheval majeur*, Galerie Louis Carré, Paris, 1966, *passim* (ill.)

Cf. George Heard Hamilton and William

Agee, *Raymond Duchamp-Villon*, New York, 1967, pp. 22–23, 86–103, fig. 69

Artemis Report, 1975–76, London, 1976, cat. no. 12 (ill.)

Cf. Judith Zilczer, "Raymond Duchamp-Villon: Pioneer of Modern Sculpture," *Philadelphia Museum of Art Bulletin* 76, no. 330, Fall 1980, esp. pp. 15–18

Cf. Angelica Rudenstine, *Peggy Guggenheim Collection, Venice*, New York, 1985, pp. 270–81

EXHIBITIONS: *Twentieth Century Paintings and Sculpture: Matisse to de Kooning*, Xavier Fourcade, Inc., New York, 1977, p. [18] (ill.)

Large Scale, Small Scale Sculpture, Xavier Fourcade, Inc., New York, 1978

Many extant preparatory studies attest to Duchamp-Villon's consuming involvement with *The Horse* over a number of years. This proto-Dada hybrid of animal and machine, in radically updating Europe's long history of equestrian sculpture, drew inspiration from both Duchamp-Villon's observation of riders and polo matches and his avowed enthusiasm for the "power and audacity" of modern engineering. In August 1914, after work on *The Horse* had reached an advanced stage, he enlisted in the army as a medical underofficer assigned to a cavalry regiment, which afforded him more experience as a horseman and perhaps intensified his efforts to finish the sculpture. Albert Elsen ("The Sculpture of Duchamp-Villon," *Artforum* 6, no. 2, October 1967, pp. 22–25), Hamilton and Agee (1967, pp. 86–103), and Rudenstine (1985, pp. 270–81) have traced the complicated evolution of drawings and studies leading to the final solution (see also above, cat. no. 19). The penultimate plaster study now in the Philadelphia Museum of Art (14½ inches high; Rudenstine, 1985, p. 279) retains a slightly organic modeling of the horse's head and neck but has the thrusting, cantilevered composition of the ultimate version as well as its translation of other anatomical elements into a machine vocabulary. Two plaster maquettes of the final composition are known (Philadelphia Museum of Art and Musée de Grenoble, each 17½ inches high; see Rudenstine, 1985, p. 274; a third belonged to John Quinn but is now lost), and show a greater refinement of surface and more precise articulation of machine imagery. Conflicting evidence points alternatively to completion of this stage by the end of 1914 and continuation of work throughout the war (see Rudenstine, 1985, pp. 271 n.1 and 273 n.6). By his death in 1918, however, Duchamp-Villon had prepared an armature for enlargement of *The Horse* to a scale of approximately one meter and had announced his intentions for a large version in steel to his brothers Jacques Villon and Marcel Duchamp and close friend and biographer Walter Pach.

The subsequent history of casts and enlargements of *The Horse* is too complex and problematic to treat fully here (the best analysis is found in Rudenstine, 1985). The first posthumous bronze cast was made by John Quinn in 1921–22 of the 17½-inch version; exact numbers and dates of later casts in this scale are uncertain, although at least two were made c. 1930–31 followed by an edition of both lead and bronze casts in the fifties by Galerie Louis Carré. Presumably about 1930–31, Villon and Duchamp executed the first enlargement to 100 centimeters based upon Duchamp-Villon's unused armature, and in 1955 an edition of six examples in this scale was cast by the Susse foundry. In 1966, Duchamp supervised a second enlargement to 150 centimeters, cast by Georges Rudier, again under the auspices of Louis Carré. Although it has raised certain questions as to the artist's original intentions, the largest version, known as *Le Cheval majeur*, has become well known through its now complete edition of nine numbered casts and an "artist's proof" (the final cast was made in stainless steel).

---

*21. *Portrait of Professor Gosset*, 1918 (cast 1960s)
Bronze, 3⅜ x 3¼ x 3⅜ (8.6 x 8.3 x 8.6)

MARKINGS: Right side of head: "Duchamp-Villon 5/9"
Right jaw: "Georges Rudier Fondeur Paris"
Bottom: "Louis Carré, editeur"

PROVENANCE: Mme Marcel Duchamp, Villiers-sous-Grez, France
To Arnold Herstand and Co., New York, 1986
To Nasher collection, 1986

LITERATURE: Cf. Walter Pach, *Raymond Duchamp-Villon: Sculpteur*, Paris, 1924, pp. 24–25, 85 (ill. p. 85; dated 1917)

Cf. George Heard Hamilton and William Agee, *Raymond Duchamp-Villon*, New York, 1967, pp. 24, 106–07 (ill.)

Cf. Judith Zilczer, "Raymond Duchamp-Villon: Pioneer of Modern Sculpture," *Philadelphia Museum of Art Bulletin 76*, no. 330, Fall 1980, pp. 21–22 (ill.)

Cf. *100 Oeuvres nouvelles 1977–1981*, Musée National d'Art Moderne, Paris, 1981, p. 35 (ill.)

EXHIBITIONS: *The Brothers Duchamp*, Arnold Herstand and Co., New York, 1986, ex-cat.

The severe stylization of skull and facial features seen in two earlier portrait busts, the *Baudelaire* and *Maggy* of 1911 and 1912, reached an extreme in the *Portrait of Professor Gosset*, Duchamp-Villon's last sculpture. While stationed as a medical underofficer at Champagne near the front, he contracted typhoid fever in late November or early December 1916, and was taken to the hospital at Châlons-sur-Marne. Over the next year his strength slowly ebbed, making it difficult for him even to draw, but despite his debilitated state he was able to start a small portrait of one of the attending surgeons, Professor Gosset. On May 20, 1918, he wrote to his friend Walter Pach:

> Je ne puis rien entreprendre de sérieux sauf quelques dessins qui me fatiguent plus que la construction d'une maison autrefois. J'ai cependant ébauché assez loin un portrait d'un des chirurgiens qui m'ont soigné et dont je ne suis pas mécontent comme point de départ. Mais il faut encore le rendre définitif et j'escompte les semaines de ma convalescence pour l'achever. Tout cela est un gros effort pour ma faiblesse [Pach, 1924, pp. 24–25].

Although Pach dated the work 1917, this letter shows that it was still in an early stage in May 1918. It is not known whether Duchamp-Villon ever brought it to what he considered a truly "definitive" state. He died in October 1918, leaving an undetermined number of small plasters measuring under four inches in height (see Pach, 1924, p. 85) and a wax cast in the same dimensions (exhibited with a plaster at the Brummer Gallery's *Memorial Exhibition of the Works of Raymond Duchamp-Villon*, 1929, cat. nos. 11, 41). One plaster cast is now in the Philadelphia Museum of Art (Zilczer, 1980, p. 21), another was formerly in the John Quinn collection (present location unknown; see Judith Zilczer, *"The Noble Buyer:" John Quinn, Patron of the Avant-Garde*, Washington, D.C., 1978, pp. 157–58), and a third is in the Musée des Beaux-Arts, Rouen. The date of the first casting in bronze is unknown, but Quinn had acquired a gilt bronze cast in the early twenties (he may have had it made from his plaster, however), and a bronze was included in the Galerie Pierre show of Duchamp-Villon's work in 1931. The Nasher cast is from a modern edition authorized by the artist's family and published by Louis Carré in the sixties. The edition totals nine plus artist's proofs.

Following the pattern of posthumous enlargements of *The Horse*, *Professor Gosset* underwent a similar transformation; directed by Jacques Villon and executed by Louis Carré in 1957, it resulted in a plaster measuring 30 centimeters and an edition of eight bronzes. Whereas the original small version was modeled with pellets of clay that impart

a rough texture, the enlarged version was smoothed to a hard, machinelike finish.

The radical reductions of form to a stark, skull-like image in *Professor Gosset* have been interpreted as Duchamp-Villon's presentiment of his impending death. It is more justifiable, however, to see *Professor Gosset* as an extension of earlier concerns with synthesized and rationalized structural order, integrating various influences including archaic art, the work of Brancusi, and African masks. A sheet of drawings from the artist's estate shows how he attempted to wed the forms of *Professor Gosset* to an architectural function (Zilczer, 1980, p. 21).

MAX ERNST (French, born Germany, 1891–1976)

22. *The King Playing with the Queen*, 1944 (cast 1954)
Bronze, 37⅞ x 33 x 21⅛ (96.2 x 83.8 x 53.7)

MARKINGS: Left side of base, lower left: "III"

PROVENANCE: Max Ernst and Dorothea Tanning
             To Nasher collection, 1984

LITERATURE: Cf. Sam Hunter, ed., *Max Ernst: Sculpture and Recent Painting*, The Jewish Museum, New York, 1966, p. 44, cat. no. 94 (ill.)

Cf. John Russell, *Max Ernst: Life and Work*, New York, 1967, pp. 204–05, 208, pl. 147

Cf. *Max Ernst Retrospektive*, Haus der Kunst, Munich, 1979, cat. no. 270 (ill.), entry by Werner Spies

Cf. Evan Maurer, "Dada and Surrealism," in *"Primitivism" in 20th Century Art*, The Museum of Modern Art, New York, 1984, pp. 561, 564 (ill. p. 568)

EXHIBITIONS: None

Preeminent among several major sculptures by Max Ernst dating from 1944 is *The King Playing with the Queen*. Then sharing a house with Dorothea Tanning and the dealer Julien Levy in Great River, Long Island, New York, Ernst experienced a burst of creative energy resulting in the assemblage of diverse forms which he cast in plaster from containers and objects found around the household. *The King Playing with the Queen*, like the contemporaneous *The Table Is Set*, uses a flat platform for the arrangement of numerous elements in a pictorial, still-life space, a compositional device with precedents in the work of Alberto Giacometti, Jean Arp, and Henry Moore. In a playful allusion to the Surrealist love for the game of chess, but also intoning darker themes of sexual manipulation and dominance, the large horned king reaches out to grasp and move the much smaller queen. His thin proportions and angular limbs have been compared to graceful African whistle carvings from Upper Volta, and his curved horns and flat face to Hopi Kachina dolls (Maurer, 1984, pp. 561, 564, 568–69). Certain types of African masks may also have had an influence (e.g., the Senufo helmet mask pictured in Hunter, ed., 1966, p. 51). A similar vocabulary of rectangular plaques, indented holes, and hollowed, scooplike shapes is found in other sculptures of the same year, including *An Anxious Friend*, *Young Man with Beating Heart*, and *Moonmad*.

Ernst was unable to have the plaster of this work cast into bronze until 1954. In all, nine casts were made, some stamped "Max Ernst," others numbered. This is cast number three. It was acquired by the Nashers directly from the collection of Max Ernst and Dorothea Tanning. John Russell relates how the plaster for *The King Playing with the Queen* was left behind in a basement when Ernst moved from Long Island to Arizona (1967, pp. 204–05). It was eventually rescued and was later acquired by Robert Motherwell.

23. *Capricorn*, 1948 (cast 1963–64)
   Bronze, 89 x 82 x 55¼ (226.1 x 208.3 x 140.3)

MARKINGS: Right side of base, far right: "0/V Max Ernst"
Right side, top of base at back: "Susse Fondeur, Paris"

PROVENANCE: From artist to Jimmy Ernst, East Hampton, New York
To Galerie Beyeler, Basel
To Joel Mallin, New York
Sold at Sotheby's, New York, May 14, 1985
To Nasher collection, 1985

LITERATURE: Cf. Sam Hunter, ed., *Max Ernst: Sculpture and Recent Painting*, The Jewish Museum, New York, 1966, p. 44, cat. no. 100 (ill.)

Cf. Lucy Lippard, "Max Ernst and a Sculpture of Fantasy," *Art International* 11, no. 2, February 20, 1967, pp. 42–43

Cf. *Max Ernst: A Retrospective*, The Solomon R. Guggenheim Museum, New York, 1975, p. 57, cat. no. 223 (ill. p. 212)

Cf. Evan Maurer, "Dada and Surrealism," in *"Primitivism" in 20th Century Art*, The Museum of Modern Art, New York, 1984, p. 565 (ill. p. 572)

Property from the Collection of Joel Mallin, Sotheby's, New York, May 14, 1985, cat. no. 101 (ill.)

EXHIBITIONS: *Skulptur im 20. Jahrhundert*, Wenkenpark, Riehen/Basel, 1980, cat. p. 94 (ill. p. 95)

Max Ernst spent the years between 1946 and 1953 with Dorothea Tanning in Sedona, Arizona, where his activity as a sculptor was directed primarily to the cement reliefs with which he adorned his house and to the construction of his monumental masterpiece, *Capricorn*, of 1948. This regal grouping of enthroned personages is both a family portrait of Ernst and Tanning—an association strengthened by the well-known photograph of the two engulfed in the sculpture's forms (Hunter, ed., 1966, p. 53)—and a kind of talisman against evil spirits, in keeping with Ernst's shamanistic interests. The "king," playing upon the chessboard imagery of the *King Playing with the Queen* (1944), sits in a stiff frontal position; in his right hand he holds a staff, which resembles Ernst's destroyed *Standing Woman* sculpture. Beside him sits the armless, equally immobile "queen," with the body of a Cycladic fiddle idol, the tail of a mermaid, and a fish for a headdress. Resting between them are two friendly creatures, one doglike and the other half human and half fish. The two have been interpreted as Ernst's family dogs, but given the upright figure's resemblance to the woman and the rather protective and tender gesture with which the male props it up for presentation, it is more likely an offspring of the two rulers, although Ernst and Tanning were childless. That Capricorn, symbolic of birth and metamorphosis, has been identified as both goat and fish explains the horned mask of the king and the associations with Neptune and sea life.

Recognizing the depth of Ernst's attachment to primitive sources, various authors have suggested a range of ancient and tribal influences for *Capricorn*, including horned Hopi Kachina dolls for the male head and the headdress of the female (Maurer, 1984, p. 565), the Cycladic model already mentioned, and certain Maori and Northwest Indian motifs (Lippard, 1967, p. 43). The phallic navel of the male and the rigid, side-by-side position of the principal figures may be echoes of Dogon carvings of seated couples. It has also been pointed out that certain forms repeat painted and carved decorations from Ernst's house at Saint-Martin d'Ardèche in the south of France (Lippard, 1967, pp. 42–43).

Ernst made the original version of *Capricorn* in cement, which gave the sculpture a dry, rough, colorless surface that suited perfectly its location in the high Arizona desert. Fragments of the cement original survive and have been exhibited (see *Max Ernst*, Byron Gallery, New York, 1970). In preparing the model for casting, Ernst made certain modifications, such as extending the tail of the female to the edge of the base and covering her thighs with scales, changing the shape of the fish on her head, and modifying considerably the form of the "baby." Much confusion has surrounded the number and sequence of casts of this work, but the definitive census can now be established. Dorothea Tanning has written (correspondence with the Nashers, 1984):

The piece was created in Sedona, Arizona, in 1948. Max made it in cement and scrap iron as a guardian for our (also handmade) house. In 1962 his dealer, A. Iolas, persuaded the de Menils to underwrite its casting in bronze in exchange for a cast. Max returned to Sedona to oversee the taking of molds by a local sculptor friend. These were sent to Touraine, France, where we were then living. That summer Max reconstituted the work in preparation for casting. . . . The first cast was exhibited at the Iolas Galerie, Paris, that autumn (1963).

The original edition consisted of six casts (numbered 0/V–V/V), but Ernst extended the edition in the mid-seventies, and four more casts were made before his death in 1976. Finally, two casts were made posthumously. Three of the last six casts were marked 00/V, E.A. I/II, and E.A. II/II, and three were unnumbered (all donated to museums). In addition, Ernst gave the town of Château-Chinon in France the right to cast another example of *Capricorn*. A plaster survives, given by Ernst along with a bronze to the Nationalgalerie in Berlin.

---

24. *Sister Souls* [*Les Ames-Soeurs*], 1961
    Bronze, 36⅝ x 12 x 12½ (90.5 x 30.5 x 31.8)

MARKINGS:
Top of base, at back: "Max Ernst E.A. 2/3"
Side of base, at back: "Susse Fondeur, Paris"

PROVENANCE:
From artist to Galerie Denise René–Hans Meyer, Düsseldorf
To private collection, Switzerland
To Thomas Ammann Fine Art, Zürich
To Nasher collection, 1985

LITERATURE:
Cf. *Max Ernst: Oeuvre sculpté 1913–1961*, Le Point Cardinal, Paris, 1961, cat. no. 43 (ill.)

Cf. Sam Hunter, ed., *Max Ernst: Sculpture and Recent Painting*, The Jewish Museum, New York, 1966, p. 51, cat. no. 120 (ill.)

EXHIBITIONS: None

As in other instances, Max Ernst resurrects in *Sister Souls* (1961) a favored theme from an earlier sculpture, the paired vertical stalks of *Lunar Asparagus* (1935), which in turn owe a possible debt to slender Easter Island clubs (see *"Primitivism" in 20th Century Art*, The Museum of Modern Art, New York, 1984, pp. 559–60, 564) and to Alberto Giacometti's destroyed *Figure in a Field* (1930). The two shafts in *Sister Souls* are topped by round flat faces, also seen in other Ernst sculptures and possibly influenced by Eskimo masks. More vegetal than anthropoid, the "sisters" sway and bend in posture, as if engaged in relaxed conversation. Stretched out on the ground below is a humorous little dog. Typically, sculpture brought out Ernst's wit far more than painting. The act of three-dimensional shaping and transformation appealed to him as relaxation or, as he once put it, was "even more a game than painting."

Sister Souls was made in Huismes, near Tours, where Ernst had moved from Paris in 1955. It was cast the same year as modeled in an edition of five bronzes numbered 1/5–5/5; apparently, there were three artist's copies (*épreuves d'artiste*), since the Nasher cast is marked "E.A. 2/3." The plaster still exists.

BARRY FLANAGAN (Welsh, born 1941)

*25. *Large Leaping Hare*, 1982
    Gilded bronze with painted tubular-steel base, 110 x 111 x 44 (279 x 282 x 112)

MARKINGS: None

PROVENANCE: From artist to Waddington Galleries, Ltd., London
To Nasher collection, 1984

LITERATURE: Cf. *Barry Flanagan: Sculpture*, British Council, London, 1982, pp. 27–28, 88, 93 (ill.)

Cf. *Sutton Manor: Permanent Exhibition, XXth Century Sculpture*, Sutton Scotney, Hampshire, 1984, pp. 72–73 (ill.)

EXHIBITIONS: *Barry Flanagan: Sculptures*, Musée National d'Art Moderne, Paris, 1983, cat. pp. 11, 84, 88, no. 88 (different cast ill.)

Deeply involved with natural form and order, Barry Flanagan has an abiding interest in the ritualistic, in hieroglyphs and pictograms, and in ancient art and thought systems as paths toward universal meaning. The hare stands as a cen-

tral, symbolic being in his personal cosmology, which draws upon wide-ranging sources. Flanagan has explained his thoughts on the animal:

> The hare, culturally, has a particular sort of place in the imagination . . . [as] surrogate figure . . . evocative of human situation or activity. . . . Thematically the choice of the hare is really quite a rich and expressive sort of mode. . . . If you consider what conveys situation and meaning and feeling in a human figure, the range of expression is in fact far more limited than the device of investing an animal—a hare especially—with the expressive attributes of a human being. The ears, for instance, are really able to convey far more than a squint in the eye of a figure, or a grimace on the face of a model [*Barry Flanagan: Sculpture*, British Council, London, 1982, pp. 88, 93].

Flanagan also acknowledges as an important influence the book *The Leaping Hare*, by George Ewart Evans and David Thomson, in which, among other cultural traditions, they discuss the Egyptian hieroglyph for hare as a symbol of being and present various sexual interpretations of its attributes.

The image of the hare seems first to have appeared in Flanagan's work in a drawing of late 1979 (*Barry Flanagan: Sculpture*, 1982, p. 88, fig. 49). From that time on, a large family of modeled hares in various attitudes and guises began to emerge. They ran, stood, balanced, even boxed. Flanagan's imagination showed a fecundity closely associated symbolically with the animal itself. The modeling was loose and animated, seemingly done with a spontaneity that suggests drawing. The first Leaping Hare was cast in November 1979. In a drawing of 1980, Flanagan introduced the mystical, altarlike pyramid that he then used in a sculpture, adding a sort of platform at the top to support one of his leaping hares (1980; 70 x 107 x 25 cm). Finally, in 1982, he produced the monumental version of this composition, as represented in the Nasher collection, eliminating the platform atop the pyramid and thus enhancing the effect of suspended balance and the contrast between organic and geometric form. This work was first exhibited in 1982 at *Documenta 7* in Kassel, West Germany. The total edition numbers five; in only two examples are the hares gilded. The Nasher cast is the so-called "artist's copy."

NAUM GABO (American, born Russia, 1890–1977)

26. *Linear Construction in Space No. 1 (Variation)*,
1942–43 (fabricated c. 1957–58)
Plexiglass with nylon monofilament, 24¾ x 24¾ x 9½ (63 x 63 x 24)

MARKINGS: End of bottom plane: "N. Gabo"

PROVENANCE: Family of the artist
              To Nasher collection, 1985

LITERATURE: Cf. Herbert Read and Leslie Martin,

Gabo: Constructions, Sculpture, Paintings, Drawings, Engravings, Cambridge, Massachusetts, 1957, pls. 77–78

Albert Elsen, *Modern European Sculpture 1918–1945: Unknown Beings and Other Realities*, New York, 1979, pp. 78, 84, fig. 78

Colin Sanderson and Christina Lodder, "Catalogue Raisonné of the Constructions and Sculptures," in Steven Nash et al., *Naum Gabo: 60 Years of Constructivism*, Dallas Museum of Art, 1985, p. 234, cat. no. 53.7 (ill. pp. 82, 120)

EXHIBITIONS: *Gabo*, Boymans–van Beuningen Museum, Rotterdam, 1958, cat. no. 16

              Modern European Sculpture 1918–1945, Albright-Knox Art Gallery, Buffalo, 1979, cat. no. 20 (ill. p. 78)

              Naum Gabo: 60 Years of Constructivism, Dallas Museum of Art, 1985, cat. no. 38 (ill.)

Gabo made the prototype of his *Linear Construction in Space No. 1 (Variation)* during the winter of 1942–43 in Cornwall, England, where he had moved with his wife to escape the Nazi bombings of London. It differs slightly from *Linear Construction in Space No. 1* (1941–42), Gabo's first sculpture to incorporate the technique of stringing; by the notches or steps on the end pieces of the plastic frame, which both enliven the profile and create a broader, more active spread of the stringing pattern. It was Gabo's practice to recreate certain favorite works in different sizes and sometimes different materials as a way of exploring further the sculptural idea and/or fulfilling other purposes such as gifts, sales, or exhibition needs. Sanderson and Lodder have cataloged eleven versions of *Linear Construction in Space No. 1 (Variation)*, all in Perspex (plexiglass) with nylon filament, and varying in height from 21.8 to c. 60–63 centimeters. Among the four largest versions are the Nasher example and others in The Phillips Collection, Washington, D.C.; a private collection in England; and the Washington University Gallery of Art, St. Louis. The dates of certain examples are difficult to establish but range from 1942–43 to 1976. Miriam Gabo, the artist's widow, recalls that the Nasher version was finished just prior to its exhibition in Rotterdam in 1958.

Gabo's use of stringing, starting at roughly the same time that Henry Moore and Antoine Pevsner adopted this new technique, developed out of his slightly earlier practice of carving or scoring striations into surfaces for a sense of movement, transparency, and expansion, and may also have been prompted by his knowledge of strung mathematical models. A renewed influence of these models in the late thirties helped him grapple with problems of topology and spatial curvature, and lies behind the increased physical and conceptual purity of his work from this period. Indeed, the basic structure of *Linear Construction in Space No. 1* and its *Variation*, with strings running diagonally across a rectangular frame to describe an elliptical central void, resembles a common mathematical diagram. Transcending any possible diagrammatic influences, however, are the extremely sensuous effects of delicate movement and radiant light that Gabo achieves in these airy plastic constructions.

Gabo exhibited a large-scale version of this sculpture in his important show with Pevsner at The Museum of Modern Art, New York, in 1948 (cat. pp. 44–45; version now in The Phillips Collection, Washington, D.C.).

ALBERTO GIACOMETTI (Swiss, 1901–1966)

27. *Spoon Woman* [*Large Woman*; *Femme cuillère*], 1926–27 (cast 1954)
Bronze, 57¾ x 20 x 7¹⁵⁄₁₆ (147 x 50.8 x 20)

MARKINGS: Rear center, top of highest base: "Alberto Giacometti 2/6"
Right side of lower base, bottom edge: "Susse Fondeur, Paris"

PROVENANCE: Nelson Rockefeller
To Harold Diamond, New York
To Mr. and Mrs. Burton Tremaine, New York and Connecticut, 1971
To Nasher collection, 1984

LITERATURE: Cf. Reinhold Hohl, *Alberto Giacometti*, New York, 1971, pp. 78–79 (ill. p. 39)

Cf. Michael Brenson, "The Early Work of Alberto Giacometti," Ph.D. thesis, Johns Hopkins University, Baltimore, 1974, no. 24, pp. 1–61 *passim*

Cf. Reinhold Hohl, "Zur Datierung von 'Femme Cuillère' et 'Le Couple,'" in *Alberto Giacometti: Plastiken, Gemälde, Zeichnungen*, Wilhelm-Lehmbruck-Museum, Duisburg, West Germany, 1977, pp. 79–80

Cf. Rosalind Krauss, "Giacometti," in *"Primitivism" in 20th Century Art*, The Museum of Modern Art, New York, 1984, pp. 504–08, 528 n. 11, 13–15 (ill. p. 509)

Cf. James Lord, *Giacometti: A Biography*, New York, 1985, pp. 93–94

EXHIBITIONS: *Twentieth Century Art from the Nelson Aldrich Rockefeller Collection*, The Museum of Modern Art, New York, 1969, cat. p. 84 (ill.)

The Tremaine Collection: 20th Century Masters, the Spirit of Modernism,

Wadsworth Atheneum, Hartford, 1984, p. 44 (ill.)

"Primitivism" in 20th Century Art: Affinity of the Tribal and the Modern, The Museum of Modern Art, New York, 1984, cat. p. 509 (ill.)

In a handwritten, illustrated list of his early sculptures (published in *Alberto Giacometti*, Pierre Matisse Gallery, New York, 1948), Alberto Giacometti referred to this work as the *Femme grande* and dated it 1932–33. His preference for this title as opposed to the already commonly known *Spoon Woman* may reflect his figurative concerns of the time. His dating can be attributed to a temporary lapse of memory, for the plaster of this work was exhibited at the Salon des Tuileries in Paris in 1927. Varying dates have been assigned to it by different scholars (see Krauss, 1984, p. 528 n. 11).

Giacometti himself, however, cleared up the problem of dating in a letter to Pierre Matisse in 1955, first published by Reinhold Hohl (1977, p. 79):

> Je vous écris surtout à propos de l'histoire de date de la "femme cuillère" (il faudra trouver un autre titre). Dans le catalogue de la première exposition chez vous j'ai écrit moi-même le date 32–33.... En fait je me suis trompé...J'ai ici chez moi un cahier fait autrefois où j'ai inscrit des croquis à l'appui à peu près toutes mes sculptures faites depuis 1925. La femme cuillère y figure avec des précisions. Elle a été faite fin 1926 début 1927 et exposée au Salon des Tuileries en 1927.

The plaster for *Spoon Woman* (private collection, Paris) measures only 47¼ inches high. At the time of casting in 1954, Giacometti must have wanted still greater stature for this already monumental figure, and he increased the height to 57¾ inches. It has not been possible to determine when the Nasher cast entered the collection of Nelson Rockefeller. Mrs. Burton Tremaine, its subsequent owner, recalls that Rockefeller installed it at the end of his dock at Seal Harbor, Maine. A total of six casts was made in 1954, and at least two others have been made since then.

Spoon Woman stands as the summation of many forces at work in Giacometti's early sculpture: Cubism (in the angular forms and overall geometric conception), primitivism (in the references to ancient fertility idols and African spoon figures), the partial figure as an expressive mode, and themes of fertility and sexuality. The figure is presented in three-quarter length, perched on a pedestal, with small blocklike head, protruding chest, pinched waist, and huge abdomen or womb in the exaggerated form of a rounded organic receptacle. The columnar pedestal can also be read, however, as legs and feet. Vertical, monumental, and immobile, *Spoon Woman* has a totemic presence that transcends in both physical and expressive impact the somewhat similarly conceived woman in Giacometti's *The Couple* of the same period.

27A. *No More Play* [*On ne joue plus*], 1931–32
Marble, wood, and bronze, 1⅝ x 22⅞ x 17¾ (4.1 x 58 x 45.2)

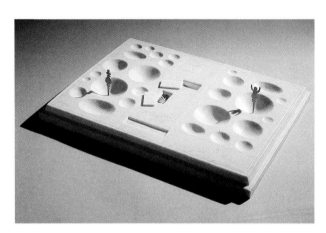

MARKINGS: Top of base, front left, inverted and reversed: "On ne joue plus"

PROVENANCE: From artist to Julien Levy, New York, 1934
To Mrs. Julien Levy, Bridgewater, Connecticut
To Nasher collection, 1986

LITERATURE: Christian Zervos, "Quelques Notes sur les Sculptures de Giacometti," *Cahiers d'Art 7*, nos. 8–10, 1932, p. 340 (ill.)

William S. Rubin, *Dada and Surrealist Art*, New York, 1968, pp. 252, 254, pl. 221

Reinhold Hohl, *Alberto Giacometti*, New York, 1971, pp. 82–83, n. 27 (ill. p. 66)

Rosalind E. Krauss, *Passages in Modern Sculpture*, New York, 1977, p. 118 (ill. p. 116)

Julien Levy, *Memoir of an Art Gallery*, New York, 1977, pp. 156–57

Paintings, Drawings, and Sculpture from the Julien Levy Collection, Sotheby's, New York, November 4 and 5, 1981, cat. no. 46 (ill.)

Rosalind Krauss, "Giacometti," in *"Primitivism" in 20th Century Art*, The Museum of Modern Art, New York, 1984, pp. 512, 513, 521, 523, 524 (ill. p. 513)

EXHIBITIONS: *Abstract Sculpture by Alberto Giacometti*, Julien Levy Gallery, New York, 1934, cat. no. 2 (ill. on exhibition announcement)

Alberto Giacometti, Art of This Century, New York, 1945, cat. no. 2

Alberto Giacometti: Exhibition of Sculptures, Paintings, Drawings, Pierre Matisse Gallery, New York, 1948, cat. no. 10

Giacometti, The Solomon R. Guggenheim Museum, New York, 1955, cat. n.n.

Alberto Giacometti, The Museum of Modern Art, New York, 1965, cat. no. 13 (ill.)

Dada, Surrealism, and Their Heritage, The Museum of Modern Art, New York, 1968, cat. no. 128 (ill. p. 118).

1936 Surrealism: Objects, Photographs, Collages, Documents, Zabriskie Gallery, New York, 1986, cat. p. 25 (ill.)

Among Alberto Giacometti's most remarkable sculptural innovations was a series of objects developed from the idea of the game board. Reversing the traditional relationship between sculpture and base, these objects make the base the central focus of the sculptor's concern. Moreover, by inviting the viewer's participation in a game of undefined rules and purposes, the game boards radically redefine the relationship between viewer and object. *No More Play* is the culmination of the series, following upon *Man, Woman, and Child* (1931) and *Circuit* (1931).

No More Play is identified in Giacometti's handwritten, illustrated list of early sculptures (*Alberto Giacometti*, Pierre Matisse Gallery, 1948, New York, n.p.) as having been executed in a preliminary plaster (given to Matta; now in The Museum of Modern Art, New York) as well as in marble. As a photograph by Man Ray indicates (*Cahiers d'Art 7*, nos. 8–10, 1932), the work dates from before the end of 1932. The marble version now in the Nasher collection figured in Giacometti's first exhibition in America, held at the Julien Levy Gallery in December 1934. On that occasion, *No More Play* was given by Giacometti to Levy, the young gallery owner whose interest in Surrealism was largely responsible for introducing the movement to this country.

No More Play contains an extraordinary depth and complexity of meaning in its elegant and deceptively simple sculptural form. A flat marble base pitted with round, craterlike depressions, the piece has an almost lunar appearance. The large cavities at the lower left and upper right have small slots cut into their bottoms into which two small figurines can fit. In Man Ray's 1932 photograph there is a figure with upraised arms at the right and one with only the barest suggestion of arms standing at left (the former is probably male, the latter female). In the center are three rectangular holes, resembling tombs. Each has a tombstone-like cover. In Man Ray's photograph, the earliest known document of the work's appearance, the top tomb is covered and the bottom two appear with lids ajar. In the bottom tomb lies a skeletonlike object; in the middle tomb, hidden in shadow, the suggestion of a serpent. In the marble, in reverse script, Giacometti inscribed the words "On ne joue plus."

Julien Levy's book of 1977, *Memoir of an Art Gallery*, describes some of the history of the small figures that people

the moonscape. He recalled that the work included two standing figurines and a serpent (he does not mention the skeleton). The figurines were twice lost, and each time, Levy reports, were replaced at his request by Giacometti. In addition, the lower grave cover was broken in 1955 and replaced by Diego Giacometti. Currently there exist nine pieces associated with *No More Play*, ranging in length from two to four inches. Another four pieces may be presumed lost. The pieces illustrated include a pair of wood figurines, a wood serpent, and a metal skeletonlike form made of a copper alloy. Not illustrated are a wood skeleton, a single wood figurine with raised arms (the arms are now broken), a pair of metal figurines (which may have been made by Alberto or Diego Giacometti and then rejected, as they do not fit into the slots at the bottom of the craters), and a single metal figurine with a round wooden base which helps to stabilize the figure in its slot. It is known through photographs that this last figure had a mate (see Hohl, p. 66). In fact, this was the pair shown at the 1955 Guggenheim exhibition.

Sources for *No More Play* might include African wooden game boards with craterlike depressions, which were known to Giacometti (see Krauss, 1984, p. 524; Hohl, p. 299, n. 27). Carola Giedion-Welcker illustrates a Swiss wooden peasant table with similar depressions (see Giedion-Welcker, *Contemporary Sculpture: An Evolution in Volume and Space*, New York, rev. ed., 1960, p. 98). Giacometti melded these references to the primitive, typical of Surrealism, with another more personal concern: the presence of death, violence, and war. In 1931 memories of crater-scarred European battlefields of World War I were vivid. *No More Play* resembles a game of chess, and like chess, it is a metaphor of organized conflict. However, the game appears to have been played out, and its full potential for destruction has been realized.

JEREMY STRICK

---

28. *Head (Skull) [Cubist Head]*, 1934
    Marble, 7⅜ x 7¾ x 8⅛ (18.8 x 19.6 x 20.5)

MARKINGS: Lower left side: "A. Giacometti"

PROVENANCE: Ernst Scheidegger, Zürich
              J. J. Klejman, New York
              Reiss Cohen Gallery, New York
              To Milton Ratner, Chicago
              To Nasher collection, 1985

LITERATURE: Cf. *Alberto Giacometti*, Pierre Matisse Gallery, New York, 1948, catalog of early works in facsimile, n.p.; studio photograph, p. 34; letter in facsimile, p. 41

              Cf. Reinhold Hohl, *Alberto Giacometti*, New York, 1971, pp. 104–05 (ill. pp. 72 and 110)

              Cf. *Die Sammlung der Alberto Giacometti-Stiftung*, Zürich, 1971, pp. 106–09 (ill.)

              Paintings, Drawings and Sculpture by Alberto Giacometti from the Ratner Family Collection, Sotheby's, New York, May 16, 1984, cat. no. 321 (ill.) (not sold)

EXHIBITIONS: *Exhibition of Sculpture, Painting, and Drawing by Alberto Giacometti*, Sidney Janis Gallery, New York, 1985, cat. no. 23 (ill.)

Alberto Giacometti's title for this work was *Tête* (Head) or *Tête crâne* (Skull); the appellation "Cubist Head" seems to have been assigned much later as a comment on the style of the piece. In Giacometti's own handwritten, illustrated list of his early sculptures, published in 1948 (*Alberto Gia-*

cometti, Pierre Matisse Gallery, New York, n.p.), he noted three versions of the *Tête* of 1934: a plaster in the Bruguière collection, Tours; a terra-cotta in the Bomsel collection, Versailles; and a stone belonging to the artist. The first two of these have not been conclusively traced. The third could be one of two marbles now known: the Nasher version or another, in a more speckled stone, in a New York private collection (*Alberto Giacometti*, The Solomon R. Guggenheim Museum, New York, 1974, cat. no. 37). An unpainted plaster passed from the artist to the Alberto Giacometti Foundation in Zürich; a painted plaster is now in the Hirshhorn Museum and Sculpture Garden, Washington, D.C. (*The Hirshhorn Museum and Sculpture Garden*, New York, 1974, p. 695); and another has been identified as belonging to a New York private collection (Bernard Lamarche-Vadel, *Alberto Giacometti*, Paris, 1984, p. 73, fig. 104; this may actually be a bronze). *Head (Skull)* was cast in an edition of at least seven bronzes, and a reportedly unique bronze variant is listed in *Alberto Giacometti*, Galerie Beyeler, Basel, 1963, cat. no. 23. An unauthorized stainless-steel cast is now in the Kunsthaus, Zürich.

Ruminations on mortality are a steady ingredient in Giacometti's Surrealist work, and the specific memento mori theme of a death's head or skull is anticipated in a painting from 1923 called *Le Crâne* (Lamarche-Vadel, 1984, fig. 33). The aggressive faceting of *Head (Skull)* is seen in certain earlier drawings such as the self-portrait of 1923–24, in the Alberto Giacometti Foundation (Lamarche-Vadel, 1984, fig. 41); reaches abstract purity in the *Cube* of 1934; and finds a reprise in the head of the figure in *Invisible Object* of 1934–35. A terminus date of 1934 for *Head (Skull)* is confirmed by its publication in *Minotaure*, no. 5, 1934. Although Diego Giacometti is known to have transferred certain of his brother's Surrealist sculptures from plaster to marble and wood, it has not been determined specifically which ones. For an etching by Giacometti closely related to the *Head (Skull)* and generally dated 1933, see Louise Averill Svendsen, *Alberto Giacometti: Sculptor and Draftsman*, American Federation of Arts, 1977, cat. no. 64.

---

29. *Two Figurines*, c. 1945
    Metal with gold leaf, each 1½ x ⁷⁄₁₆ x ⁷⁄₁₆ (3.8 x 1.2 x 1.2)

MARKINGS: Inside base of each: "I"

PROVENANCE: From artist to Maria Martins, Paris
To Lucia Donnelly, Maryland, 1972
Sold at Sotheby's, New York, May 16, 1984
To Weintraub Gallery, New York
To Nasher collection, 1985

LITERATURE: Cf. Reinhold Hohl, *Alberto Giacometti*, New York, 1971, pp. 276–77

Cf. *Alberto Giacometti: A Retrospective Exhibition*, The Solomon R. Guggenheim Museum, New York, 1974, cat. nos. 40–45 (ill.)

Impressionist and Modern Paintings and Sculpture, Part II, Sotheby's, New York, May 16, 1984, cat. no. 410 (ill.)

Cf. Bernard Lamarche-Vadel, *Alberto Giacometti*, Paris, 1984, pp. 78–79

EXHIBITIONS: None

In December 1941, Alberto Giacometti moved from Paris to Geneva, where he lived and worked in a tiny hotel room on the rue de la Terrassière. Forced by his surroundings to think small, and devoted to the problem of depicting a figure as seen from a distance, he produced a series of miniature sculptures so diminutive that they sometimes fragmented at the touch. Giacometti wrote: "Finally, in trying to accomplish a little, I began to work from memory. . . . But wanting to create from memory what I had seen, to my terror the sculptures became smaller and smaller, they only had a likeness when very small . . . and then often they became so very small that with one touch from my knife they disappeared into dust" (letter published in *Alberto Giacometti*, Pierre Matisse Gallery, New York, 1948, p. 44). A considerable number of the figurines survived, however, some of which were cast in metal. According to the Sotheby's catalog entry on the Nasher *Two Figurines* (New York, May 16, 1984, cat. no. 410), the plaster versions were formerly in the collection of Mr. and Mrs. Thomas B. Hess. The incised Roman numeral "I" inside both bases may mean that this pair was the first from an actual or intended series of casts.

---

30. *The Chariot*, 1950
    Painted bronze, 56¼ x 24¼ x 27 (142.9 x 61.5 x 68.5)

MARKINGS: Left side of square platform: "A. Giacometti 5/6"

Back of square platform: "Alexis Rudier Fondeur Paris"

PROVENANCE: Galerie Maeght, Paris
To Mr. and Mrs. Fernand Leval
Sold at Christie's, New York, November 15, 1983

To Nasher collection, 1983

LITERATURE: Cf. *Alberto Giacometti*, Pierre Matisse Gallery, New York, 1950, pp. 3, 12, 13, 32 (ill.)

Cf. Reinhold Hohl, *Alberto Giacometti*, New York, 1971, pp. 134, 135, 138 (ill. pp. 132, 295)

Impressionist and Modern Paintings and Sculpture, Christie's, New York, November 15, 1983, cat. no. 79 (ill.)

Cf. James Lord, *Giacometti: A Biography*, New York, 1985, pp. 304–07, 335

EXHIBITIONS: *Giacometti*, The Solomon R. Guggenheim Museum, New York, 1955

In a letter and some notes on his recent work published in 1950 (*Alberto Giacometti*, Pierre Matisse Gallery, New York), the artist identified the source of *The Chariot* as his personal memory of a pharmacy cart in a clinic: "1938 at the Bichat Clinic, I was . . . amazed at the . . . pharmacy wagon being wheeled around the room. In 1947 I saw the sculpture as if it had been made in front of me, and in 1950 it was already situated in the past, but this is not the sole reason which prompted me to do this sculpture." He also indicated that *The Chariot* was realized out of a need "to have the figure in empty space in order to see it better and to situate it at a precise distance from the floor," alluding to the professed visual verisimilitude of his work. Although according to James Lord he may have confused the Bichat Clinic with another (Lord, 1985, p. 306), it would seem, in any case, that other sources are more direct. In 1942–43 Giacometti had modeled *Woman with the Chariot*, a figure, very large in scale for the time, standing on a boxlike base with four small movable wheels. The scale of figure to wheels was reversed in *The Chariot*, where metaphorical movement was substituted for actual motion. There is also close similarity to the wheels, axle, and platform of an Eighteenth Dynasty Egyptian battle chariot that Giacometti saw at the Archaeological Museum in Florence (Hohl, 1971,

p. 295, fig. 56; fig. 58, an Etruscan incense burner with figure mounted on wheels, is another possible source).

The occasion for making *The Chariot* was a commission from the City of Paris to replace a memorial to Jean Macé removed by the Nazis from a square in the nineteenth arrondissement. The resulting sculpture, totally inappropriate as a commemorative object, was unceremoniously rejected. Giacometti nevertheless proceeded to have it cast in bronze, making an edition of seven, numbered 0/6–6/6. Most of the casts have a golden patina, but two are darker and hand-painted: the Nasher cast and an even more extensively painted one in a Swiss private collection. The painting adds to the delicacy and hence to the mystery of this small figure poised in space, seemingly overwhelmed by the large wheels on either side and the movement—and perhaps ancient ancestry—they symbolize. In the oil painting *Annette in the Atelier* from the same year, *The Chariot* is featured prominently in the artist's studio.

---

31. *Bust of Diego*, 1954
   Painted bronze, 15½ x 13¼ x 8¼ (39.5 x 33.7 x 21)

MARKINGS: Back, center: "Susse Fond. Paris" and "A. Giacometti 0/6"

PROVENANCE: From artist to Fondation Maeght, Saint-Paul-de-Vence, France
To Galerie Maeght Lelong, New York
To Nasher collection, 1979

LITERATURE: Cf. Jacques Dupin, *Alberto Giacometti*, Paris, 1962, p. 273 (ill.)

Cf. Bernard Lamarche-Vadel, *Alberto Giacometti*, Paris, 1984, pp. 150–52, fig. 215

William McCarter and Rita Gilbert, *Living with Art*, New York, 1985, p. 269, fig. 346

EXHIBITIONS: "Alberto Giacometti," *XXXI Esposizione Biennale Internazionale d'Arte*, Venice, 1962, cat. no. 61

Alberto Giacometti, Fondation Maeght, Saint-Paul-de-Vence, France, 1978, cat. no. 77 (ill. p. 96)

Alberto Giacometti: Ein Klassiker der Moderne 1901–1966, Bündner Kunstmuseum, Chur, Switzerland, 1978, cat. no. 132 (ill.)

Giacometti, Dallas Museum of Fine Arts, 1979, cat. no. 14

Exhibition of Sculpture, Painting, and Drawing by Alberto Giacometti, Sidney Janis Gallery, New York, 1985, cat. no. 40 (ill.)

32. *Diego in a Cloak [Diego au manteau]*, 1954
Painted bronze, 15⅛ x 13½ x 8¾ (38.5 x 34.3 x
22.2)

MARKINGS: Back, center: "Susse Fond. Paris / Alberto
               Giacometti 6/6"

PROVENANCE: From artist to Fondation Maeght, Saint-
               Paul-de-Vence, France
               To Galerie Maeght Lelong, New York
               To Nasher collection, 1979

LITERATURE: Cf. Bernard Lamarche-Vadel, *Alberto
               Giacometti*, Paris, 1984, pp. 150–52

               William McCarter and Rita Gilbert, *Living*

with Art, New York, 1985, p. 269, fig. 346

EXHIBITIONS: *Alberto Giacometti*, Fondation Maeght,
               Saint-Paul-de-Vence, France, 1978, cat. no.
               79 (ill. p. 96)

               *Alberto Giacometti: Ein Klassiker der
               Moderne 1901–1966*, Bündner
               Kunstmuseum, Chur, Switzerland, 1978,
               cat. no. 134 (ill.)

               Giacometti, Dallas Museum of Fine Arts,
               1979, cat. no. 12

               *Exhibition of Sculpture, Painting, and
               Drawing by Alberto Giacometti*, Sidney Janis
               Gallery, New York, 1985, cat. no. 42 (ill.)

---

33. *Diego in a Sweater [Diego au chandail]*, 1954
Painted bronze, 19 x 10¾ x 8¼ (48.2 x 27.3 x 21)

MARKINGS: Left side of base: "A Giacometti" and "6/6"
               (twice)
               Back of base: "Susse Fondeur Paris"

PROVENANCE: From artist to Fondation Maeght, Saint-
               Paul-de-Vence, France
               To Galerie Maeght Lelong, New York
               To Nasher collection, 1979

LITERATURE: Cf. Reinhold Hohl, *Alberto Giacometti*,
               New York, 1971, pp. 169–70, 211, 257 (ill.;
               dated 1953)

               Cf. Bernard Lamarche-Vadel, *Alberto
               Giacometti*, Paris, 1984, pp. 150–52, fig. 220

               William McCarter and Rita Gilbert, *Living
               with Art*, New York, 1985, p. 269, fig. 346

EXHIBITIONS: *Alberto Giacometti*, Kunsthalle, Bern, 1956,
               cat. no. 37

               Alberto Giacometti, Accademia di Francia,
               Villa Medici, Rome, 1970, cat. no. 31 (ill.)

               Alberto Giacometti, Fondation Maeght,
               Saint-Paul-de-Vence, France, 1978, cat. no.
               78 (ill. p. 96)

               *Alberto Giacometti: Ein Klassiker der
               Moderne 1901–1966*, Bündner
               Kunstmuseum, Chur, Switzerland, 1978,
               cat. no. 133 (ill. pp. 94, 95)

               Giacometti, Dallas Museum of Fine Arts,
               1979, cat. no. 13

               *Exhibition of Sculpture, Painting, and
               Drawing by Alberto Giacometti*, Sidney
               Janis Gallery, New York, 1985, cat. no. 41
               (ill.)

Giacometti's brother Diego was one of his most frequent models, appearing in drawings, paintings, and sculpture alike from the earliest periods of the artist's work. A particularly prolific and searching series of portrait busts dates from the early fifties, as Giacometti worked diligently to capture the essence of Diego's character and appearance with a "realism" that he felt constantly eluded him. During this period he often painted his plasters and bronzes as a means of approaching more closely his fleeting perceptions. The three bronze portrait busts of Diego in the Nasher collection are extensively and beautifully painted in muted gray and gray-green tones.

The dates of Giacometti's many portrait busts of the fifties are generally not known with precision. The three in the Nasher collection are most often ascribed to 1954, although Hohl dates the *Diego in a Sweater* to 1953 (*Alberto Giacometti*, New York, 1971, p. 257). All were cast in editions of seven bronzes numbered 0/6–6/6. This cast of the *Bust of Diego* was among the forty-two sculptures that Giacometti exhibited in his triumphant showing at the 1962 Venice Biennale's main pavilion, where he won the prize for sculpture.

---

34. *Venice Woman III* [*Femme de Venise III*], 1956
Bronze, 47½ x 13½ x 6⅞ (120.5 x 34.3 x 17.5)

MARKINGS:
Right side of base, lower left: "0/6 Alberto Giacometti"
Back of base, lower left: "Susse Fondeur Paris"

PROVENANCE:
Madame Giacometti
To Thomas Gibson Fine Art, London, by 1977
To Nasher collection, 1979

LITERATURE:
Cf. Reinhold Hohl, *Alberto Giacometti*, New York, 1971, pp. 142–43, 281 (ill. p. 119)

Cf. *Alberto Giacometti: A Retrospective Exhibition*, The Solomon R. Guggenheim Museum, New York, 1974, pp. 24–25

Cf. Bernard Lamarche-Vadel, *Alberto Giacometti*, Paris, 1984, pp. 144–45

Cf. James Lord, *Giacometti: A Biography*, New York, 1985, pp. 355–57

EXHIBITIONS:
Thirteen Bronzes: Alberto Giacometti, Thomas Gibson Fine Art, London, 1977, cat. no. 6 (ill.)

Alberto Giacometti, Fondation Maeght, Saint-Paul-de-Vence, France, 1978, cat. no. 87

Giacometti's *Venice Woman III* is so named because he made it expressly for the Venice Biennale of 1956. Having turned down Switzerland's invitation to represent his home country at the 1950 Biennale, he accepted instead the French invitation the same year but later withdrew. Another opportunity to represent France at the Biennale of 1956 was eagerly received. During the first five months of the year, he created fifteen standing female figures in a sustained, intensive campaign. The series represents a continued process of invention, destruction, and reinvention, as Giacometti modeled then destroyed then remodeled variations on the same figure, halting periodically to preserve a particular stage with a cast. In addition to the ten figures for the Biennale, all of which were later cast in bronze, Giacometti also sent five other Venice Women (later destroyed) to a simultaneous one-man show at the Kunsthalle in Bern.

All the women in the series stand erect, their legs together, arms straight down, heads disproportionately small, and feet disproportionately large. Although modeled from the mind's eye rather than life, they display qualities fundamental to Giacometti's ideas for replicating perception: for example, an emphasis on small heads and large feet to counterbalance the eye's tendency to focus on the face, the roughened surfaces to suggest the effects of light and atmosphere, and the slim proportions to show how a figure can look when glimpsed at a distance. Precedents for this figure type are found in earlier immobile, standing figures from the forties, and various external sources have also been suggested, including wooden Egyptian statues and Etruscan bronze figurines.

JULIO GONZALEZ (Spanish, 1876–1942)

*35. *Woman with a Mirror* [*Femme au miroir*], c. 1936–37 (cast c. 1980)
Bronze, 78½ x 21 x 23 (199.4 x 53.3 x 58.4)

MARKINGS: Bottom of left leg: "E. Godard Fondeur"
Back of foot: "J. Gonzalez © 1/2"

PROVENANCE: From estate of the artist to The Pace Gallery, New York
To Nasher collection, 1982

LITERATURE: Cf. Josephine Withers, *Julio Gonzalez:*

Sculpture in Iron, New York, 1978, pp. 53, 64, 87, 89, 104, fig. 109, cat. no. 117 (dated 1937)

Cf. Margit Rowell, *Julio Gonzalez: A Retrospective*, The Solomon R. Guggenheim Museum, New York, 1983, cat. no. 211 (ill.; dated c. 1937)

Jörn Merkert, Gonzalez catalogue raisonné (forthcoming, 1987), cat. no. 29 (dated c. 1936–37)

EXHIBITIONS: *Julio Gonzalez: Sculpture and Drawings*, The Pace Gallery, New York, 1981, cat. n.n. (ill.)

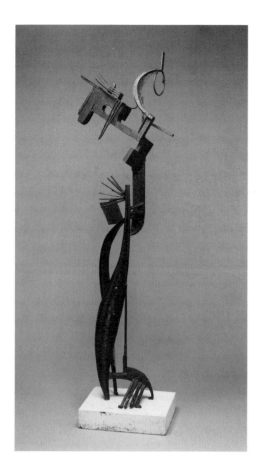

The traditional and emotionally neutral motif of a woman at her toilet figured in the art of Julio Gonzalez from the time of his earliest drawings and provided the point of departure from 1930 to 1937 for several of his most important sculptures, including the three representations of *Woman Combing Her Hair*, c. 1931, c. 1934, and c. 1936, and the *Woman with a Mirror*, c. 1936–37. All are tall, vertical, welded irons. In technique and syntax, they contain many of the most salient features of Gonzalez's sculptural innovations, his open compositional networks, his seemingly easy manipulation of iron into lively, inventive configurations; his dynamic "drawing in space," and his synthesis of abstract and representational forms. *Woman with a Mirror*, the largest of his sculptures, seems to have been constructed over a two-year period, in 1936–37. It has frequently been dated 1936 and was first exhibited in *Origines et développement de l'art international indépendant* at the Jeu de Paume, Paris, in July–October 1937. Numerous drawings connected with the sculpture date from the early months of 1937, however (indeed, some continue until December), indicating that it still must have been in progress at that time (see Josette Gilbert, *Julio Gonzalez Dessins*, Paris, 1975). An earlier, smaller sculpture called *Woman with a Mirror* (c. 1934; Rowell, 1983, cat. no. 114) shares some of the same forms, but it is more rectilinear and far less complex in morphology. In this later version of the theme, the commanding figure stands gracefully and proudly erect. One of the two long legs expands into a podlike shape to suggest the swelling curves of a feminine hip or thigh. A spray of spiky hairs at the midsection seems to indicate the pubic area. The flat plane angled outward near the top, with a hole cut in the middle and more spiky hairs attached, can be read as the head bent sharply backward, while a round mirror is held daintily aloft with a long, raised arm.

Like numerous other works in iron by Gonzalez, *Woman with a Mirror* was cast in bronze by the artist's estate on the grounds that Gonzalez had wished and intended, but could not afford, to make casts of many of his sculptures. This particular work exists in an edition of four bronzes, marked HC, EA, 1/2 and 2/2. The Nasher cast is number 1/2. The original iron is still in the estate of the artist in Paris. The casts, like the iron, pivot on a bolt just below the head. A frequently illustrated photograph shows Gonzalez together with this work in his studio (e.g. *Gonzalez*, Galerie Beyeler, Basel, 1982, cover).

BARBARA HEPWORTH (British, 1903–1975)

36. *Squares with Two Circles [Monolith]*, 1963 (cast 1964)
   Bronze, 124 x 65 x 30 (315 x 165 x 76.2)

MARKINGS: Left rear, top of base: "Barbara Hepworth 1964 3/3"
            Back of base, upper left: "Morris / Singer / Founders / London"

PROVENANCE: From artist to Gimpel Fils, London
            To Nasher collection, 1968

LITERATURE: Cf. *Barbara Hepworth: A Pictorial Autobiography*, St. Ives, 1970; rev. ed. 1978, figs. 284, 297

            Alan Bowness, ed., *The Complete Sculpture of Barbara Hepworth 1960–69*, London, 1971, cat. no. 347, pls. 6, 92–94

EXHIBITIONS: None

Sometimes referred to as *Monolith* or *Square [sic] with Two Circles*, this sculpture was given its definitive title in the Hepworth catalogue raisonné of 1971 (Bowness, 1971, cat. no. 347). The date inscribed on the base, 1964, apparently refers to the year of the bronze casting, as the plaster version of the sculpture was completed in 1963. The plaster was first exhibited in *Painting and Sculpture of a Decade 54/64* at The Tate Gallery, London, in April–June 1964 (cat. no. 79). Four numbered casts in bronze were made: 0., now at the University of Liverpool; 1., in The Tate Gallery; 2., in the Rijksmuseum Kröller-Müller, Otterlo, the Netherlands; and 3., in the Nasher collection. A maquette measuring 12¾ inches in height also dates from 1963 (Bowness, 1971, cat. no. 349; cast in an edition of ten bronzes numbered 0–9).

This work adopts the form of an upright monolithic slab, a shape that owes its favored role in the work of both Hepworth and Ben Nicholson to the powerful influence of Neolithic stone monuments found, for example, in Avebury and Carnac. The layering of flat planes with a balanced play of circle and rectangle recalls Nicholson's white reliefs of the thirties, while the tunneled-out circle was a common Hepworth device as early as the thirties and forties, when she introduced it in her sculpture to relieve mass and achieve a flow of continuous space. Despite the sculpture's geometric syntax, a sense of the natural and vital is preserved by the slightly skewed angles, poised relationship of the circles, and roughened texture. Color is used to suggest further texture but also to achieve spatial articulation: the back is uniform in tonality (mottled greens and dark golden browns); in the front, the lower square has the same dark coloration as the back, while the upper square and inside of the lower hole are a lighter green. Similar pierced, rectangular planes are seen in numerous other works by Hepworth, including drawings and paintings.

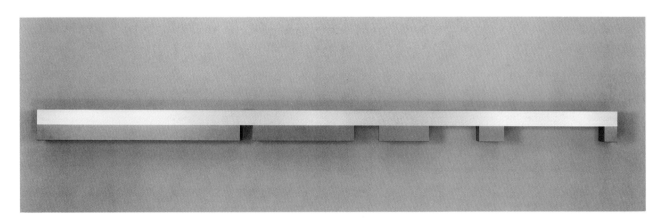

DONALD JUDD (American, born 1928)

*37. *Untitled*, June 1976
Aluminum and anodized aluminum, 8¼ x 161 x 8
(21 x 409 x 20)

MARKINGS: Back side of aluminum tube, on right end: "Judd / JO Bernstein Bros. Inc. 6-23-76"

PROVENANCE: Bonnier Gallery, New York
              Through Shaindy Fenton, Inc., Fort Worth
              To Nasher collection, 1978

LITERATURE: None

EXHIBITIONS: *20th Century Sculpture: Mr. and Mrs. Raymond D. Nasher Collection*, University Gallery, Southern Methodist University, Dallas, 1978, cat. no. 12 (ill.)

This work is based upon a smaller, damaged prototype (1964), measuring 5¼ by 75 by 5¼ inches, that was the first in the so-called Progression series (see Brydon Smith, *Donald Judd: Catalogue Raisonné of Paintings, Objects, and Wood-Blocks 1960–1974*, National Gallery of Canada, Ottawa, 1975, cat. no. 49). An expanded version from 1965 (Smith, 1975, cat. no. 60) matches the prototype and the Nasher sculpture in composition (although neither one in color) and has nearly the same dimensions as the latter.

Judd's wall-mounted Progressions developed out of his slightly earlier shelf pieces, replacing the unitary structure of the latter with several boxlike units that are notched at the top front and attached to a long square tube. They occupy a crucial place in the artist's movement away from more complicated, irregular compositions toward greater reductiveness, and encompass certain key themes that would continue to preoccupy him. The precisely finished metal boxes have the austere rectilinearity and technological surfaces that became one of Judd's trademarks. The geometric progression of elements, based upon a calculation of increased spacing between diminishing masses, expanded upon a consistent concern for mathematical sequence. In the volumetric projection off the wall lies a more concerted exploration of suspension and geometric displacement of space. The combination of colors and surfaces shows a restrained sensuousness that is also a hallmark of Judd's work.

The fabrication of these works involves an intricate system of fitting, bolting, and internal supporting of the various units. The boxes, while made to appear weighty, are hollow and open at the back, and the aluminum tube is open at both ends. This particular work was fabricated at Bernstein Brothers Sheet Metal Specialties in Long Island City. The "JO" in the inscription stands for José Otero, the metalworker who made the piece.

ANISH KAPOOR (British, born India 1954)

*38. *In Search of the Mountain I*, 1984
Wood, gesso, and pigment, 44⅞ x 44⅞ x 100 (114 x 114 x 254)

MARKINGS: None

PROVENANCE: From artist to Lisson Gallery, London
To Nasher collection, 1985

LITERATURE: "Skulptur: 9 Kunstnerne in Storbritannien," *Louisiana Review*, March 1986, p. 29 (ill.)

EXHIBITIONS: *London International Contemporary Art Fair*, London, 1985, ex-cat.

Anish Kapoor, Kunsthalle Basel, 1985, cat. n.p. (ill.)

Nouvelle Biennale de Paris, 1985, ex-cat.

The Poetic Object, The Douglas Hyde Gallery, Dublin, 1985, cat. p. 29 (ill.)

Anish Kapoor, Kunstnernes Hus, Oslo, 1986, cat. no. 1 (ill.)

Entre el Objeto y la Imagen, Palacio de Velásquez, Madrid, 1986, cat. no. 33 (ill. p. 127)

A member of the younger generation of British artists who have sought to poeticize the Minimalist object and reverse its self-referentiality with personal, even metaphysical meanings, Anish Kapoor first came to international attention in 1981–82 in a series of exhibitions on new trends in British sculpture. Since then his work has progressed from ensembles of small-scale, brightly colored shapes experienced as a field to singular, large-sized, iconic objects. They retain an intense coloration, achieved not by painting but by rubbing pigment into a gessoed wooden form, which gives them a special, mysterious aura of light and helps transform materiality into something more visionary. Kapoor's forms are varied but distinct, ranging from the organic and erotic to the more architectural and mathematical. Attempts have been made to link them with Hindu symbolism; but despite the artist's strong interest in Indian culture and religion and their correspondence in color with Indian dyes and natural pigments, they seem rather to come from an intuitive or automatist grasp of signs and forms with a lease on universal subconsciousness.

A series of works in conical shapes with serrated sides (dating from 1984–85) are ostensibly linked by title to a mountain symbolism, but they also seem sexually charged. *In Search of the Mountain I* is the earliest. Its basically male, elongated, hollow shape, colored an intense blue and serrated inside as well as out, bites aggressively into the contained and surrounding space. *Mother as a Mountain* (1985; *Kapoor*, Kunsthalle Basel, 1985, n.p.) is red and assumes a more peaklike pyramidal form, albeit with female organic overtones. *In Search of the Mountain II* (*Kapoor*, Kunsthalle Basel, 1985, n.p.) is blue and attached to the wall. Its internal surfaces are smooth and its cone shape is truncated, leaving a dark elliptical void that reverses the maleness of the first *In Search of the Mountain*. Among the wall drawings included by Kapoor in his installations (*Kapoor*, Kunsthalle Basel, 1985, n.p.) are some that explore similar forms in a loose pictographic style, showing the intuitive, spontaneous origins of his sculptural ideas.

ALAIN KIRILI (French, born 1946)

*39. *Generations*, 1985
Forged and painted iron, 85 x 58 x 33½ (216 x 147 x 85)

MARKINGS: None apparent (*Kirili*, Musée Rodin, 1985, says signed and dated "Kirili 1985")

PROVENANCE: From artist to Nasher collection, 1985

LITERATURE: *Kirili*, Galerie Adrien Maeght, Paris, 1985, p. 33 (ill.)

EXHIBITIONS: *Alain Kirili*, Musée Rodin, Paris, 1985, pp. 12–15, 26, 27 (ill.)

Generations (1985) represents both a summation of earlier forms in Alain Kirili's work and the announcement of a new

compositional direction. After exploring vertical linearity in a series of exceedingly slender iron works from 1976 to 1979, Kirili shifted to heavier shafts of metal, which are bent, hammered, or topped with abrupt geometric elements that express the strength of iron and the power of the forging process. Surfaces are left in the darkened, rough state of first emergence from the furnace. Generally freestanding and vertical, these works break from the strictures of Minimalism by invoking simplified totemic anatomies, phallic symbols such as the Oriental lingam, or ancient glyphs. In 1983 and 1984, Kirili began to complicate and multiply his imagery by joining such forms on flat or multileveled bases, occasionally adding organically modeled terra-cottas and bronzes to the composition. He also began painting selec-

tive forms and sometimes adding wooden fragments. *Generations* (1985) and *Mediterranean I, II,* and *III* (1985), in which he incorporated vertical cutout planes, are his most ambitious statements in this vein to date. A more simplified tabletop tableau from 1984, also called *Generations,* preceded the present work (*Kirili,* Galerie Adrien Maeght, 1985, p. 32). Among the antecedents of this compositional development are such works as Max Ernst's *King Playing with the Queen,* Alberto Giacometti's various horizontal groupings, and David Smith's *Voltri XIX.* Distinctive of Kirili, however, is the sense of the object as a ceremonial votive altarpiece, which develops further the implicitly solemn religious associations of his earlier work.

WILLEM DE KOONING (American, born the Netherlands 1904)

*40. *Hostess* [*Bar Girl*], 1973
Bronze, 48¾ x 38 x 25¾ (124 x 96.5 x 65.4)

MARKINGS: Underside of right foot: "de Kooning 7/7"
Right side, back of base: "Modern Art Foundry /
New York / N.Y. / ୪"

PROVENANCE: From artist to Xavier Fourcade, Inc., New York
To Nasher collection, 1980

LITERATURE: Cf. *De Kooning: Drawings/Sculptures,* catalog by Philip Larson and Peter

Schjeldahl, Walker Art Center, Minneapolis, 1974, n.p., fig. 66, cat. no. 147

Cf. *Willem de Kooning in East Hampton,* The Solomon R. Guggenheim Museum, New York, 1978, p. 26, cat. no. 95 (ill.)

Cf. Claire Stoullig, "The Sculpture of Willem de Kooning," in *Willem de Kooning: Drawings, Paintings, Sculpture,* Whitney Museum of American Art, New York, 1983, p. 242, cat. no. 278 (ill.)

EXHIBITIONS: None

In the sculptural oeuvre of Willem de Kooning, produced almost entirely between 1965 and 1974, the Nasher collection *Hostess* of 1973 along with the *Clamdigger* and *Figure Seated on a Bench* of 1972 and the *Large Torso* of 1974 stand as his major accomplishments. Initially uncomfortable with modeling in clay, in 1969 de Kooning began to work in an Italian foundry where he made a number of small bronzes. He soon expanded to a larger scale and developed an exaggerated gestural style that parallels the expressive facture of his paintings and drawings. In the *Hostess,* anatomical forms are squeezed, gouged, and freely reconfigured with an abandon that capitalizes fully on the soft, extrudable quality of wet clay. Both the style and caricatural aspect of Honoré Daumier's sculptures are recalled, but they are forced to new limits. The bizarre, "tortured" creature that results can be interpreted as threatening or demonic. Peter Schjeldahl has described her as "a loitering figure with three or four arms, upthrust nose and gash of a mouth emitting an almost audible whinnying laugh"; she is "possessed by energies quite beyond rational comprehension" and can be seen as "the destructive aspect of the Great Mother—the Hindu goddess Kali, perhaps—in contemporary guise, a Maenad of the cocktail lounge" (*De Kooning: Drawings/ Sculptures,* 1974, p. 21). Savagery, however, may have less to do with the figure than jocularity, her rolling contours perhaps materializing the convulsions of laughter with childlike, haptic spontaneity.

De Kooning had the *Hostess* cast at Modern Art Foundry, New York, in an edition of seven with two artist's proofs. Although the sculpture has been widely exhibited, it has been impossible to determine in which exhibitions, if any, this particular cast appeared prior to 1980 when the Nashers acquired it.

HENRI LAURENS (French, 1885–1954)

*41. *Grande Maternité*, 1932 (cast 1965)
Bronze, 21½ x 55 x 22½ (54.5 x 139.8 x 57)

MARKINGS: Left front of base: "HL 0/6"
Left back of base: "C. Valsuani / Cire
perdue"

PROVENANCE: Galerie Louise Leiris, Paris
Galerie Brusberg, Hanover
To Waddington Galleries, Ltd., London
To Nasher collection, 1984

LITERATURE: Cf. Werner Hofmann, *The Sculpture of*

Henri Laurens, New York, 1970, no. 143 (ill.)

Cf. *Henri Laurens 1885–1954*,
Kunstmuseum, Bern, 1985, p. 103, cat. no.
54 (ill.)

EXHIBITIONS: None

Grande Maternité is an enlargement of Laurens's *Petite Maternité* (18.5 centimeters long) from the same year. A plaster of the large version (probably the one illustrated in *Cahiers d'Art* 10, nos. 1–4, 1935, p. 52) remains in the collection of M. and Mme Claude Laurens in Paris, together with a terra-cotta of the small one. The posthumous edition of eleven bronzes issued by the Laurens family and made by Valsuani consists of seven casts marked 0/6 to 6/6, three artist's proofs, and one proof donated to the Musée National d'Art Moderne, Paris. The edition was cast over several years, and the Nasher cast dates from 1965.

Part of a series of reclining figures from 1930–32 in which Laurens returned to a theme prominent in his work of the early twenties, *Grande Maternité* evidences the degree to which Baroque rhythms and volumes had supplanted his earlier Cubist style. Common to the series is an elongated, wavelike organization of somewhat disjunctive anatomical forms. In the *Grande* and *Petite Maternités*, the distended abdomen both adds to the flow of curves and makes manifest the theme of fecundity that is a constant, but generally less overt, element of his later imagery. The influence here of Matisse's reclining nudes of the late twenties is strongly felt.

SOL LEWITT (American, born 1928)

*42. *Modular Cube / Base*, 1968
Painted steel, cube: 19⅛ x 19⅛ x 19⅛ (48.6 x 48.6 x 48.6); base: 1 x 58½ x 58½ (2.5 x 148.6 x 148.6)

MARKINGS: None

PROVENANCE: From artist to Dwan Gallery, New York
To William Rubin, New York, 1968
To M. Knoedler & Co., New York, 1982
To Nasher collection, 1982

LITERATURE: None

EXHIBITIONS: *Prospect '68*, Kunsthalle, Düsseldorf, 1968

Sol LeWitt: Sculptures and Wall Drawings, Museum Haus Lange, Krefeld, West Germany, 1968

Sol LeWitt, The Museum of Modern Art, New York, 1978, cat. no. 65 (ill.)

A consistent theme of Sol LeWitt's sculpture has been to explore the relation of modular cubes to the two-dimensional grid, as in such works as *Serial Project No. 1 (ABCD)* (1966), *Cube / Base* (1969), *Cubes with Hidden Cubes* (1977), as well as the Nasher collection *Modular Cube / Base* (see *Sol LeWitt*, The Museum of Modern Art, New York, 1978, nos. 130, 67, 139, 65). These structures situate

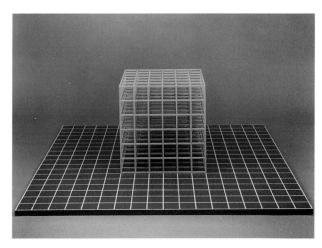

LeWitt's familiar cube forms on flat bases that are either square or rectangular and marked with grid patterns so that the three-dimensional element becomes an extension of—yet contrasts with—the two-dimensional pictorial space. Interested in mathematical structures and progressions and the different visual and physical effects they can yield, LeWitt selected the grid and the cube as constructive integers linked by "the same ratio of line (matter) to interval (space)." Logic and conceptual purity are further stressed by pristine fabrication and the use of even, white surface coatings. In the Nasher work, the basic module is six cubic units, repeated in the three dimensions of the central cube, in the symmetrical layout of the grid, and in the distance of the cube from the edge of the base.

This work was also made in a slightly smaller version (Museum of Contemporary Art, Chicago) historically dated 1967 (one year earlier than the Nasher sculpture) but fabricated in 1972. Its ratio of cube to base, but with a module of one cubic unit rather than six, was repeated in the smaller *Cube / Base* (1969).

ROY LICHTENSTEIN (American, born 1923)

*43. *Head with Blue Shadow*, 1965
　　Glazed ceramic, 15 x 8¼ x 8 (38.1 x 21 x 20.3)

MARKINGS:　　Inside front of neck: "r.f. Lichtenstein /'65"

PROVENANCE:　Leo Castelli Gallery, New York
　　　　　　　Robert and Ethel Scull, New York
　　　　　　　Leo Castelli Gallery, New York
　　　　　　　To Mr. and Mrs. Burton Tremaine, New York and Connecticut, 1966
　　　　　　　To Larry Gagosian Gallery, New York and Los Angeles, 1985
　　　　　　　To Nasher collection, 1985

LITERATURE:　Diane Waldman, *Roy Lichtenstein*, New York, 1971, pl. 129

　　　　　　　Cf. John Coplans, *Roy Lichtenstein*, New York and Washington, 1972, p. 91

　　　　　　　Edward Lucie-Smith, *Art Now: From Abstract Expressionism to Superrealism*, New York, 1977, p. 210 (ill.)

EXHIBITIONS:　*Lichtenstein*, Leo Castelli Gallery, New York, 1965

　　　　　　　Roy Lichtenstein, The Solomon R. Guggenheim Museum, New York, 1969, cat. no. 99

　　　　　　　Roy Lichtenstein: Ceramic Sculpture, text by Constance W. Glenn, Art Galleries, California State University at Long Beach, 1977, cat. no. 3, pl. 3 (ill. p. 16)

　　　　　　　The Tremaine Collection: 20th Century Masters, the Spirit of Modernism, Wadsworth Atheneum, Hartford, Connecticut, 1984, cat. p. 100 (ill.)

　　　　　　　Pop Art from the Tremaine Collection, Larry Gagosian Gallery, New York, 1985

The archetypal blonde movie star and lover was a constant persona in Lichtenstein's work from the beginning of his comic-strip style around 1961–62. Between 1964 and 1966 he gave three-dimensional form to her familiar features in a series of ten ceramic Heads (Glenn, 1977, cat. nos. 1–6, 36). At the same time, he further confounded pictorial and sculptural styles by adding graphic decoration to both this series and his ceramic Cup and Saucer still lifes. Asked if the ceramic Heads represented an attempt to extend the ambiguities of representation found in his paintings, Lichtenstein replied:

　Perhaps. I had considered painting a girl—a real girl—as a cartoon which may have given me the idea of drawing shadows on a three-dimensional surface. I guess the ceramic heads are an extension of that.

　[In putting two-dimensional symbols on a three-dimensional object] I wanted the ambiguity between realness and unrealness. Decorating them made them look unreal at the same time it pretended to make them look more real [Glenn, 1977, pp. 17, 19].

For the application of a pictorial device—the dot pattern—to sculpture, Lichtenstein's work can be compared to Pablo Picasso's painted *Glass of Absinthe* of 1914, although several other sculptors, among them Henri Laurens and Alexander Archipenko, adopted the same Cubist technique.

　Four of the ten ceramic Heads are unfinished. The others differ in the patterns and colors of the applied decoration. *Blonde I*, for example, has no distinct shadow. Others have red, black, or blue shadows and are appropriately titled. One is done strictly in black and white. The technical difficulties involved led Lichtenstein to collaborate with a professional ceramist and also a fellow artist, Hui Ka Kwong. To achieve the dot patterns, they used a flexible tape with perforations that could bend with the contours. They then masked the rest of the surface and sprayed the glazes. Lines and some areas of color were added by hand. The color—completely artificial—followed that of newspaper cartoons: "Those colors had to be consistent with the nature of the drawing and the nature of the idea, which was the drawing of an illusion so artificial that for instance you would never accept a certain area as a shadow but you would know that it was meant to represent shadow" (Glenn, 1977, p. 22).

　Preceding the ceramic Heads were two plaster mannikin heads from 1964 that Lichtenstein bought and then painted. The first of the two differs from the ceramic series in hair style and facial expression. The second (now lost) Lichtenstein built up with a plasticine compound and used as a maquette for the ceramics (Glenn, 1977, cat. nos. 28–29).

The occasional, incorrect citation of Mr. and Mrs. Michael Sonnabend in the provenance of this work seems to result from confusion with another Lichtenstein ceramic.

---

*44. *Double Glass*, 1979–80
Painted bronze, 56¼ x 41 ¹⁄₁₆ x 17¼ (142.9 x 104.3 x 43.8)

MARKINGS: Front, bottom: "2/3 r.f. Lichtenstein '79"

PROVENANCE: From artist to Leo Castelli Gallery, New York
Through Shaindy Fenton, Inc., Fort Worth
To Nasher collection, 1980

LITERATURE: Cf. Jack Cowart, *Roy Lichtenstein 1970–1980*, New York, 1981, p. 179 (ill. p. 155)

EXHIBITIONS: None

Like the slightly earlier *Goldfish Bowl* and *Cup and Saucer* (Cowart, 1981, pp. 151 and 154), Lichtenstein's *Double Glass* materializes a motif from his still-life paintings and carries on the cross-media exchanges that had characterized his work in sculpture since the ceramic Head and Cup and Saucer series of 1964–66. In his sculptures of the late seventies, a resolute flatness emerged that, together with discontinuous openings and contours, complex mixtures of shadow and reflections, and coloration at once illusionistic and abstract, produced a dialectical play between pictorial and sculptural qualities and between illusion and reality. Such strategies hark back to Cubist assemblage, but take on new force through Lichtenstein's large scale and brilliant color.

The glass vessel in general and the drinking glass in particular, with the complex potentials offered by transparency, reflections, and flattened ovoid shapes, seem to have held special appeal for Lichtenstein in his investigation of pictorial three-dimensionality. At least four versions of a single glass predate the still more complex *Double Glass*, with its interlocking forms and increased spatial ambiguities. A painting from 1974 shows a double glass produced as a mirror reflection (Cowart, 1981, p. 46), and a study for the sculpture dates from c. 1979 (colored pencil on paper; exhibited in *Roy Lichtenstein as Sculptor*, Gibbes Art Gallery, Charleston, South Carolina, 1985, cat. no. 40). As was his custom, Lichtenstein first made a painted wooden maquette of the *Double Glass* (collection of the artist), which served as the model for the bronze mold. An edition of three bronzes followed, each one painted (i.e., with no patina). Although the bronzes are marked 1979, the casting and painting was not completed until 1980, which is the date generally given for this work.

JACQUES LIPCHITZ (American, born Lithuania, 1891–1973)

45. *Seated Woman* [*Cubist Figure*; *Standing Figure*; *Sculpture*], 1916
Stone, 42½ x 11¼ x 12¼ (108 x 28.5 x 31)

MARKINGS: None

PROVENANCE: From artist to Marlborough-Gerson Gallery, New York, before 1968
To Norton Simon, Los Angeles
Sold at Sotheby Parke Bernet, New York,
May 2, 1973
To Medarco, Switzerland
To M. Knoedler & Co., New York
To Nasher collection, 1977

LITERATURE: *Important 19th and 20th Century Paintings, Drawings and Sculpture*, Sotheby Parke Bernet, New York, May 2–4, 1973, cat. no. 38 (ill.)

Deborah A. Stott, *Jacques Lipchitz and Cubism*, New York and London, 1978, pp. 129–32, 154, 237–38, 243–44, fig. 23

EXHIBITIONS: *Lipchitz: The Cubist Period 1913–1930*,

Marlborough-Gerson Gallery, New York, 1968, cat. no. 25 (ill.)

The Metropolitan Museum of Art, New York, 1968–69

The Cubist Epoch, Los Angeles County Museum of Art, 1971, cat. no. 193, pl. 307

Selections from the Norton Simon, Inc. Museum of Art, The Art Museum, Princeton University, Princeton, New Jersey, 1972–73, cat. no. 92 (ill.)

20th Century Sculpture: Mr. and Mrs. Raymond D. Nasher Collection, University Gallery, Southern Methodist University, Dallas, 1978, cat. no. 16 (ill.)

Dallas Collects: Impressionist and Early Modern Masters, Dallas Museum of Fine Art, 1978, cat. no. 112 (ill.)

Although various titles have been assigned to this work, Jacques Lipchitz confirmed in interviews that it represents a seated woman with legs crossed, her crystallized forms perched on a bench or stone (Stott, 1978, pp. 237–38). In his language of equivalences between nature and architectural abstraction, the head is turned into a faceted block with a single raised circle to symbolize mouth or eyes. When asked if the tall attached plinth represented a raised arm he replied: "Oh no, it's not an arm. It is still the head, to give volume to the head. . . . It is a desire of more completeness" (Stott, 1978, p. 238).

On stylistic grounds, the *Seated Woman* can be dated late 1916. It belongs to a series of standing and seated figures from 1916–17 that represents a transition in Lipchitz's work away from strictly geometric and planar compositions toward increased volume and figurative description. In the winter of 1916, then living in Paris, Lipchitz signed a contract with the dealer Léonce Rosenberg, which enabled him to employ a stone cutter to help with his carvings (Jacques Lipchitz, *My Life in Sculpture,* New York, 1972, p. 42). He later recalled, however, that he began the cutting of this particular sculpture himself (Stott, 1978, p. 237). His normal practice was first to make a plaster and then, based on that model, proceed to the carving of a stone, although in this case, no original plaster has come to light. A plaster that appears to have been made *from* the stone is now in The Tate Gallery, London. It includes a base and replicates the stone's rough texture. The date of its casting is problematic, and it may postdate the stone version by a considerable period of time. The surface of the plaster is marked with a network of pencil crosses seemingly in preparation for the carving of another copy, but none is known (information on the plaster from A. D. Fraser Jenkins, The Tate Gallery, London). At some time prior to 1970, the sculpture was cast in an edition of bronzes numbered up to 7/7. The bronzes also include a base.

Seated Woman was retained by Lipchitz until acquired by the Marlborough-Gerson Gallery before 1968. The Brummer Gallery is sometimes incorrectly listed in its provenance due to a confusion with a different, cast-stone work from 1916 exhibited as catalog no. 137 in *Cubism and Abstract Art,* The Museum of Modern Art, New York, 1936.

RICHARD LONG (British, born 1945)

*46. *Slate Line,* 1979
    Five pieces of Welsh slate, length approx. 336 (853)

MARKINGS: None

PROVENANCE: From artist to Anthony d'Offay Ltd., London
             To Nasher collection, 1985

LITERATURE: None

EXHIBITIONS: None

Slate Line is one of a large number of works conceived by Long in the late seventies and early eighties specifically for indoor gallery installation, unlike earlier stone sculptures that were placed in natural settings. Simple in configuration, these works are consistently composed of a single material indigenous to a particular area traversed by the artist on one of his many documented "walks" through the countryside of Great Britain and various remote locations. Brought indoors and arranged in simple geometric formations—most often lines, circles, spirals—they suggest the unity of the natural world and man's rational ability to bring about a systematic ordering of form.

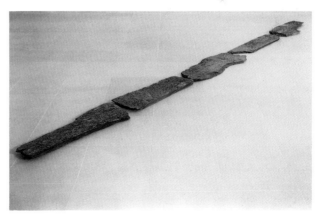

Composed of five sheets of Welsh slate quarried in Blaenau Ffestiniog in northern Wales, *Slate Line* allows the inherent sheetlike character of the slate to determine a corresponding flat, linear placement of the five stones. Guidelines for the installation of Long's works accompany each piece, such as the certificate for *Slate Line*:

> The stones are placed flat on the ground one by one, with the longitudinal axii of the stones in alignment. Each stone is placed with its lighter, weather-side uppermost. They are laid end to end, just touching but not overlapping. The stones are chosen in a random order.

While each installation may be slightly different, Long's guidelines specify weathered versus inherent color, axial alignment, and the continuity of touching rather than overlapping forms. Although strict alignments of modular elements are found in the work of Carl Andre, Long's stress on the natural differs from Andre's concern for the mathematical and industrial. The shapes of Long's configurations often suggest the straight line of a man walking, or the circular enclosure of a prehistoric ritual site, or the continuous structure of a geological formation. He made his first major stone line in Ireland in 1974. (For larger variations on the slate line, see R. H. Fuchs, *Richard Long*, The Solomon R. Guggenheim Museum, New York, 1986, pp. 147, 156.)

ARISTIDE MAILLOL (French, 1861–1944)

47. *La Nuit*, c. 1902–09 (cast 1960)
Bronze, 41 x 42 x 22½ (104 x 106.5 x 57)

MARKINGS: Top of base, left front: "Ⓜ"
Right side of base: "Georges Rudier / Fondeur Paris"
Left front of base: "E.A."

PROVENANCE: Dina Vierny, Paris
To Galerie Beyeler, Basel
To Nasher collection, 1982

LITERATURE: Cf. John Rewald, *Maillol*, London, Paris, New York, 1939, pp. 11, 12, 165 (ill. p. 56)

Cf. Waldemar George, *Aristide Maillol*, Greenwich, Connecticut, 1965, pp. 156–57 (ill.)

Cf. *Aristide Maillol: 1861–1944*, The Solomon R. Guggenheim Museum, New York, 1975, cat. nos. 43–45 (ill.)

EXHIBITIONS: *Skulptur im 20. Jahrhundert*, Wenkenpark, Riehen/Basel, 1980, cat. p. 26 (ill.)

Dates for the conception and execution of Maillol's early works are often problematic (the artist himself having generally declined to be specific when questioned about dates), and *La Nuit* is no exception. John Rewald dated it c. 1902 (Rewald, 1939, p. 165), which is now generally accepted as a terminus for the beginning phases of work. In a letter written by Maillol in 1916 (files of the Winterthur Kunstmuseum; information from Linda Konheim), he noted that he worked one entire winter in Banyuls modeling *La Nuit* in clay, and that he carved it in stone over the next two summers at Marley, although he gives no precise dates. We can conjecture that the clay version came first (probably destroyed), the stone second (now in the Winterthur Kunstmuseum), and finally the plaster that Maillol exhibited at the 1909 Salon d'Automne (Rewald, 1939, ill. p. 56). The first cast from the plaster, executed in lead by the Alexis Rudier foundry, was not made until 1939 (Albright-Knox Art Gallery, Buffalo), followed by two other lifetime casts in bronze. A total of seven posthumous casts were issued by Maillol's heir, Dina Vierny, with the Georges Rudier foundry. These include four *épreuves d'artiste* marked "E.A.," of which the Nasher cast (1960) was the second.

Judith Cladel (*Aristide Maillol*, Paris, 1937, p. 82) published the well-known anecdote about Maillol transporting *La Nuit* to the Grand Palais for the Salon d'Automne of 1909 and placing it in the center of the rotunda, a coveted location that Auguste Rodin, president of the Section de Sculpture, had envisioned for himself. When Rodin saw the installation, he magnanimously deferred to the young Maillol, complementing his work with the observation: "On oublie trop que le corps humain est une architecture, *mais vivante*. . . ." The figure's somnolent pose and weighty anatomy, confined within the ideal geometry of a cube, recall the massiveness of Egyptian sculpture, which Maillol greatly admired. Also invoked are Symbolist themes of sleep as a creative and regenerative state and the fecund powers of womanhood.

In addition to the large format, Maillol made *La Nuit* in a 7-inch version in terra-cotta, which was subsequently cast in an edition of six bronzes. An undated lithographic crayon drawing, presumably a preparatory sketch for *La Nuit*, is now in the Worcester Art Museum.

HENRI MATISSE (French, 1869–1954)

48. *Madeleine I*, 1901 (cast 1903)
Plaster, painted terra-cotta, 23¾ x 9½ x 7½ (60.3 x 24.1 x 19)

MARKINGS: Top of base, left front, in raised letters: "H. Matisse"

PROVENANCE: Private collection, Paris
To Galerie Beyeler, Basel, 1985
To Nasher collection, 1985

LITERATURE: Cf. Albert Elsen, *The Sculpture of Henri Matisse*, New York, 1972, esp. pp. 48–56 (ill.)

Cf. Alicia Legg, *The Sculpture of Matisse*, The Museum of Modern Art, New York, 1972, pp. 9–12 (ill.)

Cf. Michael Mezzatesta, *Henri Matisse: Sculptor / Painter*, Kimbell Art Museum, Fort Worth, 1984, cat. no. 3 (ill.)

EXHIBITIONS: None

Madeleine I (1901), which ranks as the earliest sculptural masterwork by Henri Matisse, was begun after but completed before its male counterpart *The Serf* (1900–03). Together they stand as a conscious demonstration of two opposing expressive modes: the serpentine, feminine ele-

gance of *Madeleine I* versus the rough, masculine forcefulness of *The Serf*. The undulating S-curves of the *Madeleine I* almost lift the figure off its base. To emphasize this sense of movement, Matisse smoothed the surfaces and cropped the arms above the elbows. Although he was undoubtedly working from a model and had previously explored the same pose in a painting from 1900 and a slightly later drawing (Mezzatesta, 1984, pp. 43, 45), the position of the figure may ultimately derive from Michelangelo's *Bound Slave*. Abandoning the smooth transition of forms and even flow of light of *Madeleine I*, Matisse produced in the *Madeleine II* of 1903 a variation with far rougher surface treatment.

Three plasters were made of *Madeleine I*, of which two survive (documentation kindly provided by Wanda de Guébriant, secretary for the Matisse estate). Unable to afford an edition in bronze, Matisse cast the first two himself in 1903, using a mold taken from the original clay model. He gave one of these to the painter Albert Marquet, who had shown a particular interest in the work (now in the Musée des Beaux-Arts, Bordeaux). The second (the Nasher cast) Matisse retained. Later, when he had the means to cast the work in bronze, Matisse commissioned a professional *mouleur* to make another plaster, which served for the pulling of the bronzes (edition of ten, plus one artist's proof) and was then destroyed. The original clay model was also destroyed.

At some point, the Nasher plaster was painted terracotta pink. According to Georges Duthuit, grandson of the artist, the sculpture disappeared from Matisse's studio under mysterious circumstances, and an illegal bronze cast of it appeared on the market c. 1954. It resurfaced in a French private collection and was purchased by the Galerie Beyeler and subsequently by the Nashers. A plaster version of *Madeleine I* appears in Matisse's painting *Still Life in Venetian Red* (1908; Pushkin Museum of Fine Arts, Moscow). Since the other early plaster was in the hands of Marquet by 1908, the one in the painting would seem to be the Nasher cast, although it is depicted as pure white.

---

49. *Head with Necklace* [*La Femme au collier*], 1907
Bronze, 5⅞ x 5⅛ x 3¾ (14.5 x 13 x 9.5)

MARKINGS: Back, lower left: "9/10 / HM"

PROVENANCE: Galerie Benador, Geneva
To Waddington Galleries, Ltd., London
To Nasher collection, 1983

LITERATURE: Cf. Albert Elsen, *The Sculpture of Henri Matisse*, New York, 1972, p. 122 (ill. p. 123)

Cf. *Henri Matisse Dessins et sculpture*, Musée National d'Art Moderne, Paris, 1975, cat. no. 10 (ill.)

Michael Mezzatesta, *Henri Matisse: Sculptor / Painter*, Kimbell Art Museum, Fort Worth, 1984, cat. no. 13 (ill.)

Cf. Pierre Schneider, *Matisse*, New York, 1984, p. 550

EXHIBITIONS: *Groups VI*, Waddington Galleries, London, 1983, cat. no. 66 (ill. p. 56)

The Sculpture of Henri Matisse, Hayward Gallery, London, 1984, cat. no. 25 (ill.)

Henri Matisse: Sculptor / Painter, Kimbell Art Museum, Fort Worth, 1984, cat. no. 13 (ill.)

This work is one of a series of very small heads modeled by Matisse between 1903 and 1907, all characterized by a sense of intimate spontaneity (see Elsen, 1972, figs. 153–66). The sketchy quality of this particular head prompted Pierre Schneider to hypothesize: "The memory of a woman glimpsed in the street inspired the *Little Head with Necklace* (1907): it was only a spark, but it brought the material substance beneath the artist's hands to life" (1984, p. 550). Despite its casual air, however, this small composition contains a close-knit family of rhymes and sequences. The rounded crescent of the crownlike hair, for example, is matched by the spread of the shoulders. The sharply cut ellipse of each eye echoes the arc of the necklace below.

And the soft, doughy curves in the chin, nose, and cheekbones spread fluidly upward into the masses of the hair. The progression of shapes is simple, firm, and clearly grasped. A certain hieratic quality enters in, perhaps resulting from Matisse's interest in primitive and archaic art, but a personal note also is sounded. Michael Mezzatesta has observed: "The small scale of the head favored experimentation as well as the quick and economical exploration of his ideas. The simplicity of the overall form and the informality of the modeling give it the freshness of a child's work. This quality is especially evident in the necklace draped over the shoulders, a piece of clay rolled thin, just as one of Matisse's children might have done" (1984, p. 67).

---

50. *Decorative Figure* [*Femme assise*; *Figure assise et accoudée*], August 1908 (cast early 1930s)
Bronze, 28⅜ x 20⅜ x 12⅜ (72 x 51.8 x 31.5)

MARKINGS: Right side of support, under arm: "aout 1908 / HM 2/10"
Top of base, right rear center: "HM"
Back side of base, at left: "C. Valsuani / Cire perdue"

PROVENANCE: Brummer Gallery, New York, 1931 (?)
To Dr. and Mrs. Harry Bakwin
Sold at Sotheby's, New York, November 13, 1985
To Nasher collection, 1985

LITERATURE: Cf. Albert Elsen, *The Sculpture of Henri Matisse*, New York, 1972, pp. 87–91 (ill.)

Cf. Jack Flam, "Matisse and the Fauves," in *"Primitivism" in 20th Century Art*, The Museum of Modern Art, New York, 1984, p. 230 (ill. p. 226)

Cf. Michael Mezzatesta, *Henri Matisse: Sculptor / Painter*, Kimbell Art Museum, Fort Worth, 1984, cat. no. 16 (ill.)

Impressionist and Modern Paintings and Sculpture, Part I, Sotheby's, New York, November 13, 1985, cat. no. 34 (ill.)

EXHIBITIONS: The Brooklyn Museum, 1935

Bronzes by Degas, Matisse, Renoir, Buchholz Gallery, New York, 1943, cat. no. 26

The Sculpture of Henri Matisse, Curt Valentin Gallery, New York, 1953, cat. no. 17 (ill.; dated 1906)

The Dr. and Mrs. Harry Bakwin Collection, Wildenstein and Co., New York, 1967, cat. no. 74 (ill.; dated 1914)

One Century: Wellesley Families Collect, Jewett Art Center, Wellesley College, 1978, cat. no. 48 (ill.)

Decorative Figure was modeled during Matisse's summer sojourn at the Mediterranean seaside village of Collioure in 1908. As with *The Serf* (1900–03) and *Madeleine I* (1901), he may have worked from a live model but took his pose from an earlier production, in this case, his 1907 painting *La Coiffure* (Mezzatesta, 1984, fig. 42). Similarly frontal and direct renditions of seated nudes are found in the small sculpture *Seated Woman* of 1904 and the well-known painting *Carmelina* of 1903. In transforming the relaxed pose and linear style of the nude in *La Coiffure* into an assertively three-dimensional, tactile composition, Matisse made certain key adjustments: the legs are swung around to form a more strictly organized diagonal continuum with the upper body; intersecting arabesques play against the geometry of the base and the vertical axis of the head, emphasizing the body's sensuous volumes; gaps are left between arms and torso to multiply the flow of outlines; and the support itself is given a simple blocky presence that works in concert with the assertive modeling of the anatomy. It has been stressed by various authors that the figure's large head, protruding breasts, and exaggerated buttocks reveal the influence of African sculpture, although absorbed into a style which, unlike Picasso's of the period, proffers a calm and pleasurable rather than aggressive emotion. It is possible that the archaizing face may derive from Etruscan art (Flam, 1984, p. 230; Mezzatesta, 1984, p. 73).

When first exhibited at the Salon d'Automne of 1908 (no. 919) and at Matisse's 1913 one-man show at the Galerie Bernheim-Jeune in Paris (no. 13), this work was called *Femme assise* and *Figure assise et accoudée*, respectively. It is not known precisely when or by whom the appellation *Decorative Figure* was first assigned, but it has remained the favored title for the sculpture and reflects the role of the arabesque in Matisse's theories on "decorative" art as well as the hedonistic appeal of the figure. John Elderfield points out that "the sensuous and voluptuous dominate Matisse's sculpture of this period, as they do his paintings, which reveal a preoccupation both with decorative figure compositions and, in still life, with the extreme arabesque" (*Matisse in the Collection of The Museum of Modern Art*, New York, 1978, p. 61).

Matisse generally cast his sculptures in editions numbered 0 to 10, but the individual castings were often considerably separated in time, and the sequence of numbers is sometimes inconsistent. Two casts of *Decorative Figure* are numbered 2/10, the Nasher example and one in another Texas private collection (ex-Wilfred P. Cohen). The Nasher cast is traditionally thought to have belonged to the Brummer Gallery, New York, by 1931, the year of an exhibition of Matisse sculptures at that gallery, but this information has not been confirmed. The second cast marked "no. 2" was made in 1952.

---

51. *Two Negresses* [*Deux Femmes; Groupe de deux jeunes filles*], 1908
    Bronze, 18⅜ x 10½ x 7½ (46.7 x 26.7 x 19)

MARKINGS: Top of base, below figure with ponytail: "Henri Matisse / HM 8/10"
             Edge of base, below signature: "C. Valsuani / cire perdue"

PROVENANCE: Brummer Gallery, New York, 1931
             To Dr. and Mrs. Harry Bakwin
             Sold at Sotheby's, New York, November 13, 1985
             To Nasher collection, 1985

LITERATURE: Alfred H. Barr, Jr., *Matisse: His Art and His Public*, New York, 1951 (paperback, 1971), pp. 138–39, 140, 141, 179 (ill. p. 366)

             Cf. Albert Elsen, *The Sculpture of Henri Matisse*, New York, 1972, pp. 83–87 (ill.)

             Cf. Jack Flam, "Matisse and the Fauves," in *"Primitivism" in 20th Century Art*, The Museum of Modern Art, New York, 1984, p. 230 (ill. p. 231)

             Cf. Michael Mezzatesta, *Henri Matisse: Sculptor / Painter*, Kimbell Art Museum, Fort Worth, 1984, cat. no. 17 (ill.)

Cf. Isabelle Monod-Fontaine, *The Sculpture of Henri Matisse*, Arts Council of Great Britain, London, 1984, pp. 14–15, cat. no. 28 (ill.)

Impressionist and Modern Paintings and Sculpture, Part I, Sotheby's, New York, November 13, 1985, cat. no. 35 (ill.)

EXHIBITIONS: *Henri Matisse Retrospective Exhibition*, The Museum of Modern Art, New York, 1931, cat. no. 158 (ill.)

              The Brooklyn Museum, 1935

              Sculpture by Painters, Buchholz Gallery, New York, 1939

              Bronzes by Degas, Matisse, Renoir, Buchholz Gallery, New York, 1943, cat. no. 20

              Henri Matisse, The Museum of Modern Art, New York, 1951–52, cat. no. 89

              The Art of Henri Matisse, Society of the Four Arts, Palm Beach, 1953, cat. no. 53

              Painting, School of France, Birmingham Museum of Art, Alabama, 1955, cat. no. 60

              The Dr. and Mrs. Harry Bakwin Collection, Wildenstein and Co., New York, 1967, cat. no. 71

              The Sculpture of Matisse, The Museum of Modern Art, New York, 1972, cat. no. 35 (ill. p. 23)

              One Century: Wellesley Families Collect, Jewett Art Center, Wellesley College, 1978, cat. no. 49 (ill.)

Two Negresses (1908) is one of Matisse's best known and most frequently published sculptures. It highlights, perhaps more than any other of his three-dimensional works, the primitivizing tendency that commingled with other influences in his oeuvre during the first decade of the century as he sought to rejuvenate stale sculptural conventions. Not only the pose but also the handling of anatomy and the overall expressiveness of this sculpture are pointedly antitraditional. The often-cited source of the pose is a photograph of two Tuareg girls from a French ethnographic magazine; the exotic flavor of the image clearly helped spur the artist's primitivizing formal response. (For other, less-convincing sources sometimes conjectured for this sculpture, see Elsen, 1972, pp. 83–85; and Flam, 1984, p. 230. Elsen plays down the significance of African art as an influence on this sculpture and on Matisse's work in general.) Although Matisse followed the photograph rather faithfully, he nevertheless transformed the image, amplifying its sense of *négritude*. The hairdos are simplified, the protrusion of buttocks and breasts is exaggerated, and other elements of the anatomies are given thicker, stronger proportions to enhance the quality of brutal beauty. The side-by-side position allowed the artist to explore concepts of duality and rhymed opposites, but it also suggests a certain sexual ambiguity (in the highly masculine anatomy of one of the figures and in the two figures' posed but perhaps amorous embrace), which helps give the sculpture potency.

Matisse completed the *Two Negresses* before the Salon d'Automne of October–November 1908, when it was shown as *Groupe de deux jeunes filles* (no. 922), with the added catalog note: "Tirages limités à 10 exemplaires numérotés." It is almost exactly contemporaneous with Brancusi's first version of *The Kiss*, which explores a different form of symmetrical face-to-face embrace.

This work was eventually cast in an edition of eleven bronzes numbered 0/10 to 10/10. Valsuani in Paris was the foundry, but the date of the casting of no. 8/10 has not been determined. Like the Nasher cast of the *Decorative Figure*, this sculpture resided for many years in the well-known Bakwin collection, and was frequently lent for exhibition.

---

52. *Large Seated Nude*, c. 1923–25
Bronze, 30½ x 31⅝ x 13⅝ (77.5 x 80.3 x 34.6)

MARKINGS: Right side of support: "9/10 HM"
Rear edge of base, at right: "C. Valsuani / cire perdue"

PROVENANCE: From artist to Ruff Steinersen, Oslo, 1950
To Heinz Berggruen, Paris, 1958
To Acquavella Galleries, New York
To Nasher collection, 1983

LITERATURE: Cf. Albert Elsen, *The Sculpture of Henri Matisse*, New York, 1972, pp. 144–53 (ill.)

Michael Mezzatesta, *Henri Matisse: Sculptor / Painter*, Kimbell Art Museum, Fort Worth, 1984, cat. no. 39 (ill.)

Cf. Isabelle Monod-Fontaine, *The Sculpture of Henri Matisse*, London, 1984, pp. 35–40, cat. no. 56 (ill.)

John Russell, "Matisse's Sculptures Take on a New Light," *The New York Times*, August 26, 1984, p. H 27 (ill.)

EXHIBITIONS: *XIX and XX Century Master Paintings*, Acquavella Galleries, New York, 1983, pp. 34–37 (ill.)

Henri Matisse: Sculptor / Painter, Kimbell Art Museum, Fort Worth, 1984, cat. no. 39 (ill.)

One of the most monumental of Matisse's sculptures, the *Large Seated Nude* is second in scale only to the artist's series of Backs and exudes, moreover, an expansive power and command of space beyond its actual size. Within Matisse's artistic development, it occupies a critical position, helping to signal, during the middle twenties, his move away from softer decorative values and his return to more concentrated form.

The story of the sculpture's protracted production is complex, and can be only partially reconstructed from photographs and documents. It has been variously dated 1922–25, 1923–25, 1924 or '25, and 1925, although most scholarly opinion now settles on c. 1923–25. A series of photographs taken of Matisse and certain of his works in his hotel-room studio in Nice, probably between 1924 and 1926 (see Elsen, 1972, figs. 194, 196–98; Monod-Fontaine, 1984, figs. 54–55), shows the *Large Seated Nude* as it evolved through at least three stages: starting as a relatively small plaster with rounded, soft volumes, it then grew in scale through plaster and clay versions, taking on a more muscular, sharply articulated anatomy, with flat planar accents, and reached at last the still more faceted, final version. An active, ongoing dialogue between two- and three-dimensional imagery is apparent throughout this evolution in the many drawings, lithographs, and paintings that explore related poses (e.g., Elsen, 1972, figs. 195, 201–03; Monod-Fontaine, 1984, figs. 47–50).

Just before or after work began on the *Large Seated Nude*, Matisse modeled a much smaller nude seated in an armchair (c. 1924; Elsen, 1972, figs. 199, 200). Matisse's sitter was Henriette Darricarrère, who had posed for many of his odalisques from 1920 on. The small sculpture and related two-dimensional images differ from *Large Seated Nude*, however, in the relaxed pose of their figures and the slack anatomy comfortably supported by armchairs or implied backrests. The tectonics of the large sculpture are much more daring, as Matisse reduced the support to a small socle that no longer holds up the back. Thus, the head and torso, cantilevered along a diagonal dramatically thrust into space, are held only by the tension of one leg locked behind the other and the figure's flexed abdominal muscles. The combination of implied muscular strength, aggressive paring of anatomy into taut planes and compact volumes, and bold rhythms of contour create one of Matisse's most powerful sculptural statements. While the pose relates naturally to earlier studies, it may also show the influence of certain heroic figures in Michelangelo's Medici Tomb and Sistine Chapel ceiling (Mezzatesta, 1984, pp. 117–18). Matisse continued the shift to a more monumental mode in ensuing works such as the painting *Decorative Figure on an Ornamental Background* (1925–26).

The plaster and clay models of the preliminary stages of *Large Seated Nude* have been lost or destroyed. The final sculpture exists in an edition of eleven casts numbered from 0/10 to 10/10.

---

53. *Tiari [Le Tiaré]*, 1930
   Bronze, 9⅝ x 7⅞ x 5⅝ (24.5 x 20 x 14.3)

MARKINGS: Rear left, bottom of back plinth: "HM 3/10"
Rear right, bottom of back plinth: "Valsuani / Cire Perdue"

PROVENANCE: Frederick Hellstrom, Minneapolis
To Paul Rosenberg, New York
To Mr. and Mrs. Richard K. Weil, St. Louis
To Galerie Beyeler, Basel, 1985
To Nasher collection, 1986

LITERATURE: Cf. Albert Elsen, *The Sculpture of Henri Matisse*, New York, 1972, pp. 170–74 (ill.)

Cf. John Elderfield, *Matisse in the Collection of The Museum of Modern Art*, New York, 1978, pp. 137–38 (ill.)

Cf. Alan Wilkinson, *Gauguin to Moore: Primitivism in Modern Sculpture*, Art Gallery of Ontario, Toronto, 1982, cat. no. 65 (ill.)

EXHIBITIONS: None

Henri Matisse modeled *Tiari* in Nice in the summer of 1930 soon after his return from a trip to the South Seas. It looks back to the format and intimate scale of his *Head with Necklace* (1907) and the organic masses of *Henrietta II* (1927). It also introduces a clever analogy between human and floral forms to evoke the sensuousness of Tahitian women, the aromatic atmosphere and indolent pleasures still so strong in the memory of his journey (see Elderfield, 1978, for a bibliography and cogent analysis of this work).

The petals, leaves, and stem of the *tiari*, or Tahitian gardenia, are fused in a visual pun with the shapes of nose, head, and hair. As if to stress even more the play between floral and human and between abstraction and reality, Matisse added an actual necklace to the first bronze cast (Baltimore Museum of Art, Cone Collection). This was the only sculpture he transferred into stone, his son Jean carving, around 1934, a white-marble version that extends the analogy with the white gardenia even further (Musée Matisse, Nice-Cimiez).

Comparisons can be drawn with the organic forms of Constantin Brancusi, who stripped away outer appearance to reach an inner purity, and with those of Jean Arp, whose sculptures seem to generate form outward from a vital nucleus. But perhaps the closest analogy, in terms of radically reforming anatomy through an agglomeration of organic shapes, is with Pablo Picasso's slightly later Boisgeloup Heads. The *Tiari*'s smooth elegance of surface separates it from Picasso, however, and makes it unique within Matisse's sculptural oeuvre for its refined purity.

JOAN MIRÓ (Spanish, 1893–1983)

54. *Moonbird [Oiseau Lunaire; The Lunar Bird]*, 1944–46 (enlarged 1966, cast 1967)
   Bronze, 90 x 80½ x 57¾ (228.5 x 204.5 x 146.7)

MARKINGS: Back of right leg, bottom: "Miro 4/5"
Back of left leg, bottom: "Susse Fondeur, Paris"

PROVENANCE: From artist to Galerie Maeght, Paris
To Nasher collection, 1972

LITERATURE: Cf. David Sylvester, *Miró: Oiseau solaire, oiseau lunaire, étincelles*, Pierre Matisse Gallery, New York, 1967, *passim*, pl. 1

Cf. *idem.*, "About Miró's Sculpture," in *Miró Bronzes*, Hayward Gallery, London, 1972, pp. 9, 11, 15–16 (ill. pp. 18–19)

Cf. William Rubin, *Miró in the Collection of The Museum of Modern Art*, New York, 1973, pp. 98, 134 (ill. p. 99)

Alain Jouffroy and Joan Teixidor, *Miró Sculpture*, New York and Paris, 1974, cat. no. 56, and also nos. 26, 29, 113 (ill.)

EXHIBITIONS: None

Moonbird and its companion *Sunbird* were the first independent works made by Joan Miró following his collaboration in 1944 with the ceramist Josep Llorens Artigas. In them he departed fundamentally from the assemblage technique of his Surrealist sculptures of the twenties and thirties. In addition to the formative experience of shaping three-dimensional ceramics, one can conjecture the possible influence in these new works of Jean Arp's biomorphic Concretions. The imagery is consistent with Miró's paintings, however, particularly the lunar symbolism and fantasy creatures of such pictures as *Triptych* (1937), *Nocturnal Bird* (1939), and the series Woman and Bird in Front of the Moon (1944). Whereas *Sunbird* strikes a horizontal position as if flying or swimming, *Moonbird* stands forcefully upright, with wings or arms raised in the traditional *amant* gesture. With its multiple personalities (animal or humanoid, bird or bull, sinister or playful, erotic or innocent), its morphology offers differing interpretations. The crescent at the top can be read as plumage, the horns of a bull, or simply a lunar symbol. The sharp projection in the center of the head may be phallic or it may be a bird's tongue, and the atavistic wings-as-arms, so important to the compositional play of curves, are equally ambiguous. In keeping with Miró's interest in ancient art, this heavyset syncretic creature with its ritualistic pose could descend from some pagan fertility idol, its sexuality now cast into a mythic and heroic dimension.

The original version of *Moonbird* was a small clay maquette, only 8½ inches high, the present location of which is unknown (perhaps destroyed). From this, Miró cast an edition of eight bronzes (Jouffroy and Teixidor, 1974, cat. no. 26) plus a terra-cotta (illustrated in *Cahiers d'Art* 20–21, 1945–46, p. 295). In 1947 a slightly larger version was carved in olive wood (Jouffroy and Teixidor, 1974, cat. no. 29; now private collection, South Africa), followed c. 1960–64 by one in obsidian (50 centimeters; Fondation Maeght, Saint-Paul-de-Vence). In 1966, Miró had the small version enlarged for a casting of monumental bronzes approximately 90 inches in height. He is known to have personally worked over and smoothed the surface of the enlarged plaster, but changes from the small version are minimal. An edition of five casts numbered 1/5 through 5/5 was planned, plus three artist's copies marked I/III through III/III, although cast no. 5/5 was never made; Miró donated one of the artist's proofs to the City of Paris and another to The Museum of Modern Art in New York. Finally, an even larger version (118⅛ inches) was carved in marble in 1968 (Jouffroy and Teixidor, 1974, cat. no. 113; Fondation Maeght, Saint-Paul-de-Vence), and a still more monumental bronze (400 centimeters) was recently cast (Pierre Matisse Gallery, New York).

---

55. *Caress of a Bird* [*La Caresse d'un oiseau*], 1967
    Painted bronze, 123 x 43½ x 19 (312.5 x 110.5 x 48.3)

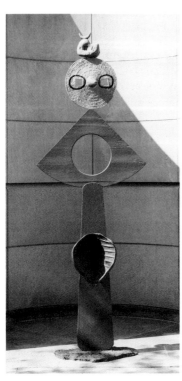

MARKINGS: Back at bottom: "Miró 4/4"

PROVENANCE: From artist to Galerie Maeght Lelong, New York
To Nasher collection, 1979

LITERATURE: Cf. Margit Rowell, *Miró*, New York, 1968, pl. 178

Cf. *Miró Sculptures*, Walker Art Center, Minneapolis, 1971, cat. no. 13 (ill.)

Alain Jouffroy and Joan Teixidor, *Miró Sculpture*, New York and Paris, 1974, cat. no. 86 (ill. p. 85)

EXHIBITIONS: *Miró Sculptures*, Seibu Museum of Art, Tokyo, 1979, cat. no. 14

Dallas Museum of Art, on loan since 1984

After producing a group of masterfully modeled sculptures in the forties, Joan Miró returned again to assemblage, employing this method almost exclusively after 1950 although sometimes combining it with modeling. All manner of found objects were pressed into service. The works generally were cast in bronze in small editions and, for a period in the late sixties, painted in bright primary colors. *Caress of a Bird* and also *Seated Woman and Child* (cat. no. 56) derive from this series.

Although Miró's titles are often poetic and improvisational rather then explanatory, this one may have been inspired by the friendly little bird perched lightly on the personage's head. In Miró's whimsical language of assembled objects cast in bronze, a straw basket or hat forms the head. A tortoise shell, another recurrent object in Miró's late work, provides a concave abdomen, the feminine meaning of which is evidenced by the usage of the same form in the 1969 *Woman* (Jouffroy and Teixidor, 1974, no.

139). Two small balls attached at the back indicate the buttocks. The body is formed by a plinth in the shape of an ironing board, and the chest and shoulders by a piece of carpentry with a hole cut in the middle. Tall, frontal, and symmetrical, the figure may have been inspired by totem carvings, but any serious suggestion of mysticism or religion is erased by Miró's playful wit. This work was cast by the Susse foundry in Paris in an edition of four.

---

*56. *Seated Woman and Child* [*Femme assise et enfant*], 1967
    Painted bronze, 48¼ x 16¾ x 16½ (122.5 x 42.5 x 42)

MARKINGS: Left rear leg: "Miró"
               Bottom of leg: "N 4"

PROVENANCE: From artist to Galerie Maeght Lelong, New York
               To Nasher collection, 1979

LITERATURE: Cf. Margit Rowell, *Miró*, New York, 1968, pl. 170

               Cf. *Miró Sculptures*, Walker Art Center, Minneapolis, 1971, cat. no. 15 (ill.)

               Alain Jouffroy and Joan Teixidor, *Miró Sculpture*, New York and Paris, 1974, cat. no. 88 (ill. p. 87)

EXHIBITIONS: *Miró Sculptures*, Seibu Museum of Art, Tokyo, 1979, cat. no. 16

The chair or stool is an objet trouvé that recurs in Miró's work between 1967 and 1969 in different guises (Jouffroy and Teixidor, 1974, nos. 122 and 136). In *Monsieur et Madame* and *Man and Woman in the Night* it substitutes for male and female anatomy. Here it can be read in two ways, either as a sturdy perch for an owl-like creature balanced on its top rung and keeping a watchful eye on its small red "baby" below or as the morphology of a woman. In this case, the flat plaque at the top becomes the woman's head

(with hat?) and the egglike baby now sits in her lap. In either interpretation, the playful analogizing, bright colors and tactile play of molten, irregular form versus carved regularity all proclaim the most ingenuous and pleasurable of Surrealist strategies.

This work was cast by the Clementi foundry outside of Paris in an edition of four, of which the Nasher cast is fourth. Another cast was installed as part of a fountain at the Fondation Maeght, Saint-Paul-de-Vence (Rowell, 1968, pl. 170).

HENRY MOORE (British, 1898–1986)

*57. *Time-Life Screen: Maquette No. 2*, 1952
    Bronze, 7⅛ x 12¾ x 1 (18.1 x 32.4 x 2.5)

MARKINGS: None

PROVENANCE: Sovereign Arts, London
               To Martin Ackerman, London
               To William Pall, New York
               To Shaindy Fenton, Inc., Fort Worth
               To Nasher collection, 1977

LITERATURE: Herbert Read, *Henry Moore: Volume Two, Sculpture and Drawings 1949–1954*, London, 1955; rev. ed., 1965, cat. no. 340, pl. 65 (plaster)

               Cf. Philip James, ed., *Henry Moore on Sculpture*, New York, 1967, p. 235, fig. 97

Cf. Alan Wilkinson, *The Moore Collection in the Art Gallery of Ontario*, Toronto, 1979, p. 122, no. 91 (ill.)

EXHIBITIONS: *20th Century Sculpture: Mr. and Mrs. Raymond D. Nasher Collection,* University Gallery, Southern Methodist University, Dallas, 1978, ex-cat.

In 1952, Henry Moore received a commission for a large reclining figure for the terrace of the new Time-Life Building on Bond Street in London. While working on this figure, he was approached by the architect to produce, in addition, a carved-stone screen for the third floor of the building's Bond Street exterior. There ensued a series of four maquettes and a working model in plaster (Read, 1965, nos. 339–43), followed by four upright abstract sculptures that Moore carved in Portland stone in his garden at Hoglands to be inserted into the four apertures in the building's stone screen (Read, 1965, no. 344, pls. 69–74). Moore wrote of this project:

> It seemed to me that the "Screen" should look as though it was part of the architecture, for it is a continuation of the surface of the building—and is an obvious part of the building.
>
> The fact that it is only a screen with space behind it, led me to carve it with a back as well

as a front, and to pierce it. . . .

I rejected the idea of a portrayal of some pictorial scene, for that would only be like hanging up a stone picture [James, ed., 1967, pp. 231–35].

The first maquette presented five evenly spaced apertures with vertical organic motifs, but it was rejected by Moore as "too obvious and regular a repetition of the fenestration of the building" (James, ed., 1967, p. 235). In the second maquette, as in the Nasher collection bronze, the rhythm of motifs and the sizes of openings are varied considerably, but Moore found the spacing "too vertical." In the third maquette he introduced horizontal elements, and in number four he hit upon the slightly varied rhythm of four vertical motifs that served as the basis for the final version. The highly organic, irregular forms in the first maquette had evolved in the final one into blockier patterns of interweaving flattened shapes somewhat reminiscent of Pre-Columbian carvings and glyphs (see Alan Wilkinson, *Gauguin to Moore: Primitivism in Modern Sculpture*, Art Gallery of Ontario, Toronto, 1982, p. 295). Moore's idea that the four stone carvings in the screen be mounted on turntables so they could be rotated regularly, thus showing their three-dimensional nature, was rejected for structural and safety reasons.

Maquette No. 2 exists in an edition of nine unnumbered and unmarked bronzes. The original plaster (estate of the artist) is illustrated in Read (1965, pl. 65).

---

*58. *Maquette for Large Torso: Arch*, 1962 (cast 1971)
Bronze, 4⅛ x 3⅛ x 2¹³⁄₁₆ (10.5 x 8 x 7.1)

MARKINGS: Top of base at rear: "Moore 7/9"
Below base: "Moore"

PROVENANCE: From artist to Patrick Cramer, Geneva
To Greenberg Gallery, St. Louis
To Nasher collection, 1978

LITERATURE: Cf. David Finn, *Henry Moore: Sculpture and Environment*, New York, 1976, pp. 342–45 (ill.)

Alan Bowness, *Henry Moore: Sculpture and Drawings, Vol. 4, Sculpture 1964–73*, London, 1977, cat. no. 503a (ill.)

Cf. Alan Wilkinson, *The Moore Collection in the Art Gallery of Ontario*, Toronto, 1979, p. 179, no. 160 (ill.)

EXHIBITIONS: *20th Century Sculpture: Mr. and Mrs. Raymond D. Nasher Collection,* University Gallery, Southern Methodist University, Dallas, 1978, ex-cat.

Arch forms entered Henry Moore's art with a variety of allusions: architectural, skeletal, biomorphic, and geological. Here there is a particularly strong reference to human or animal bones, especially the pelvic arch. Thus, the work's sturdy, open stance, despite the torso notation in the title, carries an anatomical association with the girth of the hips and the fertility of the pelvic region. Alan Bowness has dated the maquette 1962 (1977, cat. no. 503a). This version was cast in an edition of nine bronzes in 1971. A larger version, measuring 78½ inches, dates from 1962–63 and was cast in an edition of six (Bowness, *Henry Moore: Sculpture and Drawings, Vol. 3*, New York, 1965, cat. no. 503, pls. 159–62). Finally, a series of three bronzes plus one fiberglass cast were executed in a still more monumental scale (approximately 20 feet) in 1969 (Bowness, 1977, cat. no. 503b, and Wilkinson, 1979, cat. no. 160). In its two large-scale incarnations, this was the first sculpture by Moore that invited one to walk through it, thus establishing a different means of experiencing its three-dimensionality.

59. *Three Piece No. 3: Vertebrae [Working Model for Three Piece No. 3: Vertebrae; Three Piece Sculpture: Vertebrae]*, 1968
Polished bronze, 41⅛ x 93 x 48 (104.5 x 236.2 x 122), including base

MARKINGS: Top of base, front left: "Moore 4/8"
Left side of base, upper right: "H. Noack Berlin"

PROVENANCE: From artist to Gimpel Fils, London, 1968
To Nasher collection, 1968

LITERATURE: Cf. David Sylvester, *Henry Moore*, The Tate Gallery, London, 1968, p. 141, fig. 140, cat. no. 142

Alan Bowness, *Henry Moore: Sculpture and Drawings, Vol. 4, Sculpture 1964–73*, London, 1977, cat. no. 579, pls. 88–91

Cf. Alan Wilkinson, *The Moore Collection in the Art Gallery of Ontario*, Toronto, 1979, p. 202, no. 180 (ill.)

Cf. *The Tate Gallery 1978–80: Illustrated Catalogue of Acquisitions*, London, 1981, p. 141, no. T2303 (ill.)

EXHIBITIONS: None

This work evolves from Henry Moore's long-standing fascination with bones, vertebrae, and flint stones as sources of his forms and from his breakup of the human figure into disjointed horizontal segments, first seen in the early thirties. He stated in 1980 that each form in the sculpture resembled the joins between vertebrae, and that what interested him was the concept of creating a series or progression of similar elements (*The Tate Gallery 1978–80*, 1981, p. 142). Also of interest to him was the idea of nestled or interlocking shapes that could be varied in their spacing and relationships; and in the installation of the largest casts of this work, he experimented with slightly different sequences. Although direct references to the reclining figure have been minimized, the sculpture still evokes the figurative, and stimulates internal, bodily responses to its touching, opposing, and enveloping movements. Alan Wilkinson (1979, pp. 193 and 202) demonstrates the close relationship between some of its elements and flint stones that Moore kept in his studio.

A small maquette for this work (7½ inches long) exists in an edition of nine bronzes (Bowness, 1977, cat. no. 578). A plaster in the same scale belongs to the artist's estate and was shown in the 1968 Henry Moore exhibition at The Tate Gallery, London (cat. no. 140, fig. 140). Of the midsize, 90-inch version, such as the one in the Nasher collection, eight bronzes exist, including examples at the Art Gallery of Ontario, Toronto; the Memorial Art Gallery of the University of Rochester; The Tate Gallery, London; and the Hirshhorn Museum and Sculpture Garden, Washington, D.C. This version was also first exhibited at the 1968 Tate show (cat. no. 142). Moore produced a large, 24-foot, 6-inch version in an edition of three bronzes now located at the First National Bank of America in Seattle, the Israel Museum in Jerusalem, and the Dallas City Hall (Bowness, 1977, cat. no. 580). This version was prominent in the installations of the acclaimed Henry Moore exhibitions in Florence and Paris in 1972 and 1977 (see Bowness, 1977, pl. 93, and Stephen Spender, *Henry Moore: Sculptures in a Landscape*, n.d., pl. 59).

In 1967, Mr. and Mrs. Nasher visited Henry Moore at his studio and saw the small working maquette mentioned above. They decided at that time to buy the work once it was cast in full scale.

---

60. *Two Piece Reclining Figure No. 9*, 1968
Bronze, 56⅜ x 96 x 52 (143.2 x 243.8 x 132.1), including base

MARKINGS: Top of base, rear right: "Moore 3/7"
Right side of base: "H. Noack Berlin"

PROVENANCE: From artist to Gimpel Fils, London, 1968
To Nasher collection, 1968

LITERATURE: Alan Bowness, *Henry Moore: Sculpture and Drawings, Vol. 4, Sculpture 1964–73*, London, 1977, cat. no. 576, pls. 82–85 (Nasher cast listed as NorthPark National Bank)

Cf. Alan Wilkinson, *The Moore Collection in the Art Gallery of Ontario*, Toronto, 1979, p. 201, no. 179 (ill.)

Cf. *The Tate Gallery 1978–80: Illustrated Catalogue of Acquisitions*, London, 1981, pp. 140–41, no. T2301 (ill.)

Cf. *Henry Moore: The Reclining Figure*, Columbus Museum of Art, Columbus, Ohio, 1984, cat. nos. 51, 51a (ill.)

EXHIBITIONS: None

Dating from the same year as *Three Piece No. 3: Vertebrae* (cat. no. 59), this work represents another side of Moore's late work and treats a number of themes central to his development: abstraction of the reclining figure into shapes evocative of landscape or internal structures of bones and joints, division of the figure into two primary masses held in dynamic opposition, the contrast of rounded versus flattened shapes, the tension of forms that nestle or barely touch, and activation of the figure through tunneled holes. In this case, the upper body reminds one of rock formations weathered by wind and water. Its globular protrusions con-

trast with the flat shelf of the tops of the legs, which connect with the pointed lower legs like a beam that reaches across to fit snuggly into the hollowed curve of the abdomen. Thus, a variety of movements, shapes, and associations commingle in an overall composition that nevertheless sacrifices no coherency. Alan Wilkinson (1979, p. 201) points out similarities with the "smooth functional forms" and locking torso of *Three Piece Reclining Figure No. 2: Bridge Prop* (1963).

As was almost always the case in Moore's work, this large figure started as a small maquette (from 1967), which was cast in an edition of nine bronzes (not listed in Bowness, 1977). A plaster of the full-scale version now resides in the Art Gallery of Ontario, Toronto (see Wilkinson, 1979, p. 201). The bronze edition of this version numbers seven. A fairly close precedent for this composition is found in the *Two Piece Reclining Figure No. 2* (1960), where the two forms are completely separated and more roughly worked.

---

61. *Reclining Figure: Angles*, 1979 (cast 1980)
Bronze, 48¼ x 90¼ x 61¾ (122.5 x 229.2 x 156.8), including base

MARKINGS: Rear, at side of base: "H. Noack Berlin"
Right rear corner of base: "Moore 4/9"

PROVENANCE: From artist to Nasher collection, 1981

LITERATURE: Alan Bowness, *Henry Moore: Sculpture and Drawings, Vol. 5, Sculpture 1974–80*, London, 1983, cat. nos. 673–75, pls. 54–59

Cf. *Henry Moore: The Reclining Figure*, Columbus Museum of Art, Columbus,

Ohio, 1984, cat. nos. 62, 66 (ill.)

EXHIBITIONS: None

In the ongoing dialogue between abstraction and figuration that characterizes Henry Moore's late work, this sculpture represents one of his more naturalistic statements. Enacting again the signature theme of the reclining woman, Moore articulated this long, lithesome figure with a series of sharp angles pushing outward against its contours (hence the subtitle): the high inverted Vs forming the knees, the sharp angle of the left elbow and shoulder, the pointed breasts, and the sharp cut of the hair. The massing of the figure is unusually simplified and fluid, moving from the archlike legs into the twisted torso and culminating in the raised, observant head. A particularly close comparison can be made with Moore's earlier *Draped Reclining Figure* (1952–53).

A small maquette dating from 1975 and measuring 9¼ inches long was cast in an edition of nine bronzes (Bowness, 1983, cat. no. 673). An intermediate version (36 inches in length) from 1975–77 also exists in an edition of nine (Bowness, 1983, cat no. 674), and the large-scale version (86 inches), represented in the Nasher collection, was cast in an edition of nine plus an artist's proof, which remains the property of the Henry Moore Foundation. A finished watercolor-and-crayon drawing of *Reclining Figure: Angles* formerly belonged to Thomas Gibson Fine Art, London, and similar motifs appear in numerous drawings and prints from the same period.

BARNETT NEWMAN (American, 1905–1970)

62. *Here III*, 1965–66
Stainless and Cor-Ten steel, 125 x 23½ x 18⅝ (318 x 60 x 47)

MARKINGS: Top: "Barnett Newman / 1965–66 B/3
Treitel-Gratz / N.Y.C."

PROVENANCE: Estate of artist
To Harold Diamond, New York
To The Mayor Gallery, London
To Mr. and Mrs. Daniel Dietrich
To The Mayor Gallery, London
To Nasher collection, 1985

LITERATURE: Cf. Barbara Reise, "The Stance of Barnett Newman," *Studio International* 179, no. 919, February 1970, p. 55 (ill. p. 59)

Cf. Harold Rosenberg, *Barnett Newman: Broken Obelisk and Other Sculptures*, Seattle and London, 1971, pp. 13, 15, 32, 33 (ill.)

Cf. Thomas B. Hess, *Barnett Newman*, The Museum of Modern Art, New York, 1971, pp. 119, 120 (ill.); reprinted in *Barnett Newman*, The Tate Gallery, London, 1972, pp. 71–72

Cf. Harold Rosenberg, *Barnett Newman*, New York, 1978, p. 78, pl. 233

EXHIBITIONS:
None

Barnett Newman's three sculptures in the Here series, designated I, II, and III, date respectively from 1950 (original plaster; cast in 1962 and, with base added, in 1971), 1965, and 1965–66. As has often been observed, these works materialize the narrow vertical zips, voids, or stripes, with all their weighty implications of oneness, vertical ascension, and sublimity, that are so characteristic of Newman's paintings. In *Here I* a broad plinth, its edges treated with painterly roughness, is contrasted with a narrower, sleek, sharp-edged shaft, both of which are set into low mounds that heighten the metaphor of ritualistic space. Returning to the same theme fifteen years later, Newman produced *Here II*, a trinity of Cor-Ten shafts, each now with a truncated pyramidal base, which themselves are attached at carefully balanced intervals to an irregularly cut floorplate. In *Here III*, the shaft, now singular and commanding, is made from stainless steel and joined to a Cor-Ten base with a rough margin cut around

the bottom. The weightiness of the base is counteracted by lifting it slightly off the ground with a low, recessed, inner base. The resulting sense of suspension joins with the reflectivity of the silver to make this the most ethereal and spiritual of the three Heres and to relate it particularly closely to the wide white verticals in the Stations of the Cross, Newman's series of fourteen paintings dating from roughly the same time.

No plaster or maquette for this sculpture ever existed. According to Annalee Newman (conversation with the author, 1986), the artist worked from drawings and stayed closely involved in the fabrication, which took place at the Treitel-Gratz Company in Long Island City, New York. Thomas Hess records that work began in 1965, and that Newman's main problem was to decide whether the plinth should seem to stand on top of the base or sink within it. By exposing his weld along the top of the base, Newman chose the first option (Hess, 1972, p. 71). Although Hess states further that the measurements of the sculpture were fixed in advance, Mrs. Newman recalls that the exact height was determined only during the process of fabrication. Whereas *Here I* and *Here II* exist in editions of two, Newman decided to produce *Here III* (and subsequent sculptures) in an edition of three: now located in the Kunstmuseum Basel, Whitney Museum of American Art, New York, and the Nasher collection. Because of his demanding standards, the replication of this work, particularly the rough-cut base, caused him serious problems (Hess, 1972, pp. 71–72). At least one of the three examples he placed outdoors at the home of his friend, Harold Diamond, for weathering. Photographs of it taken at that time, which are frequently reproduced (e.g., Rosenberg, 1978, pl. 233), were made by Newman himself.

ISAMU NOGUCHI (American, born 1904)

63. *Gregory* [*Effigy*], 1945 (cast 1969)
Bronze, 69¼ x 16⅛ x 16⅜ (175.9 x 41 x 41.6)

MARKINGS: Back side of platform: "Isamu Noguchi 1945–69" and "4/8"
Left side of platform: "Susse Fondeur, Paris"

PROVENANCE: From artist to Cordier and Ekstrom, Inc., New York
To Nasher collection, 1969

LITERATURE: Cf. Dorothy C. Miller, *Fourteen Americans*, The Museum of Modern Art, New York, 1946, p. 42 (ill.)

Cf. Sam Hunter, *Isamu Noguchi*, New York, 1978, p. 79 (ill. pp. 178, 230)

Nancy Grove and Diane Botnick, *The Sculpture of Isamu Noguchi, 1924–1979: A Catalogue*, New York and London, 1980, cat. no. 242B (ill.) (incorrectly listed as not inscribed)

EXHIBITIONS: *Selections from the Nasher Collection*, North Texas State University, Denton, 1975

Twentieth Century Art from Fort Worth Dallas Collections, Fort Worth Museum of Art, 1974 (ill., n.p.)

20th Century Sculpture: Mr. and Mrs.
Raymond D. Nasher Collection,
University Gallery, Southern Methodist
University, Dallas, 1978, cat. no. 19 (ill.)

The original version of *Gregory* (or *Effigy*, as it was titled when first exhibited) was carved in purple slate (collection of the artist; Grove and Botnick, 1980, cat. no. 242A). Part of a sizable group of stone, biomorphic totem figures from the mid-forties, it was included in the 1946 exhibition *Fourteen Americans* at The Museum of Modern Art, New York, which marked Noguchi's first public triumph. Characteristic of the work of this period are the thin, flat planes of stone, elegantly smoothed and shaped, which fit intricately together in a tall, self-supporting configuration. Noguchi had rejected the "artificiality" of welded or cast joints, and sought to give expression to the aesthetic qualities inherent in his materials:

> In seeking materials to work with, I wanted to use them as I found them without trying to change the nature of a substance through melting (casting), pasting (welding), painting (patina), or otherwise.
>
> About 1944, I came to realize that the most available form of marble in New York was in slabs, since most of it was cut that way for surfacing buildings. . . . The very limitations of the medium imposed a kind of honesty; to find the minimum

means for construction and expression rather than the myriad possibilities that metal welding soon came to involve [Isamu Noguchi, *A Sculptor's World*, New York and Evanston, 1968, pp. 27–28].

The biomorphism that was so strong a stylistic ingredient of Noguchi's work at this time, and so basic a feature of his well-known set designs for the Martha Graham dance company, derives from Picasso's bone figures of the late twenties and Surrealist sources such as Yves Tanguy and Joan Miró, as does also the self-conscious mythic content so clear from his titles of the period, such as *Kouros*, *Effigy*, *Avatar*, and *Metamorphosis*. With regard to the latter, Noguchi reported to Patsy Nasher in 1979 that the title *Gregory* came from a character in a short story by Franz Kafka, undoubtedly Gregor Samsa in "The Metamorphosis."

A small maquette frequently preceded a final sculpture in Noguchi's work, and presumably one existed for *Gregory* (now lost; several similar maquettes visible in the 1946 studio photograph published in Hunter, 1978, p. 82). Casting took place at the Susse foundry in Paris in two different sessions, one in the mid-sixties when the first three out of eight casts were made (numbered 1/8–3/8), and one in 1969, when the edition was completed. Noguchi mistakenly numbered the second series 2/6 through 6/6, however, and had to correct these markings at the Modern Art Foundry in Long Island City after the sculptures were shipped to the United States.

CLAES OLDENBURG (American, born Sweden 1929)

*64. *Mannikin Torso: Two-Piece Bathing Suit*, 1960
Cloth soaked in plaster over wire frame and painted,
32½ x 14¾ x 4½ (83 x 37.5 x 11)

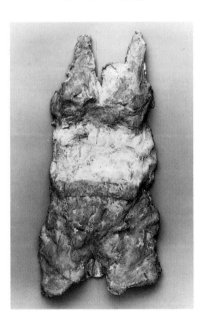

MARKINGS: Verso: "C.O. 1960 N.Y.C."

PROVENANCE: Renée Lachowsky, Brussels
Shaindy Fenton, Inc., Fort Worth
To Nasher collection, 1982

LITERATURE: Cf. Claes Oldenburg and Emmett Williams, *Store Days: Documents from the Store (1961) and Ray Gun Theater (1962)*, New York, 1967, *passim*

Barbara Rose, *Claes Oldenburg*, The Museum of Modern Art, New York, 1969, cat. no. 14, pp. 62–70, *passim*

Cf. Grace Glueck, "Soft Sculpture or Hard—They're Oldenburgers," *The New York Times Magazine*, September 21, 1969, pp. 107–08

EXHIBITIONS: *The Store*, Ray Gun Manufacturing Company, New York, 1961–62

Claes Oldenburg, The Museum of Modern Art, New York, 1969, cat. no. 14

Claes Oldenburg, Stedelijk Museum, Amsterdam; Städtische Kunsthalle Düsseldorf; The Tate Gallery, London; 1970, a traveling exhibition organized by the International Council of The Museum of Modern Art, New York, 1970, cat. no. 21 (ill.; inverted in Amsterdam catalogue)

Mannikin Torso: Two-Piece Bathing Suit, along with numerous other painted objects made from cloth, plaster, and wire, was included in Oldenburg's now-famous environmental installation, *The Store*. Opened in December 1961 in the artist's studio/exhibition/performance space at 107 East Second Street, New York, which he dubbed the "Ray Gun Manufacturing Company," *The Store* amassed articles representative of those in small shops that Oldenburg passed every day in his rundown Lower East Side neighborhood. Food displayed in cafeterias, cheap clothing, signs, utensils, dummies—all were recreated with jocular realism and jammed together in a kaleidoscope of form and color. With typical Oldenburgian wit, *The Store* opened for the Christmas rush. Many of the items indeed were sold, and the project can be counted as the young artist's first public success. The relief *Red Tights* was purchased by The Museum of Modern Art, New York, and was his first work to enter a museum collection.

Having renounced abstraction as a premise for his art, Oldenburg had inaugurated in 1959 a series of installation works. The first, *The Street*, was similar to *The Store* in its recreation of a contemporary urban environment but focused far more pessimistically on elements of decay and degeneration. A smaller-scale, preliminary version of *The Store*, consisting mostly of plaster wall reliefs, had been presented by Oldenburg in a group exhibition, *Environments, Situations, Spaces*, at the Martha Jackson Gallery in May 1961. By leasing his Lower East Side space, however, he pointedly rejected the traditional "uptown" gallery setting in favor of a more populist and realistic atmosphere. When *The Store* closed in January 1962, he continued to use the space as a setting for theatrical happenings. Oldenburg wrote and helped perform a number of pieces, including *Injun I*, which was photographed showing *Mannikin Torso* as a prop on the wall (see Coosje van Bruggen, *Claes Oldenburg: Mouse Museum/Ray Gun Wing*, Cologne, 1979, p. 26).

---

*65. *Pile of Typewriter Erasers*, 1970–75
Canvas filled with kapok, painted in acrylic, 7 x 28 x 22 (18 x 71 x 56), variable

MARKINGS: In pencil on top of one eraser: "Oldenburg / 74"

PROVENANCE: From artist to Leo Castelli Gallery, New York
Shaindy Fenton, Inc., Fort Worth
To Nasher collection, 1977

LITERATURE: Cf. Barbara Haskell, *Claes Oldenburg, Object into Monument*, Pasadena Art Museum, 1971, pp. 120–24

Cf. Martin Friedman, *Oldenburg: Six Themes*, Walker Art Center, Minneapolis, 1975, pp. 69–77

EXHIBITIONS: *Oldenburg: Six Themes*, Walker Art Center, Minneapolis, 1975, checklist no. 230

20th Century Sculpture from the Mr. and Mrs. Raymond D. Nasher Collection, University Gallery, Southern Methodist University, Dallas, 1978, cat. no. 21 (ill.)

Within his repertory of commonplace objects converted into art, the typewriter eraser has been one of Oldenburg's most mutable and fancifully evocative images. Notable for its distinctive, somewhat odd shape and its simplified structure of circle and inverted triangle, it first appeared in 1968 as a prop in Oldenburg's script for a happening commissioned by *Esquire* magazine entitled "The Typewriter" (Claes Oldenburg, "My Very Last Happening," *Esquire* 71, no. 5, May 1969, pp. 154–57). The immediate inspiration for the use of this image was apparently a magazine advertisement featuring a typewriter eraser that Oldenburg clipped out and added to the notebooks he keeps for reference. It may also have biographical significance, however, since as Martin Friedman relates (1975, p. 11), items such as the typewriter and eraser were part of Oldenburg's childhood memories of visits with his father, then Swedish consul general in Chicago, at the consulate headquarters where he entertained himself with the office equipment.

Oldenburg has explored the structural, abstract, and coloristic possibilities of the eraser form in all areas of his work: it appears in cardboard studies, in soft versions, in metal, in proposals for monuments and a plethora of drawings, and assumes many different guises, including windmill, waterfall, tornado, seated or reclining figure, even Sphinx and Medusa (see Haskell, 1971, pp. 120–24; Friedman, 1975, pp. 70–77). Each permutation is essentially a different work, but contributes to the development of the overall iconography or theme. There are several versions of soft erasers in different positions from 1970, which is always given as the starting date for work on *Pile of Typewriter Erasers* but was probably only the conceptual beginning. The date of actual fabrication is normally cited as 1975, although when Mrs. Nasher took one of the segments of the sculpture to Oldenburg's studio and asked him to sign it, he added "1974." In this sculpture, five small canvas elements show how a family of erasers can stack together and embrace one another, much as in the well-known watercolor drawing and lithograph of the same subject (1970 and 1975, respectively; see Friedman, 1975, p. 76).

---

66. *Typewriter Eraser*, 1976
Ferro cement, stainless steel, and aluminum, 89 x 90 x 63 (226 x 229 x 160)

MARKINGS: Back of steel clasp: "Oldenburg / Typewriter Eraser Copyright © 1976 Claes Oldenburg / 2/3 Work executed by

"Lippincott North Haven Conn"

PROVENANCE: From artist to Leo Castelli Gallery, New York
To Nasher collection, 1978

LITERATURE: Cf. Barbara Haskell, *Claes Oldenburg, Object into Monument*, Pasadena Art Museum, 1971, pp. 120–24

Claes Oldenburg, *Photo Log: May 1974– August 1976*, Stuttgart and London, 1976, pls. 88–89, 98, 100–07

Nancy Foote, "Oldenburg's Monuments to the Sixties," *Artforum* 15, no. 5, January 1977, p. 56 (ill.) (this example?)

EXHIBITIONS: *Claes Oldenburg*, Leo Castelli Gallery, New York, 1976 (this example?)

20th Century Sculpture from the Mr. and Mrs. Raymond D. Nasher Collection, University Gallery, Southern Methodist University, Dallas, 1978, cat. no. 21 (ill.)

One of Oldenburg's earliest ideas for the typewriter eraser image involved a proposal for a monument at a site across from the Art Students League in New York City:

> [My] line of approach was thinking about what might fall out of an office building. If one imagined a typewriter eraser falling, the result might be a bent typewriter eraser, a fine antiheroic subject. Since a real typewriter eraser is too light to bend in a fall, I imagined a giant one. . . . This particular object has no accepted "rest" position and I had to determine one [Haskell, 1971, p. 122; small model illustrated].

The colossal monument Oldenburg envisioned was never realized, but in 1970 he created *Heroic Sculpture in the Form of a Bent Typewriter Eraser*, which is 84 inches high (Haskell, 1971, p. 121). The circular part of the eraser lies flat on the floor, and the brush, executed in rope, stands straight up in differentiated strands like hair or stalks.

The technical means to realize additional works on that scale in durable materials came through Oldenburg's collaborative association with Lippincott, Inc. Although he had worked with Lippincott since 1969 on a number of other projects, it was not until the mid-seventies that Oldenburg brought them a small model of a typewriter eraser in cardboard and copper tubing with the intent of producing an edition on a monumental scale. The first version, manufactured from stainless steel, concrete, and aluminum, was 90 inches high, in an edition of three (number 1, private collection, Los Angeles; number 2, Nasher collection; number 3, collection of Mr. and Mrs. Sidney Lewis). In this version, the eraser portion rests on the base at a diagonal, with the brush curving upward, its strands individually bent and slightly different in each work. In 1977, Oldenburg produced an edition of eighteen plus five artist's proofs of the same composition in the same materials but 36 inches in height (documentation from Lippincott, Inc., and the Leo Castelli Gallery, 1986). See Claes Oldenburg, *Photo Log*, 1976, for a series of photographs made at the factory that show the execution of the larger version.

MIMMO PALADINO (Italian, born 1948)

*67. *A Surrounded Figure* [*Assediato*], 1983
Bronze, 55⅜ x 47¼ x 50⅜ (140.6 x 120 x 128)

MARKINGS: Left rear, top of base: "M Paladino VII.1983"
Left side, at back: "Fonderia d'Arte / Luigi Tommasi / . . . [*illegible*]"

PROVENANCE: From artist to Waddington Galleries, Ltd., London
To Nasher collection, 1984

LITERATURE: Cf. *Mimmo Paladino*, Sperone Westwater Gallery, New York, 1983, n.n. (ill.)

Nena Dimitrijevic, "Sculpture after

Evolution," *Flash Art* no. 117, April–May 1984, p. 25 (ill.; mistitled *Hortus Conclusus*)

EXHIBITIONS: *Mimmo Paladino*, Waddington Galleries, Ltd., London, 1984, cat. no. 4 (ill. p. 15)

A New Romanticism: Sixteen Artists from Italy, Hirshhorn Museum and Sculpture Garden, Washington, D.C., 1985, cat. no. 38 (ill.)

Compared to Paladino's usual darkly expressive imagery, with its mysterious pagan rituals and teeming psycho-battles, *A Surrounded Figure* seems calm, classical, even Elysian. In a painting from the same year titled *La Tempesta* (*Paladino*, Sperone Westwater Gallery, 1983, n.n.), a hairless ghostly figure sits astride a small fawnlike creature, stirring up a maelstrom of dismembered animals and humans. Here, a similar figure kneels prayerfully beside an ancient urn and three now very tame fawns, which seem to share with him a common spirit. One hand is raised slightly with fingers spread. With the other he reaches into

the urn, perhaps to bring forth food or an offering. His own masklike face and the string of masks he wears over his shoulder confirm his shamanistic or priestly status, evidenced also by his spiritual communion with the animals. The trunk at the back has various enigmatic symbols and human and animal forms attached. Scarification on the flanks of the animals is matched by long scars down the man's back. Although embodied in far less emotional terms, Paladino's familiar themes of mythological mystery, of past as part of the present, and of primal relationships between man and nature are very much at work.

Perhaps best known as a painter, Paladino frequently weds the pictorial and sculptural in constructed, heavily painted reliefs. Even in his fully three-dimensional work in wood and bronze, color always plays an important role. In the case of *A Surrounded Figure*, four bronze casts were made, each of which he patinated differently in a range of descriptive colors. The original plaster of this work is seen in a photograph of Paladino taken in his studio (*Paladino*, Sperone Westwater Gallery, 1983, n.n.).

ANTOINE PEVSNER (French, born Russia, 1884–1962)

*68. *Dynamic Projection at Thirty Degrees* [*Projection dynamique au 30e degré*], 1950–51 (cast after 1960) Bronze, 37⅛ x 74¼ x 36 (94.2 x 188.5 x 91.5)

MARKINGS: Back, lower right: "Pevsner 3/3" and "Susse Fondeur Paris"

PROVENANCE: Alix de Rothschild, Paris
Galerie Natalie Seroussi, Paris
To Galerie Beyeler, Basel
To Nasher collection, 1983

LITERATURE: Cf. René Massat, *Antoine Pevsner et le Constructivisme*, Paris, 1956, n.p. (ill.)

Cf. Barbara Butler, "Antoine Pevsner in Paris," *Arts* 31, no. 5, February 1957, pp. 25f. (ill.)

Carola Giedion-Welcker and Pierre Peissi, *Antoine Pevsner*, Neuchâtel, 1961, cat. no. 107, addendum no. 107 (ill.)

Cf. George Heard Hamilton, *Painting and

Sculpture in Europe 1880 to 1940, Baltimore, 1967, pp. 232–33, pl. 138b

EXHIBITIONS: None

Dynamic Projection at Thirty Degrees is related to Antoine Pevsner's Developable Surface series of freestanding sculptures, the first bronze *Surface développable* dating from as early as 1936, followed by *Projection dans l'espace* of 1938–39. These works, with their projections of twisting, ribbed surfaces, seem to have originated in drawings and paintings of a few years earlier (Giedion-Welcker and Peissi, 1961, nos. 72, 73), in which networks of radiating lines trace complex movements in space. Similar genuses of movement are given solid form in the ensuing sculptures, in which linear radiation is preserved either by soldering rods or wires at regular intervals along a plane or, as in the original version of *Dynamic Projection at Thirty Degrees*, fusing these rods to create a curving planar surface. This was a painstaking technique invented by Pevsner, involving long working hours and extreme heat. The formal vocabulary is related to the striations that his brother Naum Gabo added to his sculptures about the same time, as well as to Gabo's slightly later strung sculptures.

The concept of the "developable surface," involving projecting and unfolding movement in space, derives from mathematical models providing physical embodiment of algebraic equations. Pevsner's actual compositions, however, were for the most part intuitive rather than mathematical. In this example, the theme involves a strong diagonal thrust at approximately 30°, with various countervailing movements around it. The original bronze version of the sculpture is now in the Musée National d'Art Moderne, Paris (gift of Mme Pevsner; included in Pevsner retrospective, Musée National d'Art Moderne, Paris, 1957, cat. no. 49). Two other bronze casts exist: at the Caracas University Center, in Venezuela, and the Baltimore Museum of Art (casts number one and two, respectively). It is known that the second cast was made by the Susse foundry, Paris, in 1960 (information provided by Brenda Richardson, Baltimore Museum of Art), so the third cast, also by Susse, must have been made between 1960 and the time of the addendum (date unknown) to Carola Giedion-Welcker's Pevsner monograph of 1961, in which it is listed.

PABLO PICASSO (Spanish, 1881–1973)

69. *Head of a Woman [Tête de femme; Marie-Thérèse Walter]*, 1931–32 (cast 1973)
Bronze, 34 x 14⅜ x 19¼ (86.4 x 36.5 x 49)

MARKINGS: Platform, back center: "Cire perdue C. Valsuani" and "1/2"
Inside base: "Epreuve fondue en bronze en janvier 1973"

PROVENANCE: From artist to Galerie Louise Leiris, Paris
To Nasher collection, 1986

LITERATURE: Cf. Romuald Dor de la Souchère, *Picasso in Antibes*, New York, 1960, no. 145 (ill.)

Cf. Albert Elsen, "The Many Faces of Picasso's Sculpture," *Art International* 13, no. 6, summer 1969, pp. 31–33 (ill.)

Cf. Alan Bowness, "Picasso's Sculpture," in *Picasso in Retrospect*, New York, 1973, no. 232 (ill.), pp. 141–42 (dated 1932)

Cf. Christa Lichtenstern, *Picasso "Tête de Femme,"* Städelsches Kunstinstitut, Frankfurt-am-Main, 1980, *passim*

Cf. Werner Spies, *Picasso: Das plastische Werk*, rev. ed., Stuttgart, 1983, pp. 149–57, no. 132 (ill.; dated 1931)

William Rubin, "Picasso," in *"Primitivism" in 20th Century Art*, The Museum of Modern Art, New York, 1984, pp. 325–28 (ill.)

EXHIBITIONS: *Unterlinden I*, Musée Unterlinden, Colmar, 1975, cat. no. 42

XXXVIII Esposizione Internazionale d'Arte, Venice, 1976

Espace-Lumière dans des sculptures du Cubisme à aujourd'hui, Château de Ratilly, Treigny, France, 1977, cat. no. 6

Exposition Picasso, Museum of the City of Tokyo, 1977, cat. no. 147

Modern European Sculpture 1918–1945: Unknown Beings and Other Realities, Albright-Knox Art Gallery, Buffalo, 1979, cat. no. 52

Pablo Picasso: A Retrospective, The Museum of Modern Art, New York, 1980, cat. p. 286 (ill.)

Hommage à D.-H. Kahnweiler, National-galerie Berlin, 1983

"Primitivism" in 20th Century Art, The Museum of Modern Art, New York, 1984, cat. pp. 325–28 (ill.)

Of the many works from the early thirties expressing Pablo Picasso's strong emotions toward his new love Marie-Thérèse Walter, the six large busts modeled at Boisgeloup between the summers of 1931 and 1932, known collectively as the Boisgeloup Heads, are among the most powerful. The head in the Nasher collection is the third in the series. Under the influence of Julio Gonzalez's technical methods and assistance, Picasso's sculpture for the previous three years had been primarily open-framework constructions or assemblages. After converting one of the stables at his newly purchased Château de Boisgeloup, near the village of Gisors, northwest of Paris, into a sculpture studio in May 1931, he returned to modeling in clay and plaster, a choice of mediums that in itself may have been a response to his new lover (Rubin, 1984, pp. 325–26). A serenely classical plaster bust of Marie-Thérèse appears in a painting entitled *The Lamp* of June 1931, providing evidence for an approximate date of the first of the Boisgeloup Heads (Spies, 1983, cat. no. 128). In a painting from December titled *The Sculptor*, another bust appears, which now includes the sitter's breasts and a more contorted physiognomy and relates closely to the second Boisgeloup Head (Spies, 1983, cat. no. 131). Extrapolating from this sequence, the third large head can be convincingly dated 1931–32, a placement adopted by William Rubin (1984, p. 326) *pace* Werner Spies's date of 1931 (1983, cat. no. 132). Here the shoulders and chest are eliminated and the head is perched high on a roughly worked stand, with facial features even more exaggerated into rounded, tumescent masses that begin to incorporate in their organic fullness both a male and female sexual symbolism. The head thus becomes an emblem of love-making, of male and female coupling, and of the violent erotic impulses aroused in Picasso by his model. In the fourth head (Spies, 1983, cat. no. 133), the areas of cheek, nose, and hair swell into autonomous masses, while the fifth and sixth heads (Spies, 1983, cat. nos. 110, 111) take the deconstructing abstractions of the series to new heights that are almost incomprehensible without the previous examples. The arched fusion of nose and forehead in certain of these works has been attributed by various authors to the influence of African Nimba masks, which also seem important for the overall profile and height of busts two and three and their associative linkage with eroticism and fertility (see esp. Rubin, 1983, pp. 325–28). The bold manipulation of facial features has precedents in Matisse's Jeannette series of 1910–16, and a somewhat similar biomorphic vocabulary is seen in Matisse's *Tiari* of 1930. The incorporation of found objects in the stand for the third head, reflecting Picasso's freewheeling creative processes, in which any material could be pressed into the service of art, was a carryover of his assemblage technique.

A first plaster study and a second, more advanced plaster maquette for this work are in private collections in Europe (Spies, 1983, cat. nos. 132 Ia and Ib). The first bronze, executed in the early thirties, is now in the Musée Picasso, Paris (Spies, 1983, cat. no. 132 IIa). Two additional bronze casts were made in 1973; these differ slightly from the first at the base of the neck: no. 1 is the Nasher cast, and no. 2 is in the Städelsches Kunstinstitut in Frankfurt (Spies, 1983, cat. no. 132 IIb). Finally, a cement cast, now in the Musée d'Antibes, was made in 1937 and stood with two other cement Boisgeloup Heads at the Spanish Pavilion of the 1937 World's Fair in Paris (Spies, 1983, cat. no. 132 III). It is known from recorded conversations with Brassaï that Picasso originally did not wish to have the Boisgeloup Heads cast into bronze, as he preferred the lightness and buoyancy of white plaster (see Rubin, 1984, p. 340 n. 203).

---

70. *Pregnant Woman* [*La Femme enceinte*], 1950, second version 1959
Bronze, 42¾ × 11⅜ × 13¼ (108.5 × 29 × 33.7)

MARKINGS: On platform, rear left: "15.3.59"
On platform, rear right: "2/2 Cire perdue / C. Valsuani"

PROVENANCE: From artist to Paloma Picasso, New York and Paris
Galerie Louise Leiris, Paris
To Saidenberg Gallery, New York, 1969
The Pace Gallery, New York
To Nasher collection, 1983

LITERATURE: Cf. Françoise Gilot and Carleton Lake, *Life with Picasso*, New York, 1964; reprint 1981, p. 295

Cf. William Rubin, *Picasso in the Collection of The Museum of Modern Art*, New York, 1972, p. 243, no. 171 (ill.)

Cf. Robert Rosenblum, *The Sculpture of Picasso*, The Pace Gallery, New York, 1982, pp. 7, 46, cat. no. 42 (ill.)

Werner Spies, *Picasso: Das plastische Werk*, rev. ed., Stuttgart, 1983, pp. 212–13, no. 350 (ill. pp. 248, 249)

EXHIBITIONS: *Picasso: Sculpture, Ceramics, Graphic Work*, The Tate Gallery, London, 1967, cat. no. 105 (ill.) (cast 2/2 ?)

Françoise Gilot, Picasso's companion in the forties and fifties, has sketched the historical background of this inventive, composite sculpture:

After we settled in Vallauris [1948], Pablo occasionally made small objects in plaster or terra cotta at Madame Ramié's [village ceramic shop], but it wasn't until after he had bought the atelier in the rue du Fournas [Spring 1949] that he began to make sculpture of any consequence. Next to his new atelier was a field where some of the potters threw debris.... Often on his way to work, Pablo would stop by the dump to see what might have been added since his last inspection.... The object he found became the mainspring of a new sculpture.

One of the first sculptures Pablo made in the perfume factory [rue du Fournas] was the *Pregnant Woman*. He wanted me to have a third child. I didn't want to because I was still feeling very weakened even though a year had passed since Paloma was born. I think this sculpture was a form of wish fulfillment on his part. He worked over it a long time, I suppose from a composite overall image he had of the way I had looked while I was carrying Claude and Paloma. The breasts and distended abdomen were made with the help of three water pitchers...all picked up from the scrap heap. The rest was modeled. The fact that the figure was only about half the normal size gave it a grotesque appearance [Gilot and Lake, 1981, pp. 293, 295].

With his punning use of ceramic pots to create an image of woman as vessel, Picasso fashioned a personal fetish object much like ancient fertility goddesses, one that paid homage to pregnancy but also sublimated his own frustration and desire for another offspring. It is one of his most successful works that combines modeling and found objects. In the first version of the sculpture, executed in 1950, there is greater roughness in the working of the figure, making for a marked contrast between most of the body and the expanding, smooth volumes of the abdomen and breasts. The first version is known in a plaster and three bronze casts (Spies, 1983, cat. no. 349 I and II), which were

made several years after the plaster.

In 1959, Picasso returned to the sculpture, smoothing out the modeling of the body and adding nipples to the breasts, a belly button, and feet and toes, before making two more bronze casts. The plaster of this version is in a private collection (Spies, 1983, cat. no. 350 I); a first, unnumbered bronze is in the Musée Picasso, Paris; and the second cast, numbered 2/2, is in the Nasher collection (Spies, 1983, cat no. 350 II). A photograph of Picasso at work on the first plaster of this sculpture is published in Rosenblum (1982, p. 46).

IVAN PUNI (Jean Pougny) (Russian, born Finland, 1892–1956)

71. *Construction Relief*, c. 1915–16
Painted wood and tin on wood support, 22⅞ x 18⅜ x 3½ (58 x 46.7 x 9)

MARKINGS: Lower right (in Cyrillic): "I V Puni"

PROVENANCE: Anna Leporskaya, Leningrad
Leonard Hutton Galleries, New York
To Nasher collection, 1986

LITERATURE: None

EXHIBITIONS: None

The scarcity of early sculptures by Ivan Puni and of three-dimensional works by other members of Russia's avant-garde makes the emergence of this painted wood-and-metal relief particularly welcome. It was formerly in the collection of Anna Leporskaya, a one-time student of Kasimir Malevich and the wife of another Malevich pupil. Christina Lodder speculates (correspondence with the author, 1986) that since Leporskaya and her husband were members of UNOVIS in

Vitebsk, where Puni lived and taught in 1919, they may have received the relief at that time or possibly later through Malevich, who was also a friend of Puni's. The work is signed prominently in Russian script, an unusual feature among Puni's known reliefs, which would be explained, however, if it were a gift.

The old-fashioned decorative material is also unusual; Puni has wittily placed nineteenth-century stylistic motifs in an uncompromisingly modern context. In his exploitation of diverse textural and material values for expressive ends, the influence of Tatlin's "culture of materials" is acknowledged. On a wooden backboard, whose beveled rear edges suggest it may originally have been a drawer bottom, are joined various wooden and metallic fragments that extend outward into space approximately three inches. The rough surfaces and loose application of paint stress the raw, "found" nature of Puni's materials, while the shapes and color areas are elegantly articulated. At the center is a section of a tin container, which probably held cookies or candy, with floral decoration, a heraldic symbol of two eagles, part of a date ("18...") , and remnants of various inscriptions in Cyrillic: "Fa..." (possibly for Fabrika), "George Bor...," "St. Petersburg. Khar..." (Kharkov), and "Request..." The other tin fragments bear typical southern-Russian decoration.

Puni produced his earliest recorded sculpture, the well-known relief *The Card Players* (lost, probably destroyed), in St. Petersburg in 1913–14 following a first sojourn in Paris, where he had absorbed the fundamentals of Cubist structure. His paintings, collages, and relief sculptures of this period exhibit a dense layering of small geometric elements. From 1915 onward, however, the influence of Malevich's Suprematism is apparent in the increasing sparseness and rigor of his compositions. Between 1914 and 1919 he is thought to have made over thirty reliefs (see H. Berninger and J.-A. Cartier, *Pougny: Catalogue de l'oeuvre*, I, Tubingen, 1972, p. 195), most of them lost and/or destroyed. When Puni emigrated to Germany in 1920, he carried with him the drawings and maquettes for numerous sculptures, some of which he later reconstructed. The corrugated element in the Nasher relief recalls certain works from 1915–16 (Berninger and Cartier, 1972, nos. 110, 113), and the truncated cone came into use about the same time (Berninger and Cartier, 1972, nos. 102, 104), suggesting a similar date for the Nasher relief. It could conceivably have been made later, however, around 1919, when Puni's work sometimes took on a more decorative cast (Berninger and Cartier, 1972, nos. 57–64).

AUGUSTE RODIN (French, 1840–1917)

72. *Eve*, 1881 (cast before 1932)
   Bronze, 68 x 17¼ x 25½ (173 x 44 x 65)

MARKINGS: Back of base, lower right: "Alexis Rudier /
Fondeur Paris"
Top of base, right rear: "A. Rodin"

PROVENANCE: Pierre Gilbert, Paris and Nanteau-sur-
Essonne, c. 1932
Sold by his heirs at Sotheby Parke Bernet,
Monte Carlo, November 25, 1979
To Galerie Beyeler, Basel
To Nasher collection, 1982

LITERATURE: Cf. Albert Elsen, *Rodin*, New York, 1963,
esp. p. 49 (ill.)

Cf. John Tancock, *The Sculpture of Auguste
Rodin*, Philadelphia, 1976, pp. 148–57 (ill.)

Cf. Jacques de Caso and Patricia B.

Sanders, *Rodin's Sculpture: A Critical Study
of the Spreckels Collection*, Rutland,
Vermont, and Tokyo, 1977, pp. 143–47 (ill.)

*Importantes Sculptures des XIXe et XXe
siècles*, Sotheby Parke Bernet, Monte Carlo,
November 25, 1979, cat. no. 71A (suppl.;
ill.)

EXHIBITIONS: *Skulptur im 20. Jahrhundert*, Wenkenpark,
Riehen/Basel, 1980, cat. p. 20 (ill.)

The history of Rodin's production of *Eve*, one of his most
famous works, is well known: its original invention as a
companion figure to Adam flanking the *Gates of Hell*, commissioned in 1880; its subsequent separation from the *Gates*
and casting as an independent sculpture; the strong influence of Michelangelo's *Eve* in the Sistine Chapel for Rodin's
conception; and the anecdote of the model for the figure
becoming pregnant and leaving Rodin's employ before the
work was completed, supposedly causing him to leave areas
around the head and abdomen rough and unfinished. Another possible source, less widely discussed, is Jean-Antoine
Houdon's *Winter*, a replica of which entered the Louvre in
1881 (see de Caso and Sanders, 1977, p. 147 n.3). The self-
enveloping pose of Houdon's figure, although more mun-
dane in motivation, is remarkably close to that of the *Eve*.

By removing Eve from a biblical context, Rodin expanded her metaphorical range, making her expressive not
just of the anguish of original sin but also of the general
spiritual malaise that can torment the human soul. The
sculpture became one of his most frequently requested
works for purchase, and was repeated in several sizes and
materials. Most numerous are the life-size (c. 170 centimeters) and half life-size (c. 76 centimeters) versions, which
differ in certain details. The smaller *Eve* was exhibited in
London in 1883, while the life-size version was not shown
publicly until 1889, helping to support the theory that the
smaller version actually came first (de Caso and Sanders,
1977, p. 144). John Tancock (1976, pp. 155–56) catalogs
fifteen early bronze casts of the life-size *Eve*, exclusive of
the Nasher cast, most of them marked with the name of the
Alexis Rudier foundry. An undetermined number of modern
casts have also been made. Four plasters in the large scale
are recorded.

---

73. *Head of Balzac*, 1897
   Plaster, 7½ x 8 x 6½ (19 x 20.3 x 16.5)

MARKINGS: Left rear, edge of hair: "A Rodin"

PROVENANCE: Margit Chanin, Ltd., New York, by 1963
To Lester Avnet, New York
To Stanley Moss and Co., New York
To Nasher collection, 1985

LITERATURE: Albert Elsen, *Rodin*, New York, 1963, p. 91 (ill.)

Athena Tacha Spear, *Rodin Sculpture in the
Cleveland Museum of Art*, Cleveland, 1967,
pp. 9–30, pl. 27, esp. p. 91 (plaster cast
no. 1); supplement, 1974, pp. 112–19 S, 124–25 S

Cf. Albert Elsen et al., *Rodin and Balzac:*

Rodin's Sculptural Studies for the Monument to Balzac from the Cantor, Fitzgerald Collection, Beverly Hills, 1973, *passim*, pl. 41

Cf. John Tancock, *The Sculpture of Auguste Rodin*, Philadelphia, 1976, pp. 431, 457, fig. 76

Cf. Jacques de Caso and Patricia B. Sanders, *Rodin's Sculpture: A Critical Study of the Spreckels Collection*, Rutland, Vermont, and Tokyo, 1977, pp. 237–41

EXHIBITIONS: *Rodin*, The Museum of Modern Art, New York, 1963, p. 91 (ill.)

This *Head of Balzac* corresponds to Athena Tacha Spear's "type W" in her classification of the many discrete studies of the head and features of Honoré de Balzac prepared by Auguste Rodin during the protracted evolution of his large-scale *Monument to Balzac* (Spear, 1967, 1974, *passim*). He had received the commission for a sculpture commemorating this great nineteenth-century writer in 1891 from the Société des Gens de Lettres in Paris. With·characteristic thoroughness, Rodin steeped himself in his subject through lengthy investigation. Work on the commission passed through two stages between 1891 and 1898, but Rodin's conception changed continually, as evidenced by the many surviving studies of both the head and full figure, progressing from a relatively naturalistic depiction of a young man to a more romantic image of an aged visionary. For an attempt to place the individual heads, which number over twenty, in a chronological sequence, see Spear (1967, 1974). The study in the Nasher collection was made late in the series and approaches closely the final sculpture, with its wild shock of hair, roughly modeled features, and deep-set eyes. Although it was generally Rodin's practice to make more than one plaster cast of each of his works, the Nasher plaster is the only one thus far identified of this type in this scale (affirmed by Albert Elsen in correspondence, 1981). Nor has it been possible to trace the provenance of this piece beyond Margit Chanin. The popularity of this general type, however, is indicated by the range of casts in other materials and dimensions. Numerous bronze casts are known (Spear, 1967, pp. 91–92; 1974, pp. 124–25 S), and an enlarged plaster (19½ inches), formerly in the McCrory Corporation Collection, is now in the Milwaukee Art Museum. In addition, there are four stoneware casts measuring approximately 18 inches, as well as two bronze casts of this version. A special feature of the Nasher plaster is the varnished surface, which has aged to a rich amber tonality.

MEDARDO ROSSO (Italian, 1858–1928)

74. *Ecce Puer* [*Behold the Child; Portrait of Alfred Mond*], 1906
Wax over plaster, 16⅜ x 13⅜ x 11¹/₁₆ (41.6 x 34 x 28.2)

MARKINGS: In red inside the hollow cast (nearly illegible): "Danila Rosso Parravicini"

PROVENANCE: Danila Rosso Parravicini, Milan
To Lords Gallery Ltd., London, 1969
To Nasher collection, 1986

LITERATURE: Cf. Margaret Scolari Barr, *Medardo Rosso*, New York, 1963, pp. 58–59, 65 (ill. frontis. and p. 57)

Cf. *Medardo Rosso 1858–1928*, Frankfurter Kunstverein, Frankfurt-am-Main, 1984, cat. nos. 31–32 (ill.)

Cf. Jole de Sanna, *Medardo Rosso o la Creazione dello Spazio Moderno*, Milan, 1985, *passim*, esp. pp. 136–37

EXHIBITIONS: *Pioneers of Modern Sculpture*, Hayward Gallery, London, 1973, cat. no. 188 (ill. p. 32)

This is one of the few commissioned works by Rosso. Always eager in his later years for greater exposure and publicity, the artist responded to exhibition opportunities wherever he found them, and in 1906, traveled to London for a showing with the International Society (February–March) and later a one-man exhibition at the Eugene Cremetti Gallery (December). Before the end of the year he produced this portrait head of a young boy, identified by Margaret Barr, through correspondence with a relative of the sitter, as Alfred William Mond, then five or six years old (Barr, 1963, p. 58 and n. 159; the boy's sister wrote in 1961: "I recognized the photograph at once as being the portrait of my brother Alfred William Mond as a very young boy. . . . The wax model was in our home in Hyde Park Square certainly until after 1918. The bust was certainly not in the house at the time of my mother's death [1941] and I have no idea of what became of it"). The child was the son of Emile Mond, nephew of Dr. Ludwig Mond, whose famous art collection was acquired by the National Gallery, London, in 1910.

While staying with the Mond family as a guest, Rosso

studied the boy daily but became increasingly frustrated by his inability to capture Alfred's features in clay. Finally, during an evening reception, Rosso glimpsed the child staring at the proceedings from behind curtains, and inspired by this fleeting vision, the artist worked all night until he completed the portrait. He gave the family a wax version, which they did not consider a particularly good likeness, and later made an undetermined number of wax, plaster, and bronze casts from his model.

Rosso spoke of this work, with its tender, delicate, veiled image of youth, as one of his eight favorite accomplishments (Carlo Carrà, *La Mia Vita*, Milan, 1943, p. 277). Striations down the sides of the face seem to suggest the folds of the curtains as they pulled against Alfred's face on the night of the reception. In the soft amber surface of the wax versions, the head seems to be illuminated by dim candlelight, realizing brilliantly Rosso's efforts to capture the visual effects of space, light, and atmosphere.

At least nine wax casts of this work have been identified, along with several in both plaster and bronze. This one comes from the collection of the artist's granddaughter, Danila Rosso Parravicini, as did the wax cast in the Hirshhorn Museum and Sculpture Garden, Washington, D.C. The nose has been slightly indented and the wax has aged to a particularly deep yellow. The inscription on the inside plaster surface was added by the granddaughter at the time she sold it to Lords Gallery, London.

GEORGE SEGAL (American, born 1924)

75. *Rush Hour*, 1983 (cast 1985–86)
    Bronze, 73 x 74 x 67 (185 x 188 x 170)

MARKINGS: None

PROVENANCE: From artist to Sidney Janis Gallery, New York
             To Nasher collection, 1986

LITERATURE: Cf. *New Sculpture: George Segal*, Sidney Janis Gallery, New York, 1984, cat. no. 1 (ill.)

Cf. Sam Hunter and Don Hawthorne, *George Segal*, New York, 1984, cat. no. 199 (ill. p. 266)

Cf. *George Segal*, Galerie Maeght Lelong, Paris, 1985, cat. no. 4 (ill. cover and p. 23)

EXHIBITIONS: None

George Segal was commissioned to make his first bronze in 1976. Since then, he has produced his distinctive tableaux of life-size figures in both the familiar white plaster and in bronze casts of varying coloration, using the latter in an ambitious series of outdoor sculptures that give public voice to themes frequently more weighty than those in his intimist indoor works. He has said that he has a "personal prejudice against enormous, impersonal monuments" and tries instead to maintain "human scale, personal feeling, personal intensity" (Malcolm Carter, "The F.R.D. Memorial," *Art News* 77, October 1978, p. 56). His subjects range from the biblical and literary to the sociopolitical, but they also include glimpses of everyday life. *Rush Hour*, with its procession of six weary urbanites, has been compared to Rodin's *Burghers of Calais* (1884–95), both for its clustered composition and its mood of penetrating despair. Solitary, despite being caught in a crowd, and numbed with fatigue, these hostages of modern routine march inexorably and hopelessly forward. When *Rush Hour* was first exhibited (*George Segal*, Sidney Janis Gallery, 1984, cat. no. 1), the figures were seen against a long wall to which a row of fluorescent tubes was attached, suggesting the entrance to a subway or some other public place. In subsequent installations the background was removed, bringing the figures more resolutely into the space of the viewer.

From a planned edition of five, two bronze casts of this work have been made, both at the Johnson Atelier, Mercerville, New Jersey. The original plaster, after its first exhibition in an all-white state, was painted by Segal a dark blue-black. The first bronze, now in the Frederick Weisman collection, Los Angeles, was given a patina of the same color. For the second cast, Segal chose an even more somber brownish-black patina, applying it himself. Its mottled richness and visible stains and drips are meant to blend in the natural weathering process.

RICHARD SERRA (American, born 1939)

76. *Inverted House of Cards*, 1969–70
    Cor-Ten steel, assembled: 55¼ x 101¾ x 101½ (140 x 258.4 x 258); each sheet: 55¼ x 55¼ x 1 (140 x 140 x 2.5)

MARKINGS: None

PROVENANCE: From artist to Ace Gallery, Venice, California
             To Nasher collection, 1979

LITERATURE: Cf. *Richard Serra, Arbeiten 66–77*, Kunsthalle Tubingen, 1978, cat. no. 75

Cf. *Richard Serra: Interviews, Etc. 1970–1980*, The Hudson River Museum, Yonkers, New York, 1980, *passim* (ill. p. 136)

Cf. Rosalind Krauss, *Richard Serra / Sculpture*, The Museum of Modern Art, New York, 1986, pp. 19–25

EXHIBITIONS: *Richard Serra*, Ace Gallery, Venice, California, 1970

Inverted House of Cards, and its correlate, *House of Cards*, developed out of Serra's Prop series of 1968–69, with its themes of leaning and propped structures, self-support, and the tenuous equilibrium of massive elements. In slightly earlier works, an interest in the process and inherent material properties of sculpture had led to configurations in lead and rubber that enacted a series of verbs relating to forming and shaping: to roll, to fold, to scatter, to hang, etc. In the Prop series, he engaged a wall or the corner of a room and the floor in the dynamics of supporting the sculptural elements. *House of Cards*, also known as *One Ton Prop* (1969), rejects the pictorial allusions of these wall-related compositions through its self-bracing structure seen fully in the round (Krauss, 1986, fig. 8). Four square plates

of lead, leaning together to form a cube, touch only at their top corners. Held together by the angle of incline and the force of gravity, the structure threatens by virtue of its precarious balance.

An even more dramatic equilibrium is achieved in the *Inverted House of Cards* (1969–70) in which the plates project finlike out of a central intersection. Again, they touch only at the top corners in a pivotal relationship that hardly seems strong enough to support the weight of the individual members. Indeed, when first executed in low-quality lead, the work was unstable and required repouring. Serra subsequently made another version in lead (now in the Museum für Gegenwartskunst, Basel), one in steel (formerly Galerie m, Bochum, current location unknown), and one in Cor-Ten (Nasher collection). In 1969, he also erected a monumental variation out of 8-by-10 foot steel slabs at the Kaiser Steel plant in Fontana, California, as part of his Skullcracker series (Krauss, 1986, pl. 35; later disassembled), and seven years later returned to this design in a version made from 75-by-90-inch steel plates that was installed as part of the exhibition *Ars 83* in Helsinki and is now in the Museum Folkwang, Essen.

Serra later partially attributed the idea of stacked verticality realized in these works to the influence of Brancusi, whose sculpture he was able to study in the reassembled Brancusi studio at the Musée National d'Art Moderne in Paris during a year abroad in 1964–65:

> In 1969 I built the *House of Cards*, which in retrospect seems to have been influenced by the drawing in those pieces by Brancusi where verticality is defined by a central axis but not vertical line. The four planes of the *House of Cards* inclined. Brancusi's *Architectural Project* (1918) was of basic importance to me. In this work, three diverse parts were placed on top of one another. This piece bears a central relationship to the general problem of stacking vertically . . . Vertical progression upward . . . struck me as something other than assemblage [*Interviews*, 1980, p. 46].

JOEL SHAPIRO (American, born 1941)

*77. *Untitled*, 1983
   Bronze, 85¾ x 60 x 36 (218 x 152 x 91)

MARKINGS: Bottom of vertical element, at base: "1/3 Shapiro 83"

PROVENANCE: From artist to Paula Cooper Gallery, New York
   To Nasher collection, 1984

LITERATURE: Cf. *Joel Shapiro*, Stedelijk Museum, Amsterdam, 1985, p. 53, cat. no. 27 (ill. pp. 20, 53)

EXHIBITIONS: *Ars 83*, The Art Museum of the Ateneum, Helsinki, 1983

   Joel Shapiro, Institute of Contemporary Art, Boston, 1984, checklist n.n.

The original version of this work was made in wood (collection of Paula Cooper, New York), and four bronzes were cast, including an artist's proof, the Nasher collection example, and casts in the Edward Broida collection, Los Angeles, and in a private collection, London. The Nasher cast, like the others in the group, preserves in fine detail the grain, knots, and irregularities of the original wooden surface, while adding a golden-bronze color and a durability that works in tension with the illusion of wood.

Similar ambivalence was fundamental to Shapiro's small block figures and tiny bronze houses of the mid-seventies, playing abstraction against representation, actual against implied scale, romanticism against restraint. By the early eighties, his figures had grown considerably in size, with large blocky limbs and torsos that recall the geometry of David Smith's Cubi series while still describing figures,

mostly in unstable, leaning, or balanced poses that defy gravity and take the floor into active spatial partnership. Often the paring of anatomy or doubling of parts pushes the images toward further formal purity. The present work is part of this development. Rising through space at a sharp angle, it seems at first totally abstract. With knowledge of its predecessors, however, it can be seen as the vestige of a long-legged figure bending forward at the waist. It is one of Shapiro's largest sculptures to date and one of his most simplified and linear. In order to hold its precarious position, it is attached to a plate that is sunk into the ground. Although no casts of this work were included in exhibitions at the Paula Cooper Gallery, the Nasher cast was shown in Helsinki in 1983 and Boston in 1984. When the artist's proof of this work was exhibited in *Joel Shapiro*, Stedelijk Museum, Amsterdam, 1985, it was subtitled *Malone*.

DAVID SMITH (American, 1906–1965)

78. *House in a Landscape* [*Rural Landscape with Manless House*], 1945
   Steel, 18⅛ x 24½ x 6¾ (46 x 62 x 17)

MARKINGS: Back edge of upper ledge: "David Smith 1945"

PROVENANCE: From artist to Mrs. Alexander Brook, Sag Harbor, New York
Jane Wade, Ltd., New York
To George Irwin, Quincy, Illinois, 1967
To Ronsco Fine Arts, New York
To Nasher collection, 1986

LITERATURE: Rosalind Krauss, *Terminal Iron Works: The Sculpture of David Smith*, Cambridge, Massachusetts, and London, 1971, p. 41, fig. 28

David Smith, *David Smith*, Garnett McCoy, ed., New York and Washington, 1973, fig. 29 and p. 69

Rosalind Krauss, *The Sculpture of David Smith: A Catalogue Raisonné*, New York and London, 1977, cat. no. 181 (ill.)

EXHIBITIONS: *The Sculpture of David Smith*, Willard and Buchholz galleries, New York, 1946

David Smith, American Association of University Women, 1946–47, cat. no. 23

Noguchi & Rickey & Smith, Indiana Universit Art Museum, Bloomington, 1970, cat p. 46 (ill.)

Selections from the Collection of Mr. George M. Irwin, Krannert Art Museum, University of Illinois, Champaign, 1980, cat. p. 30

House in a Landscape was included in Smith's dual exhibitions at the Willard and Buchholz galleries in New York

in 1946, and several years later, in a Guggenheim Fellowship report, he proudly noted that it had been sold through his dealer to Gina Knee (Mrs. Alexander Brook), a painter, for $750.

Like the closely related *Home of the Welder* and *Reliquary House* from the same year, *House in a Landscape* presents a Surrealist-inspired tabletop tableau in which various ideographic and symbolic forms interact in a psychological narrative of deeply personal meaning. *Home of the Welder* has been interpreted as a meditation by Smith on his métier, on the codependence of creativity and sexuality, and the bondage that both represent for him as man and artist. *House in a Landscape* contains some of the same imagery, and while seeming at first to be lighter in mood, also holds dark messages of yearning, loss, and sexual frustration.

Set on a flat ground plane, the intersecting axes of two trees and a thin vertical house define the outer limits of a boxlike space. From the secondary title, we know that the scene is rural and that the house is decidedly "manless." Indeed, the two immediately apparent figures are both women. On the platform with a framing window cantilevered from the side of the house crouches a pliable, Picassoid, headless female that recalls the reclining woman in *Home of the Welder*. Above, several curved, spiky forms seem to represent curtains blowing in the wind. With one hand, this partial figure reaches out to grasp a phallic ball atop a column, clearly a symbol of the missing male. On the opposite side of the house, within a raised window outline, sits another woman—watching and waiting. More curious is the easily overlooked human profile formed by the cutout front edge of the house, with a long molded attachment on the side shaped into a type of Egyptian eye and a little arm below that grasps another ball. Altogether then, three women inhabit this lonely residence, looking outward expectantly or longingly into the landscape, occupying themselves with male symbols. While Smith's spe-

cific meanings remain uncertain, one can conjecture, given the date and the impact that the war had upon his emotional life, that his quest for a personal symbolism is here infused with sadness over the many American households that had recently lost their husbands and brothers. *House in a Landscape* thus emerges as one of Smith's most moving statements from this period of introspective, cathartic analysis, and one of modern art's key responses to World War II.

---

79. *The Forest*, 1950
   Polychromed steel, 36⅝ x 36¾ x 4½ (40 x 38 x 11.4)

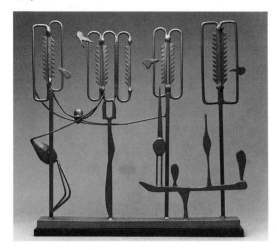

MARKINGS: Left side of metal base: "David Smith / 1950"

PROVENANCE: Estate of artist
Marlborough-Gerson Gallery, New York
Mr. and Mrs. Patrick J. Smith, New York
Sold at Christie's, New York, May 1, 1985
To Nasher collection, 1985

LITERATURE: *Art News* 50, no. 3, May 1951, pp. 42–43

David Smith, "Progress Report on Guggenheim Fellowship, 1950–51," in *David Smith*, Garnett McCoy, ed., New York and Washington, 1973, pp. 68–69, fig. 38

Rosalind Krauss, *The Sculpture of David Smith: A Catalogue Raisonné*, New York and London, 1977, cat. no. 231 (ill.)

Contemporary Art, Christie's, New York, May 1, 1985, cat. no. 15 (ill.)

EXHIBITIONS: *David Smith*, Willard Gallery, New York, 1951

David Smith, The Solomon R. Guggenheim Museum, New York, 1969, cat. no. 33 (ill.)

The Forest represents a theme in David Smith's development going back to such works as *Amusement Park* (1938) and *Helmholtzian Landscape* (1946), in which ideographic landscape and figurative elements are presented in an open, frontal, rectangular format. Polychromy enhances further the pictorial quality of these hybrid sculpture-tableaux, which seem to evolve from Smith's exploration of emotionally charged tabletop scenarios, influenced by Alberto Giacometti and Max Ernst, as well as his interest in ancient writing and pictography. This "picture" format takes on a newly resolute flatness and geometry with *The Forest* and *The Letter*, also from 1950. Although such works seem to inveigh against the basic condition of sculpture's three-dimensionality, and suffered criticism for this quality when first exhibited (*Art News*, May 1951, pp. 42–43), it is the tension they create between surface and depth and their crisp articulation of tangible forms in real space that account for their strong character.

Allusions to landscape ran through Smith's iconography of the forties and fifties as a quiet, pastoral balance to his more personal and psychological themes, and showed his enduring attachment to land and place. In *The Forest*, commercially made sawtoothed implements are welded back-to-back to suggest foliage, and numerous little birds are appended to the treetops. At the lower right, joined in Smith's familiar format of a raised horizontal base with vertical attachments, several other organic shapes suggest another, shorter clump of vegetation. At the left, several long limbs stretching between a head and torso show a lithesome figure holding onto or swinging from the overhead branches. Enhanced by pink, green, and silver coloration, the sculpture's mood is one of disarming joy and pleasure. In describing this and several other works of the same period soon after they were done, Smith said that they "carry out my mainstream concept in celebration of the beauties from my own point of view" (see *David Smith*, Garnett McCoy, ed., 1973, p. 68).

---

80. *9/15/53*, 1953
   Steel on iron base, 21¾ x 40¼ x 12¾ (55.2 x 102.2 x 32.4)

MARKINGS: Underside of base: "David Smith / 9.15.1953"

PROVENANCE: From artist to George and Joyce Wittenborn, Scarsdale, New York

Estate of Barbara Westcott, Rosemont, New Jersey
Dr. Guido Goldman, Cambridge, Massachusetts
Sold at Sotheby's, New York, May 2, 1985
To Nasher collection, 1985

LITERATURE: *David Smith 1906–1965: A Retrospective Exhibition*, Fogg Art Museum, Cambridge,

Massachusetts, 1966, checklist no. 242

Rosalind Krauss, *The Sculpture of David Smith: A Catalogue Raisonné*, New York and London, 1977, cat. no. 292 (ill.)

Contemporary Art, Sotheby's, New York, May 2, 3, 1985, cat. no. 25 (ill.)

EXHIBITIONS: *David Smith*, Willard Gallery, New York, 1954, diagram no. 9

From the Collection of Mr. and Mrs. L. B. Westcott, Summit Art Center, New Jersey, 1974, cat. no. 62

David Smith, Storm King Art Center, Mountainville, New York, 1976

The Drawings of David Smith: Themes and Variations, Fort Worth Art Museum, 1986, ex-cat.

For an exhibition at the Willard Gallery in New York in 1954, David Smith made two ink drawings illustrating schematically the nineteen sculptures to be included, one of which was then possibly used as the model for a poster (see *David Smith: Painter, Sculptor, Draughtsman*, New York, 1982, fig. 2, and Cleve Gray, *David Smith by David Smith*, New York, 1968, p. 38). In these two diagrams, *9/15/53* is

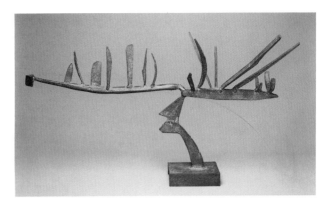

included as no. 9. Like several other works, it is titled only with its date.

Compositionally, *9/15/53* relates closely to a number of sculptures in the Agricola series, most notably numbers *V* and *IX*, both from 1952 (Krauss, 1977, cat. nos. 269, 273). In all these works, a horizontal ground line is lifted on a short, vertical base. Attached to its upper edge are other linear elements which, in Smith's symbolic sign language, suggest grain, leaves, or limbs blowing gently in the wind, thereby tying them closely to the agricultural theme. The horizontal disposition of vertical elements in a shallow pictorial space can be traced in Smith's work back to the thirties and is related to his ongoing attempt to reconcile pictorial and sculptural states.

---

81. *Tower Eight*, 1957
    Silver, 46½ x 13 x 10⅝ (118 x 33 x 27)

MARKINGS: Top of base at back: "10 11 57 David Smith"

PROVENANCE: Katherine White Reswick, Bratonahl, Ohio
Private collection, California
To M. Knoedler & Co., New York, 1984
To Nasher collection, 1984

LITERATURE: Rosalind Krauss, *The Sculpture of David Smith: A Catalogue Raisonné*, New York and London, 1977, cat. no. 437 (ill.)

EXHIBITIONS: (?) *David Smith: Sculpture in Silver*, Widdifield Gallery, New York, 1957

Paintings Sculpture, Fine Arts Associates, New York, 1959

Sculpture & Sculptors Drawings, Fine Arts Associates, New York, 1959

Cleveland Museum of Art, 1962 (temporary loan)

David Smith, The Solomon R. Guggenheim Museum, New York, 1969, cat. no. 61 (ill.)

The Drawings of David Smith: Themes and Variations, Fort Worth Art Museum, 1986, ex-cat.

Tower Eight represents a marriage in the work of David Smith between the linear schematizations of such sculptures as *Agricola I* (1951–52) and *Timeless Clock* (1957) and the vertical anatomical abstractions of his Tank Totem series. Its ancestry is therefore both Cubist and Tribal-Surrealist, but it also includes Pablo Picasso's welded sculptures of 1928–31 as well as the more linear of Julio Gonzalez's personages. *Tower Eight* can be compared, for example, with Picasso's *Head of a Woman* of 1931, where three bent angle irons lift high a composite head of metal planes, rods, bars, and two kitchen colanders. The Smith is not dissimilar in silhouette, including even the opposition of curves at the top (breasts?, or a breast and the back of a head?), but reduces with greater insistence all solid planes and volumes into outlines, leaving only thin tabs or flanges to indicate mass and the direction of an adjoining surface. Unlike many of Smith's linear works from the fifties which adopt a frontal pictorial format, *Tower Eight* "draws" its volumes in depth and demands a three-dimensional reading, offering different compositional aspects and superimposed forms from different points of view. Indeed, it is difficult to determine which prospect Smith intended as the front. A somewhat similar morphology is seen in the much larger *Tower I* of 1962–63.

Smith made a number of sculptures in silver in the forties and fifties, including five in 1957 (see Krauss, 1977, cat. nos. 414–15, 420, 436–37), when two were exhibited at the Widdifield Gallery in October of that year (the lack of a catalog makes it difficult to determine which two). He must have found the material interesting for its shiny reflectiveness but prohibitively expensive, for he stopped using it after 1957. Stainless steel, found in his work from the forties onward but given particularly crucial expression in the sixties, allowed similar effects but was much less expensive and permitted work on a larger scale.

82. *Untitled (Voltri)* [*For Gian Carlo*], June 1962
   Steel, 41¼ x 14⅝ x 7⅛ (104.8 x 37.1 x 18.1)

MARKINGS: On circular base: "Dida Becca to
              G.C.M. / David Smith 6–62"

PROVENANCE: From artist to Gian Carlo Menotti, 1962
              To Lawrence Rubin Gallery, New York, 1971
              To Nasher collection, 1971

LITERATURE: Giovanni Carandente, *Voltron*, Philadephia,
              1964, p. 48 (ill.)

              *David Smith 1906–1965: A Retrospective
              Exhibition*, Fogg Art Museum, Cambridge,
              Massachusetts, 1966, checklist no. 459

              David Smith, "Report on Voltri," *David
              Smith*, Garnett McCoy, ed., New York and
              Washington, 1973, p. 158

              Rosalind Krauss, *The Sculpture of David
              Smith: A Catalogue Raisonné*, New York
              and London, 1977, cat. no. 583 (ill.
              reversed with no. 584)

EXHIBITIONS: *Sculpture in the City*, Festival of Two
              Worlds, Spoleto, Italy, Summer 1962

              Selections from the Nasher Collection,
              North Texas State University, Denton, 1975

              *20th Century Sculpture: Mr. and Mrs.
              Raymond D. Nasher Collection*, University

Gallery, Southern Methodist University,
Dallas, 1978, cat. no. 24 (ill.)

*The Drawings of David Smith: Themes and
Variations*, Fort Worth Art Museum, 1986,
ex-cat.

Gian Carlo Menotti, the composer and organizer of the
Spoleto Festival, was instrumental in inviting David Smith
to Italy in 1962 to make works for a sculpture exhibition
associated with the festival, an invitation that resulted in
Smith's well-known Voltri series. To encourage Smith, Menotti promised to dedicate a work to Smith's two daughters,
Candida and Rebecca, then six and eight years old (see
Carandente, 1964, p. 11). He also arranged for the Italian
national steel company, Italsider, to provide working space,
materials, and assistants in the town of Voltri. Out of gratitude for Menotti's central role in what became one of the
most fruitful projects of his life, Smith gave him this work
from the Voltri series and added the inscription "Dida Becca
to G.C.M.," meaning "Candida and Rebecca to Gian Carlo
Menotti." Writing to the Nashers in 1982, Menotti recalled:

> The David Smith sculpture you have did indeed
> belong to me. [He] gave it to me in Spoleto as a
> gift.... It is quite true that David first came to
> Spoleto on my promise that I would one day ded-
> icate one of my works to his two daughters. . . .
> The work ("Martin's Lie") is still a manuscript, but
> when it is published, it will bear on the title page
> the promised dedication.

Typical of the Voltri series in general, this work is made
from various old tools and scrap metal found in the abandoned factory that Smith used as a studio. Here he has
welded them into a rather ferocious-looking standing figure.
The spreading arms of a divider form the legs; a circular
rim or gasket the body; a pair of long tongs the spine; and
two calipers the double beaks at the top. Similar forms are
found in the equally anthropomorphic but much larger *Voltri XX*. Closer in feeling and scale are two sculptures which,
like this one, were made at the end of the Voltri series and
were not included by Smith in the sequence of titles with
numerals and the "Voltri" prefix: *Compass Circle* and an
untitled work (Krauss, 1977, cat. nos. 581, 584). He apparently considered this group stylistically distinct. One
sees them disassembled but taking shape on a large layout
table in a photograph of Smith at work in the factory setting
(Carandente, 1964, p. 25). In a note about this particular
table Smith wrote: "After *Voltri XXII*, five pieces of a different
scale came from the layout table. One owned by Carandente, one my daughters gave to Menotti, and an iron ballet
dancer for Mike Pepper's daughter Jori" (*David Smith*,
McCoy, ed., 1973, p. 158).

---

83. *Voltri VI*, June 1962
   Steel, 98⅞ x 102¼ x 24 (251 x 260 x 61)

MARKINGS: On platform above wheels, on one side:
              "David Smith–1962"
              On other side: "Voltri–VI"
              On left vertical blade: "June 10 / 1962 /

Andiamo Spoleto"
On right vertical blade: "David Smith /
Voltri / Hi Sally"

PROVENANCE: From artist to Nelson A. Rockefeller
              Through Harold Diamond, New York, and
              Shaindy Fenton, Inc., Fort Worth
              To Nasher collection, 1978

LITERATURE: Giovanni Carandente, *Voltron*, Philadephia, 1964, p. 49 (ill.)

Rosalind Krauss, *Terminal Iron Works: The Sculpture of David Smith*, Cambridge, Massachusetts, and London, 1971, pp. 50–53 (ill.)

David Smith, "Report on Voltri," *David Smith*, Garnett McCoy, ed., New York and Washington, 1973, p. 162

E. A. Carmean, Jr., "David Smith: The Voltri Sculpture," in *American Art at Mid-Century: The Subjects of the Artist*, Washington, D.C., 1978, esp. pp. 218, 221, 232–35 (ill.)

EXHIBITIONS: *Sculpture in the City*, Festival of Two Worlds, Spoleto, Italy, Summer 1962

Twentieth Century Art from the Nelson Aldrich Rockefeller Collection, The Museum of Modern Art, New York, 1969, cat. pp. 33, 103 (ill.)

American Art at Mid-Century: The Subjects of the Artist, National Gallery of Art, Washington, D.C., 1978, cat. pp. 216 (checklist no. 3), 218, 221, 232–35 (ill.)

Voltri VI belongs to the Herculean series of steel sculptures that Smith produced in Voltri, Italy, in 1962 as a contribution to the Festival of Two Worlds at Spoleto. Edward Fry has succinctly described the genesis of the series:

> During the month of June of 1962, as the guest of an Italian metallurgical concern [Italsider], Smith produced 26 sculptures [Krauss, 1977, actually identifies 27; see p. 101] in a disused factory at Voltri, near Genoa. This entire Voltri series was then exhibited at Spoleto during the summer of 1962. So prolific an outpouring of monumental sculpture was without precedent in the history of modern art.

The Voltris (like their offspring, the Voltri-Bolton series), constitute a distinct genre within

Smith's late work, and may properly be treated as a separate entity. Although there is considerable diversity within the group, reflecting Smith's multiple stylistic interests in the early 1960's, all are welded assemblages of often massive segments of steel scrap, and many are of monumental proportions. As might be expected, a considerable number are essentially standing personages and in some cases are explicitly anthropomorphic. Others, notably the three large chariots (*Voltris VI, VII*, and *XIII*) are radical extensions of ideas only summarily developed previously [*David Smith*, The Solomon R. Guggenheim Museum, New York, 1969, cat. no. 87].

The most thorough examination to date of the Voltri series, with information on the commission (originally requiring that only two sculptures be produced) and Smith's working conditions, and with numerous photographs of the factory/studio and works in progress, was made by E. A. Carmean (1978, pp. 217–41). A facsimile of Smith's letter to David Sylvester, dated November 12, 1962, describing his experience at Voltri is published by Giovanni Carandente (1964, pp. 11–15), and Smith's further observations on his work in Italy are found in *David Smith*, edited by Garnett McCoy (1973, pp. 161–63).

The three chariots comprise a subset within the Voltri group. All have undercarriages with two high wheels. Converted carts or dollies from the steel factory used to transport forgings from the ovens, they support from their axles a long horizontal spine with bar and platform, or "spoon." Attached to the platform are thin, vertical planes, frontally arranged, which Smith referred to as clouds because of their curving margins left untrimmed from the rolling mill. When Smith began the Voltri series, he dreamed of using a flatbed railway car as the foundation for a huge sculpture. This proved impractical, but the chariots preserve the essence of the idea. They also recall Smith's use of wheels in certain earlier sculptures, which look back in turn to Giacometti's two Chariots, and also invite comparison with ancient chariots, a classical correlation with particular relevance considering Smith's residency in Italy and other classical allusions in the Voltri series.

The clouds in *Voltri VI* are both the most simplified and monumental in the group. The two forms rise in perfect alignment, separated by a thin vertical relief with opposing concave curves at either side. Smith described the work as "a tong with wheels and two end clouds. One cloud rests in the spoon— each cloud end goes up from the tongue unsupported" (*David Smith*, McCoy, ed., 1973, p. 162). In this tall, wafer-thin expanse, bitten into on each side and split down the center, there is both majesty and a trembling fragility that plays against the cold geometry and mechanization of the base. The sculpture seems on the one hand a crude sailing vehicle, and on the other, the proud climax of a triumphal procession.

The finish of the metal is purposefully rough and industrial, heightened by an allover burnishing of the clouds. As a final touch, Smith scrawled a long inscription on one side, not with a blowtorch as is sometimes reported but rather with a grinder. The "Sally" of the inscription must refer to some unknown friend. Smith had personalized the inscription on at least one other Voltri, the untitled work also in the Nasher collection.

TONY SMITH (American, 1912–1980)

**84. *The Snake Is Out*, 1962 (fabricated 1981)
Painted steel, 180 x 278 x 226 (457 x 716 x 574)

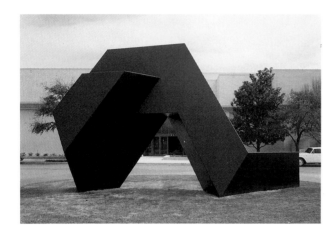

MARKINGS: None

PROVENANCE: The Pace Gallery, New York
              To Nasher collection, 1984

LITERATURE: Cf. Lucy Lippard, *Tony Smith*, New York,
              1972, pp. 8–10, pl. 36

              Cf. *Tony Smith: Ten Elements and
              Throwback*, The Pace Gallery, New York,
              1979, pp. 14–15 (ill.)

              Tony Smith: Paintings and Sculpture, The
              Pace Gallery, New York, 1983, p. 33 (ill.)

              *Tony Smith Selected Sculptures: 1961–1973,
              Part I*, Xavier Fourcade, Inc., New York,
              1985, n.p. (ill.)

EXHIBITIONS: Doris Freedman Plaza, 60th Street entrance
              to Central Park, New York, 1982–83

              245 Park Avenue, New York, 1983–84

The Snake Is Out exemplifies a group of works that Tony Smith constructed in the early sixties from tetrahedral and octahedral shapes. Trained as an architect, in the late fifties he turned his attention to sculpture based on elementary modular forms. The tetrahedron and octahedron permitted, he felt, an exciting variety of structures with "far greater flexibility and visual continuity than rectangular organizations." These possibilities took him "further and further from considerations of function and structure and toward speculation in pure form (*Tony Smith: Two Exhibitions of Sculpture*, Wadsworth Atheneum, Hartford, and The Institute of Contemporary Art, Philadelphia, 1966–67, n.p.). Like *Willy* from the same year, *The Snake Is Out* effects a complicated play between solid and void and between horizontal and vertical projections that cannot be fully apprehended from any single perspective. Both works derive their titles from impressions of things crawling: *Willy* from a character in Samuel Beckett's play *Happy Days* (1961) and *The Snake Is Out* from its morphological similarity to a snake.

The Snake Is Out was executed in a number of versions and in a variety of materials over more than a decade. In 1967 a full-scale, 15-foot-high, wood mock-up was installed outdoors on the plaza of Lincoln Center in New York under a protective ledge (see The Pace Gallery, 1979, ill. p. 14). At this time, an edition of three steel versions in the same scale was planned for fabrication at Industrial Welding, Newark, New Jersey. Number one of three, now in Albany, New York, as part of the Albany Mall Project, was first shown in New York City in 1967 when, along with seven other Smith sculptures, it received the favorable attention of critics (see Hilton Kramer, "Art: A Sculpture Show in Bryant Park," *The New York Times*, February 2, 1967, ill.). In 1970, Smith published *The Snake Is Out* in an edition of nine 15¼-inch-high bronzes. The second of the 15-foot-high versions in steel, now installed on the campus of Rice University, Houston, was fabricated in 1979 (see Pace Gallery, 1979, ill. p. 15). The third, the version in the Nasher collection, was fabricated in 1981 and installed in Doris Freedman Plaza at the Sixtieth Street entrance to Central Park, New York, from July 1982 to March 1983, and subsequently in front of 245 Park Avenue, New York, from July 1983 to April 1984, when it was purchased by the Nashers (documentation from The Pace Gallery, 1986).

---

*85. *For Dolores* [*Flores para los muertos*], c. 1973–75
Carrara marble, 44¼ x 44¾ x 45¼ (112.4 x 113.7 x 114.9)

MARKINGS: None

PROVENANCE: Jane Smith, South Orange, New Jersey, and
              New York
              To Nasher collection, 1985

LITERATURE: Cf. Eleanor Greene, "The Morphology of
              Tony Smith's Work," *Artforum* 12, no. 8,
              April 1974, p. 58

              Cf. "Statements by Sculptors," *Art Journal*
              35, no. 2, Winter 1975–76, pp. 128–29

EXHIBITIONS: None

Tony Smith's interest in scientific principles of growth and form led to the study of cellular and molecular structure, translated in many of his paintings into rounded shapes and lateral linkages. In the early seventies, diagrams of so-called Fermi surfaces—three-dimensional surfaces representing the motion and energy of electrons in metal that were developed by the great Italian physicist Enrico Fermi—inspired a series of maquettes resulting in two marble sculptures, *For Dolores* and *Fermi* (for the latter, see *Tony Smith*, The Pace Gallery, New York, 1983, pp. 24–25; now in a private collection, California). Both call to mind molecular chains. Smith in 1975 said of this group:

> There are studies already carved, or now being carved, in Carrara marble at Pietrasanta [by the firm of Sicea Marmi]. These are derived from Fermi surfaces, and although conforming to modular grids, their aspects are more voluptuous than those of previous work. These pieces are intended for indoors. . . . They are, therefore, of domestic size.

He also spoke of his desire for a huge outdoor version that people could literally walk under (*Art Journal*, 1975–76, pp. 128–29). The artist's widow, Jane Smith, from whom the Nashers acquired *For Dolores*, retains two details of the work, one in plaster and one in styrofoam.

The title, *For Dolores*, is one of many in Smith's oeuvre dedicated to a friend or associate, in this case, a design student at Bennington College. The alternate title makes reference to a line from Tennessee Williams's *A Streetcar Named Desire* spoken by a Mexican vendor: "Flores. Flores. Flores para los muertos." Both underline an important personal and emotional resonance in Smith's work that invigorates its systematic and geometric forms.

---

*86. *Ten Elements*, 1975–79 (fabricated 1980)
Painted aluminum, tallest element 50 (127); shortest element 42 (107)

MARKINGS: None

PROVENANCE: From artist to The Pace Gallery, New York
To Nasher collection, 1984

LITERATURE: Cf. *Tony Smith: Ten Elements and Throwback*, The Pace Gallery, New York, 1979, pp. 5, 8, 9 (ill. pp. 36–38)

EXHIBITIONS: None

Ten Elements differs from most of Tony Smith's earlier work in its use of irregular geometric solid forms and its dispersed and random placement. It is allied, however, to an arrangement of five elements titled *Wandering Rocks* dating from 1967. Indicative of Smith's admiration for the formal yet random placement of stones in a Japanese garden, *Wandering Rocks* and *Ten Elements* address the issue of the integration of sculpture into its environment and hint also at Smith's veneration of simple, geometric, primitive dwellings such as those found in the American West, at Macchu Picchu, or in the French countryside (see The Pace Gallery, 1979, p. 9).

While the seeming irregularity of the solids comprising *The Wandering Rocks* can be structurally analyzed according to certain themes and variations, no such system underlies the relationships in *Ten Elements*. With constantly shifting rhythm, the planes of the solids slice in different directions, challenging one's sense of continuous, illusionistic space. As Sam Hunter has observed:

> Smith made each piece singular, with its own idiosyncratic identity, and yet he has arranged them as a loosely related grouping with something of the randomness of nature. While the pieces do not have the visual complexity of his larger and more ambitious constructions, they are actually more novel and unpredictable in invention. With their sheer faces, abrupt truncations and sharply angled planes, they resemble leaning cubes, tippy steles and warped pyramids. All sense of hierarchal order has been dissolved [The Pace Gallery, 1979, pp. 8–9].

No definitive plan for installation of *Ten Elements* exists. Rather, instructions call for a random placement that adds further to its air of unpredictability.

Executed first in wood and shown in this material at The Pace Gallery in 1979, *Ten Elements* was fabricated in aluminum by Lippincott, Inc., in 1980. Although an edition of three aluminum versions was planned, only number one, now in the Nasher collection, was made (documentation from The Pace Gallery, New York, and Lippincott, Inc., North Haven, Connecticut, 1986).

FRANK STELLA (American, born 1936)

*87. *Washington Island Gadwall*, 1980–81
Mixed media on aluminum, 154 x 225 x 26 (391 x 572 x 66)

MARKINGS: None

PROVENANCE: From artist to M. Knoedler & Co., New York, 1981
To Nasher collection, 1981

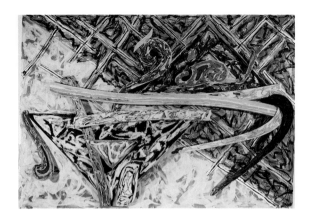

LITERATURE: Cf. *Stella since 1970*, Fort Worth Art
Museum, 1978, pp. 72–87

EXHIBITIONS: Dallas Museum of Art, on extended loan
since 1981

Washington Island Gadwall is the largest and one of the last metal reliefs from Stella's Exotic Bird series, the titles of which come from James Greenway's *Extinct and Vanishing Birds of the World* (1967), conjuring images of shimmering, brightly colored plumage. Stella had projected a total of twenty-eight works in this series, based on drawings completed in 1975. Each work was to be executed, with the help of assistants, in three versions: one the same size as the drawing, one three times larger, and one five-and-a-half times larger. The full series of twenty-eight reliefs, however, was never completed (*Washington Island Gadwall* is number fifteen), nor was this particular work executed in any other size.

Stella's first sculptures in metal date from 1974–75 when it became apparent to him that the increasing scale of his reliefs, as in the Polish Village series (1970–74), forbade the continuation of construction in wood and cardboard. Not only was honeycombed aluminum lighter, providing greater ease of handling and allowing more complicated compositions, but he could also expand his surface treatments, adding etching and burnishing to his use of paint, scumbling, and glitter. The materials and techniques went hand in hand with a propensity toward an increasingly dynamic treatment of color and space, resulting in the Exotic Bird series in frenetically integrated compositions that startled an art world accustomed to more restrained geometry in Stella's work and redirected the history of relief sculpture toward painterly expressiveness. In the succeeding Indian Bird and Circuit series, these dynamics became even more exuberant and three-dimensional.

In *Washington Island Gadwall*, the background plane is divided diagonally down the center and the two halves are tipped up, giving a sense of folding or collapsing movement. Two large triangles then break into cutout spaces in the background at different angles, while supporting an array of intersecting and superimposed strips, curlicues, triangles, and forms based on drafting curves. Each element in this cacophonous assemblage is boldly painted in a loose handwriting of tones from de Kooning pink to dark greens and black, further increasing the visual energy.

---

*88. *Diepholz II*, 1982
Mixed mediums on aluminum and fiberglass, 106½ x
120 x 24 (271 x 305 x 61)

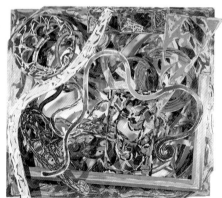

MARKINGS: None

PROVENANCE: From artist to M. Knoedler & Co., New York
To Park International, Bedford, New York
To M. Knoedler & Co., New York
To Nasher collection, 1985

LITERATURE: Cf. Noel Frackman, "Tracking Frank Stella's
Circuit Series," *Arts* 56, no. 8, April 1982,
pp. 134–37

EXHIBITIONS: None

Stella's Circuit reliefs, most dating from 1980–82, followed the Exotic Bird and Indian Bird series and preceded the South African Mine reliefs of c. 1982–83. They are named for cities throughout the world known for either grand-prix or lesser automobile races, and the looping, serpentine linear elements do indeed evoke the curves, speed, and intricacy of winding racetracks. A total of twenty-four works was planned for the series, each with a maquette and four enlargements (measuring one-and-a-quarter, three, four-and-three-quarter, and five times the size of the model), but only twenty-two were constructed.

Like his earlier painted-metal reliefs, Stella's Circuit series merges painting and sculpture into brightly colored three-dimensional constructions. Several important developments separate these works, however, from the Exotic Bird and Indian Bird series. In the earlier works, despite their aggressive structuring into space, Stella retained a rectangular backboard that invokes the traditional picture plane. In the Circuit series, he follows a more open and free-form approach, setting up increasingly dynamic relationships with the wall and surrounding space. The structures extend farther outward, a more diverse vocabulary of shapes is utilized, and magnesium and fiberglass are added to the aluminum of the previous series, creating more varied surfaces.

Diepholz exists in a number of sizes, including four versions of the one-and-a-quarter enlargement, and two of the four-and-three-quarter enlargement, of which this is number two.

JOHN STORRS (American, 1885–1956)

89. *Study in Architectural Forms [Forms in Space]*, 1927
    Steel, 31 3/16 x 7 5/8 x 4 5/8 (79.2 x 19.4 x 11.7)

MARKINGS:
Inside corner, bottom: "John Storrs /
[Paris](?) 1927"

PROVENANCE:
From artist to Edith Gregor Halpert
Sold at Sotheby Parke Bernet, New York,
March 14–15, 1973
To Nasher collection, 1973

LITERATURE:
The New York Times, February 12, 1928,
sec. 8, p. 15 (ill.)

*Highly Important 19th and 20th Century
American Paintings, Drawings, Watercolors
and Sculpture from the Estate of the Late
Edith Gregor Halpert*, Sotheby Parke
Bernet, New York, March 14–15, 1973, cat.
no. 166 (ill.)

EXHIBITIONS:
John Storrs, Arts Club of Chicago, 1927

John Storrs, Brummer Gallery, New York, 1928

John Storrs, The Downtown Gallery, New
York, 1965, cat. no. 26 or 28

42nd Anniversary Exhibition, The
Downtown Gallery, New York, 1967

John Storrs Retrospective, Corcoran Gallery
of Art, Washington, D.C., 1969

Art Deco and Its Origins, The Heckscher
Museum, Huntington, New York, 1974, cat.
no. 122

*John Storrs: A Retrospective Exhibition of
Sculpture*, Museum of Contemporary Art,
Chicago, 1976–77, cat. pp. 10–18

Although this work has generally been dated *circa* 1927, a close reading of the partially obscured inscription confirms the 1927 date and yields a possible interpretation of the preceding word as "Paris." During the twenties and thirties, Storrs divided his time between France and the United States, having bought a château in Mer, close to Orléans, in 1921 and having become one of the few American artists of the period to attain a truly international reputation. In the twenties his work appeared in exhibitions in Paris at the Galerie Briant Robert, Musée du Jeu de Paume, Galerie Durand-Ruel, Galerie Charpentier, and at Léonce Rosenberg's gallery, and in 1926 Storrs sold a sculpture entitled *Forms in Space* to the French government. Closely tied in spirit and form to the exciting emergence in America of a new, high-rise architecture, and also to certain native-American traditions of sculpture and decoration, Storrs's work is linked equally to the machine aesthetic of European artists such as Fernand Léger and Amédée Ozenfant, to Cubist stylistic conventions, and to the sleek geometric patterns of Art Deco. This successful fusing of traditions gave his art a strength and flavor that found support on both sides of the Atlantic.

Storrs's use of tall, narrow, simplified shafts bound in architectural compositions first occurred about 1920 in drawings and works such as the now lost *Forms in Space, No. 1*, a large stone sculpture from 1920–23. An apparently coincidental relationship exists with sculptures by certain Russian and Dutch artists of the same period, including Kasimir Malevich and Georges Vantongerloo, although in comparison Storrs's work retains a slightly precious quality owing to his carefully finished surfaces, penchant for fine materials (polished metals, a variety of stones), and consistent decorative touches. While some of his towers verge on pure abstraction, others like the Nasher sculpture are more literal in evoking modern skyscrapers. A closely related work is the *Forms in Space* (c. 1927) in The Metropolitan Museum of Art, New York, which has the same double-pronged top and a similar mounting rhythm of notched forms and bilateral symmetry. According to the catalog of the 1973 sale of the Halpert collection, *Study in Architectural Forms* was included in the 1965 Storrs exhibition at Halpert's Downtown Gallery. In the checklist of that show it can be identified with no. 26, *Forms in Space No. 1* (c. 1926), or more likely with no. 28, *Forms in Space No. 3* (c. 1927).

MARK DI SUVERO (American, born China 1933)

*90. *In the Bushes*, 1970–75
    Painted steel, 142 x 126 x 81 (361 x 320 x 206)

MARKINGS: None

PROVENANCE: The artist and Richard Bellamy, New York
Through Hansen-Fuller Gallery, San
Francisco
To Nasher collection, 1976

LITERATURE: *Mark di Suvero*, Whitney Museum of
American Art, New York, 1975–76, p. 80 (ill.)

EXHIBITIONS: *20th Century Sculpture, Mr. and Mrs.*

Raymond D. Nasher Collection, University Gallery, Southern Methodist University, Dallas, 1978, cat. no. 4 (ill.) (as *From the Bushes*)

Starting in the mid-sixties, Mark di Suvero began to develop I-beam constructions of which this work, like the earlier *Blue Arch for Matisse* (1965) and *Homage to the Viet Cong* (1971), represents a scaled-down, forcefully condensed example. Alternative to the artist's larger compositions that incorporate diverse materials and complex directional patterns, all three sculptures delimit open, leaning arches formed in an angular vocabulary of bolted or welded I-beams. Here the arch is collapsed with an inward thrust and intersection of I-beams at the left. The technique is rooted in Constructivism and the iron sculpture of David Smith, but di Suvero's frank use of heavy-duty building ma-

terials and rugged configurations is distinctly personal, invoking the power of industry and architectural construction while also achieving a strong rhythmic quality that recalls the structural brushwork of Franz Kline. The coloration of *In the Bushes*, a contrast of red and untreated steel, also sets it apart stylistically.

Richard Bellamy, di Suvero's longtime friend and dealer, has explained the dating and title of this work (conversation with the author, 1986). In 1970, di Suvero was working on large outdoor pieces in a space near the Pasadena Museum in California. He did a substantial amount of work on *In the Bushes* at that time, but then set it aside, putting it "in the bushes," so to speak. Soon after, di Suvero left for Europe and placed the sculpture in storage. Upon his return in 1974, he found a studio in Petaluma, California, and completed work on *In the Bushes*. The Nashers first saw it when visiting the artist at Petaluma in January 1976. The sculpture was to have been installed at the Dag Hammarskjöld Plaza in New York as part of the di Suvero retrospective at the Whitney Museum of American Art in the winter of 1975–76, but ultimately no sculptures were placed in that location, and *In the Bushes* was simply illustrated in the exhibition catalog.

Painting

JEAN DUBUFFET (French, 1901–1985)

*91. *Conjugaison*, November 1975
Acrylic on paper mounted on cloth, 52⅜ x 119¾ (133 x 304.2)

MARKINGS: Lower left: "J.D. 76"

PROVENANCE: From artist to Galerie Beyeler, Basel
To Waddington Galleries, Ltd., London, 1976
To William Pall Gallery, New York, 1977
To Nasher collection, 1977

LITERATURE: Max Loreau, *Catalogue des travaux de Jean Dubuffet*, fasc. XXXII, "Théâtres de mémoire," Lausanne, 1982, no. 6 (ill.; dated November 25, 1975)

EXHIBITIONS: None

Conjugaison belongs to the Théâtres de mémoire, a series that Dubuffet began in late 1975, drawing liberally upon earlier imagery but breaking new ground compositionally and conceptually in his exploration of perception and memory. The name of the series alludes to a study published in 1966 called *The Art of Memory*, which traces certain classical mnemonic systems. Using the collage technique to trigger free association, Dubuffet further activated the labyrinthine structure of his Hourloupe series, filling individual cells with small pictograms or abstract patterns in a variety of styles to create a turbulent space of jostling, overlapping, writhing notations. Bold color and brushwork add to the rushing tempo. Any semblance of the continuity of time or space is destroyed by constant abrupt transitions, absorbing the viewer into an allover web of perceptions. Dubuffet noted:

> In these assemblages there appear commingled sites and scenes which are the constituent parts of a moment and act of looking. Of looking with the mind, we should say, if not the immediate looking with the eyes. One must not confuse what the eyes apprehend with what happens when the mind takes it in. . . . The mind totalizes; it recapitulates all the fields; it makes them dance together [Andreas Franzke, *Dubuffet*, New York, 1981, p. 247].

Conjugaison fits tightly in its imagery into the sequence of Dubuffet's work from 1975. The precise dating to November 1975 in the Loreau catalogue raisonné (1982, fasc. XXXII) indicates that Dubuffet's inscription of 1976 on the front is incorrect.

ALBERTO GIACOMETTI (Swiss, 1901–1966)

*92. *Three Figures [Trois Personnages-Atelier; Three Figures in the Street]*, 1949
Oil on canvas, $18\frac{5}{16}$ x $22\frac{1}{16}$ (46.5 x 56)

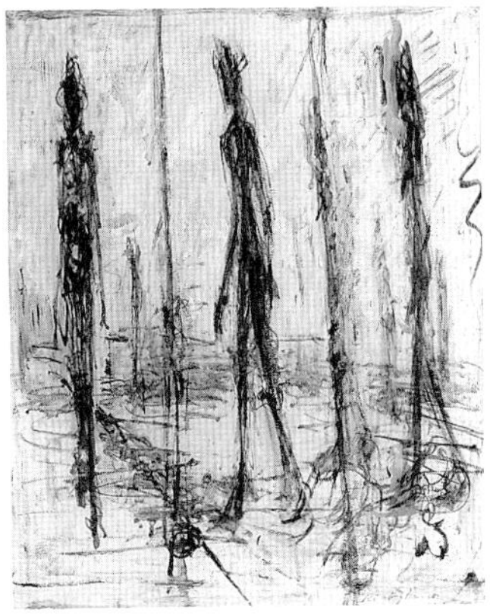

MARKINGS: Lower right: "Alberto Giacometti 1949"

PROVENANCE: From artist to Louis Clayeux, Paris
Amzallag collection
Mr. and Mrs. Adrien Maeght, Paris
To Nasher collection, 1985

LITERATURE: Reinhold Hohl, *Alberto Giacometti*, New York, 1971, p. 296, fig. 71

Bernard Lamarche-Vadel, *Alberto Giacometti*, Paris, 1984, fig. 119

EXHIBITIONS: *Alberto Giacometti*, Accademia di Francia, (ill.) Villa Medici, Rome, 1970, cat. p. 31, no. 6

Alberto Giacometti, The Seibu Museum of Art, Tokyo, 1983, cat. no. 53

Alberto Giacometti, Galerie Adrien Maeght, Paris, 1984, cat. n.p. (ill.)

This well-known painting first belonged to Louis Clayeux, Giacometti's longtime friend, supporter, and dealer and the artistic director from 1948 to 1965 of the Galerie Maeght, Paris. It has been interpreted as depicting figures both in a studio and in an outdoor street scene (Hohl, 1971, p. 296). The latter notion aligns it closely with such sculptural figure groupings as *The City Square* (1948–49) and *Three Men Walking* (1949). Giacometti was fascinated with the compositional and psychological potentials of random, passing movement by isolated figures in open, ambiguous spaces, having treated the same theme not only in sculptures but also in numerous drawings, prints, and paintings from as early as 1947 (see *Alberto Giacometti*, The Museum of Modern Art, New York, 1965, pp. 87, 96; James Lord, *Alberto Giacometti Drawings*, Greenwich, Connecticut, 1971, nos. 43, 45, 63, 69). In certain of these works, the grouping of three striding figures resembles closely that in the Nasher painting. Unusual in the painting, however, is the way the composition is squared off by vertical lines into three triptychlike panels. These dividing lines stress the frontal plane of the painting's surface and space and contrast with the sense of internal depth created by receding diagonals and smaller, loosely brushed figures in the distance. They add also to the ambiguity of locale that has resulted in differing titles.

HANS HOFMANN (American, born Germany, 1880–1966)

*93. *String Quartet*, 1959–60
Oil on canvas, $50\frac{1}{8}$ x $40\frac{1}{4}$ (127.3 x 102.2)

MARKINGS: Lower right: "60 / Hans Hofmann"

PROVENANCE: Samuel Kootz Gallery, New York
To Nasher collection, 1966

LITERATURE: Sam Hunter, *Hans Hofmann*, New York, 1963, p. 30, pl. 134

Art News 73, no. 9, November 1974 (ill. front cover)

EXHIBITIONS: *Twentieth Century Art from Fort Worth Dallas Collections*, Fort Worth Art Museum, 1974 (ill. n.p.)

Hans Hofmann: A Retrospective Exhibition, Hirshhorn Museum and Sculpture Garden, Washington, D.C., and Museum of Fine Arts, Houston, 1976–77, cat. no. 51 (ill. p. 89)

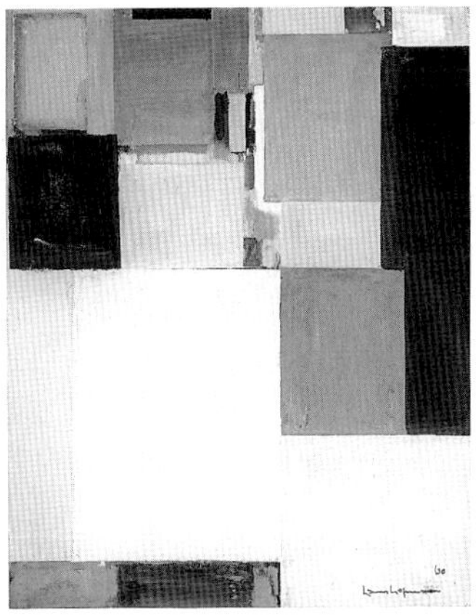

Hans Hofmann's signature style of constructing pictorial space by interposing blocks or "slabs" of color with other blocks and/or painterly passages of varying pitch and depth had reached full development by the late fifties. A number of paintings from 1959–60, including *String Quartet*, pursue as a central theme the disposition of a dominant yellow square that projects very strongly outward against differing recessive combinations of blue, green, and red (e.g., Hunter, 1963, pls. 104, 110, 116). In *String Quartet*, the push-pull relationships are notably poised and sedate, each color block overlapping its neighbor in a clear spatial ordonnance, with an application of paint that is relatively smooth and even and a careful balancing of primary colors against more poignant secondary hues. Writing in 1963, Sam Hunter commented on this picture:

String Quartet of 1960 contrasts a brilliant, dominant yellow square, tempered by an elongated rectangle of faint green, with a rich complexity of small, tiered planes of greyed and darkened color. The intricacy and richness of color vibration, and the sensitive discrimination of nuanced values, so characteristic of Hofmann's recent years, support the conviction he has stated in conversation and amplified throughout his writings: "In color, the finest shades can create the most enormous contrast; color offers the most expansive possibilities as a creative means" [Hunter, 1963, p. 30].

A color photograph by Arnold Newman of Hofmann in his Provincetown studio in 1960, which appeared on the cover of *Art News* in November 1974, shows *String Quartet* placed prominently on an easel in an unfinished state. The photograph provides a fascinating glimpse into Hofmann's working methods and a record of certain of the constructive choices behind *String Quartet*. At that point the painting bore the date "59," later changed to "60." It was quite thinly painted still, with colors considerably paler than their final state. Although the structure of the painting was basically fixed, several rectangles of colored paper were pinned to the upper quadrant in an exploration of small, lively planes that approximate rather closely the final composition. Along the left edge the color dynamics were changed considerably, with two blocks of light and dark green substituted for a more shrill plane of mauve-pink. In all, the painting took on greater depth, richness, and contrast.

ELLSWORTH KELLY (American, born 1923)

*94. *Block Island II*, 1960
Acrylic on canvas, 88 x 66 (224 x 168)

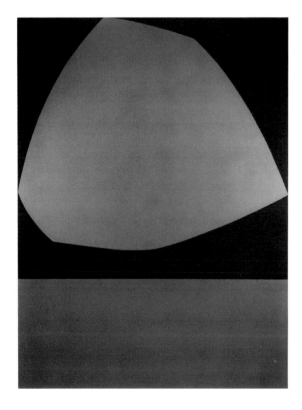

MARKINGS: None

PROVENANCE: Betty Parsons Gallery, New York
Marquise of Dufferin and Ava, London and Ireland
To M. Knoedler & Co., New York, 1985
To Nasher collection, 1985

LITERATURE: John Coplans, *Ellsworth Kelly*, New York, n.d., p. 63

EXHIBITIONS: *The 1961 Pittsburgh International Exhibition of Contemporary Painting and Sculpture,* Carnegie Institute, Pittsburgh, 1961–62, cat. no. 194 (ill.)

Painting and Sculpture of a Decade 54/64, The Tate Gallery, London, 1964

New Acquisitions, M. Knoedler & Co., New York, 1985

Ellsworth Kelly has noted (correspondence with the author, 1986) that he made three paintings and one collage study on the Block Island theme following a visit there in 1958. The collage (1958; 12 x 9 inches) comprises basically the same composition and color relationships of green on black over blue as the Nasher painting but in a lighter tonality (unpublished; collection of the artist). *Block Island Study*, an oil on canvas (1959; 24 x 18 inches), is the same composition in a larger format done in the more saturated color of the final version (Coplans, n.d., pl. 129; collection of the artist). Two oil studies in a sketchbook retained by the artist were done at this point to help him find the proper green and blue (unpublished). In *Block Island I* (1959; oil on canvas, 88 x 66 inches, private collection), Kelly expanded the format still further and shifted the black background to white. An installation photograph from his exhibition at the Betty Parsons Gallery in New York in 1959 shows both *Block Island Study* and *Block Island I* (Coplans, n.d., p. 293). The final work in the series, *Block Island II*, repeats the format and design of *Block Island I*, but returns to the original color combination in saturated tones.

This series belongs to a group of works from c. 1959–61 in which Kelly explored the spatial dynamics of an irregular, slightly rounded polyhedron touching at several points the edges of a rectangular ground (see Coplans, n.d., pls. 130, 145). In still other works he pursued further the configuration of a curved form floating above a wide horizontal band (e.g., *Charter*, 1959, Yale University Art Gallery, and *High Yellow*, 1960, University of Texas at Austin).

As Kelly's works often are based on an extreme distillation of natural forms, it is difficult not to see in the Block Island series a reference to an island floating in the sea, the green and blue enhancing one's sense of landscape, water, and sky. While the combination of chromatic richness and purist design is an enduring feature of Kelly's style, his use of Arplike irregular shapes gave way to more rigorous geometry. *Block Island II* won fourth prize in the painting category at the 1961 Carnegie International.

WILLEM DE KOONING (American, born the
Netherlands 1904)

*95. *Untitled VIII*, 1976
Oil on canvas, 59¼ x 55 (150.5 x 140)

MARKINGS: Verso, lower right: "de Kooning"

PROVENANCE: Edgar Kaufmann, Jr.

Mr. and Mrs. Robert Mnuchin
To Xavier Fourcade, Inc., New York
To Nasher collection, 1985

LITERATURE: Jack Cowart, "De Kooning Today," *Art
International* 23, no. 3–4, Summer 1979,
p. 10 (ill.)

EXHIBITIONS: *De Kooning: New Paintings 1976*, Xavier
Fourcade, Inc., New York, 1976, cat. no. 8
(ill.)

Produced in a midsize format, the oil known as *Untitled
VIII* typifies the painterly lushness and complex spatial dynamics marking Willem de Kooning's work from about 1974
to 1980. The more structured figure-ground relationship notable in his earlier paintings, even the fully abstract ones,
had given way to a complete fusion of landscape, figure,
and abstract elements in one continuous, turbulent space.
A suggestion of landscape survives in *Untitled VIII* through
the use of darker colors and a denser concentration of cal-
ligraphic strokes below a midpoint "horizon" line and a
lighter, more open and recessive treatment at the top. The
colors, glistening in their range of reds, pinks, blues, and
pearl white, are fully typical of the period and reflect in
part the influence of the artist's oceanside landscape in East
Hampton, New York, where he has lived since 1963.

FERNAND LEGER (French, 1881–1955)

*96. *The Construction Workers* [*Les Constructeurs*], 1950
Gouache on paper, 30 x 21¼ (76 x 54)

MARKINGS: Lower right: "FL / 51" (later addition?)

PROVENANCE: From artist to the Musée Fernand Léger,
Biot, France
To Galerie Louise Leiris, Paris
To Galerie Beyeler, Basel, and Thomas
Gibson Fine Art, London
To Nasher collection, 1986

LITERATURE: Cf. Peter de Francia, *Fernand Léger*, New
Haven and London, 1983, pp. 199–202
(ill.)

EXHIBITIONS: *Fernand Léger*, Nouveau Musée du Havre,
1968, cat. no. 37, pl. VI

Fernand Léger, Grand Palais, Paris, 1971–
72, cat. no. 179 (ill.)

Léger, Kunsthalle, Berlin, 1981, cat. no. 258

*Aftermath: France 1945–1954, New Images
of Man*, Barbican Centre, London, 1982,
cat. no. 31

Fernand Léger, Fundación Juan March,
Madrid, 1983, cat. no. 82

Paper, Thomas Gibson Fine Art, London,
1985, cat. pp. 30–31 (ill.)

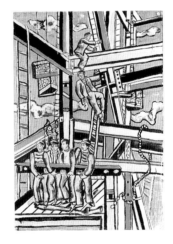

This work is a study for one of Léger's most important construction compositions, the definitive version of which is
now in the Musée Fernand Léger (1950; oil on canvas, 118⅛
inches x 78¾; see de Francia, 1983, pl. 50). Several other
drawings are known from this relatively early stage (e.g., J.
Cassou and J. Leymarie, *Fernand Léger: Drawings and
Gouaches*, Greenwich, Connecticut, 1973, no. 268) and a
more finished study is in The Solomon R. Guggenheim
Museum, New York (1950; oil on canvas, 61 x 44⅞ inches;
see *Fernand Léger*, Albright-Knox Art Gallery, Buffalo, 1982,
cat. no. 71). The Guggenheim study follows the Nasher
composition quite faithfully (one figure is eliminated; the
rope at the lower right is made much longer and more
convoluted as a foil for the architectural geometry), and
translates directly into the final canvas (where the rope is
shortened again and replaced on the platform by a log, and
the whole composition is tighter and more finished). The

position of the present work in this step-by-step progression and the faint, rather tentative nature of the inscription point to the possibility that Léger added his initials at a later time, together with an incorrect date of 1951. Numerous variations on this primary composition exist, some with a group of workers positioned on the ground, others focusing more tightly on a section of the superstructure, still others with a more abstract architectural design (see Cassou and Leymarie, 1973, pp. 179–81; *Léger*, Grand Palais, 1971–72, pp. 128–31).

In Léger's efforts after the war to produce an art with social conscience, one with the gravity of Davidian Neo-classicism that could deal with contemporary social and political reality, the theme of construction, both from the point of view of architectural transformation and heroism of the worker, was of central importance. Numerous closely related essays on the subject date from 1950–51, all with large-scale figures seen against a scaffolding of I-beams and bright colors. The initial stimulus for these works was visual. On a drive to Chevreuse, Léger was struck by a scene of construction workers building three huge pylons: "Lost in the rigid, hard, hostile surroundings the men appeared tiny. I wanted to render this in my paintings without making any concessions" (see de Francia, 1983, pp. 198–99).

ROY LICHTENSTEIN (American, born 1923)

*97. *Reclining Bather*, 1977
   Oil and acrylic on canvas, 60 x 90 (152.4 x 228.6)

MARKINGS: Verso, left center: "r.f. Lichtenstein / '77"

PROVENANCE: From artist to Leo Castelli Gallery, New York
                       To Nasher collection, 1978

LITERATURE: None

EXHIBITIONS: *20th Century Sculpture: Mr. and Mrs. Raymond D. Nasher Collection*, University Gallery, Southern Methodist University, Dallas, 1978, ex-cat.

                       Roy Lichtenstein: Recent Work, Lowe Art Museum, University of Miami, Coral

Gables, Florida, 1979, cat. p. 22 (ill. p. 16)

In the series of quotations from older artists and styles that marked Lichtenstein's paintings of the seventies, Surrealism appeared as a theme in 1976–77 and brought with it a new complexity, involving not direct, one-to-one quotation or parody but, rather, a hybrid mixing of motifs from disparate sources, including Lichtenstein's own earlier work. These "chance encounters" of wide-ranging iconographies were all subordinated to the laws of his own formally cool style, but had nevertheless a dreamlike, irrational, and perhaps personally metaphoric quality. Both *Reclining Bather* of 1977 and the larger *Reclining Nude* from the same year (Jack Cowart, *Roy Lichtenstein 1970–1980*, New York, 1981, p. 108) take as their primary motif a female nude on a beach, whose amoebic anatomy invokes both Salvadore Dali's melting forms and the contours and tunnels of Henry Moore's reclining women. In *Reclining Nude* the head is a Magrittelike transparency with only lips and hair poised in space, while the *Reclining Bather* has a downward-hanging head with an inverted vertical eye over ruby red lips in a pun on Pablo Picasso that reappears in several other paintings of this period. In the foreground are a starfish and snail that recall the pictographic styles of Alexander Calder and Joan Miró, and in the background a Mirólike ladder reaches upward into the sky. This is paired with displaced interior motifs from Lichtenstein's sculpture of the period, a mirror and a lamp, while the floppy clouds against a striated sky recall his landscapes of the sixties. This painting would in turn directly influence Lichtenstein's three-dimensional work: his bronze *Mermaid* of 1978–79 paraphrases its lamp and bather.

MORRIS LOUIS (American, 1912–1962)

*98. *Aleph Series VI*, Spring 1960
   Acrylic on canvas, 78⁹⁄₁₆ x 104¾ (199.5 x 266)

MARKINGS: None

PROVENANCE: From artist to André Emmerich Gallery, New York
                       To private collection, London
                       To Waddington Galleries, Ltd., London
                       To Rutland Gallery, London
                       To William Pall Gallery, New York
                       To Nasher collection, 1975

LITERATURE: Michael Fried, *Morris Louis*, New York, 1970, pl. 92

Diane Upright, *Morris Louis: The Complete Paintings*, New York, 1985, cat. no. 265 (ill. p. 157)

EXHIBITIONS: *Morris Louis: A Group of Paintings of the Late Spring of 1960*, André Emmerich Gallery, New York, 1967, cat. n.p.

Morris Louis's Aleph series, comprising nine large canvases with central bursts of color whose individual "flows" seem to radiate centrifugally outward, is generally thought to date from the spring of 1960. In the catalogue raisonné of Louis's oeuvre, however, Diane Upright groups this series on stylistic grounds with paintings from 1959 and 1960 in which individual rivulets of color oppose one another vertically up the sides of the canvas (Omega series), then reorient themselves around its circumference (two Circum paint-

ings), and finally cluster in the center with outward orientation (*Spawn*). Upright infers that the Aleph series, tied closely to *Spawn* in style as well as in the technique of working from all four sides of the canvas, must date very soon thereafter (Upright, 1985, cat. nos. 261–69). Furthermore, she suggests a chronological order for the Aleph paintings, again on the basis of composition, that differs from the order of their titular numbers. Her sequence (VII, I, III, II, VI, IV, V, *Aleph*, *Last of a Series*) progresses from the painting with the most clear, individualized fingers of color, to those with increasingly dark and dense overlappings in the center, and finally to those in which the flows take on more of a vertical orientation. The exploration in paintings in this period of separated hues and individual rivulets of form, as opposed to broad superimposed "veils," led by the summer of 1960 to the well-known Unfurled series. Louis had used the word Aleph in earlier titles (e.g., Upright, 1985, cat. no. 137). It derives from the first letter of the Hebrew alphabet.

PABLO PICASSO (Spanish, 1881–1973)

*99. *The Studio* [*L'Atelier*], 1961–62
Oil on canvas, 29 x 36 (73.7 x 91.4)

MARKINGS: Front, lower right: "Picasso"
Verso, upper right: "27.11.61 / 24.12 / II 25.– / 24.1.62 / 31.–"

PROVENANCE: From artist to David Douglas Duncan, 1962
To Galerie Rosengart, Lucerne
To Nasher collection, 1985

LITERATURE: None

EXHIBITIONS: None

Although it has escaped notice in the literature, this picture is a fully resolved essay on a theme of central importance to Pablo Picasso throughout his career, the relationship between artist and model as a metaphor for creativity and the questioning role of art versus empirical fact. Here the artist

in silhouette is separated by a surrounding band of color from the secluded, haremlike realm of seated and reclining nudes in proffering poses, which he observes almost as a voyeur. That Picasso rarely painted from live models underscores the nonbiographical, philosophical nature of the theme. Precedents for this composition are seen in two works from 1953 and 1954 (Christian Zervos, *Pablo Picasso*, Paris, 1965, XVI, nos. 96 and 200). A group of drawings dating from a year after *The Studio* come still closer in composition (Zervos, XXIII, nos. 122–26), replicating the same high window, middle-ground bed, marginal placement of the artist, and in one case, the same diamond-patterned rug. A similarity with the poses and general ambience in Picasso's 1954–55 series of variations on Delacroix's *Women of Algiers* (Zervos, XVI, nos. 353–60) reinforces the suggestion of a hermetic, feminine, luxuriant world in which artist/man is a foreigner.

A certificate signed by the photographer David Douglas Duncan in 1985 attests that he received *The Studio* directly from Picasso. Christian Zervos, cataloger of Picasso's oeuvre, did not know of its existence, and it seems never to have been exhibited prior to entering the Nasher collection in 1985. The series of dates inscribed on the back indicate that Picasso worked on it in several stages from late 1961 to early 1962. A Duncan photograph (Nasher archives) shows Picasso in Duncan's house at Castellaras, near Mougins in the south of France, seated in a large room with Jacqueline Picasso and two friends, all studying and seemingly discussing this painting. When Jacqueline Picasso saw the painting on a visit to the Nasher home in 1985, she remarked that she still had the blue canopy seen in the background.

---

*100. *The Kiss* [*Le Baiser*], October 1969
Oil on canvas, 38⅛ x 51³⁄₁₆ (96.8 x 130)

MARKINGS: Upper left: "Picasso"
Verso, upper right: "24.10.69 / II"

PROVENANCE: Private collection, France
To Galerie Schmit, Paris
To Galerie Marwan Hoss, Paris
To Galerie Beyeler, Basel
To Nasher collection, 1985

LITERATURE: Rafael Alberti, *A Year of Picasso Paintings: 1969*, New York, 1971, p. 68, no. 58 (ill.)

Christian Zervos, *Pablo Picasso* 31, Paris, 1976, no. 483 (ill.)

EXHIBITIONS: *Pablo Picasso: 1969–1970*, Palais des Papes, Avignon, 1970, cat. no. 103 (ill.)

Reviving a theme found in his earlier periods and styles, late in life Picasso produced an extensive series of paintings on the Kiss, featuring closeup, bust-length views of heads almost violently pressed together in the act of kissing. Any sense of tenderness is lost in the orgasmic ferocity of these embraces, which sometimes seem to verge on rape. The painter's aged, bald, long-haired alter ego, so suggestive of an ancient warrior, acts out a powerful virility belying his years. In the Nasher picture, the thick brushwork and undulating forms seem to push and heave, further intensifying the sense of forceful pressure. The two heads merge in a single amalgam, with eyes wide open in total consciousness and a shared, winding profile, tracking penetration and withdrawal. A nearly monochromatic palette of grays and blacks adds to the somber mood. The woman, with large eyes and dark, long hair, is clearly Picasso's wife Jacqueline.

Rafael Alberti (1971, nos. 56–70) published Picasso's lengthy series of paintings on the Kiss dating from October to December 1969, accompanying them with subjective, poetic interpretations. Gert Schiff (*Picasso: The Last Years, 1963–1973*, New York, 1983, pp. 50–53) examined the theme of the Kiss in the broader context of lovemaking scenes in Picasso's late work, showing how the artist drew upon a variety of sources including Henri Rousseau, Ingres, and his own rustic peasants of the teens for differing interpretations of the procreative act, from primal and innocent to erotic to symbolic of artistic creation.

The red signature on this painting and others of the same period was reputedly made with red fingernail polish belonging to Jacqueline Picasso.

---

*101. *Man and Woman [Homme et femme]*, August 1971
Oil on canvas, 76⅝ x 51⅛ (194.6 x 130)

MARKINGS: Reverse, upper left: "18.8.71"

PROVENANCE: From artist to Claude Picasso, Paris
To Paloma Picasso, Paris and New York
Stephen Shalom, New York, by 1981
The Pace Gallery, New York
To Nasher collection, 1982

LITERATURE: Rafael Alberti, *Picasso: Le Rayon ininterromptu*, Paris, 1974, fig. 136

Christian Zervos, *Pablo Picasso* 33, Paris, 1978, no. 148 (ill. p. 56)

Gert Schiff, *Picasso: The Last Years, 1963–1973*, New York, 1983, pp. 63–64, no. 93, fig. 199, pl. 50

EXHIBITIONS: *Exposition Picasso: 1970–1972, 201 Peintures*, Palais des Papes, Avignon, 1973, cat. no. 119 (ill. p. 138)

Picasso: The Avignon Paintings, The Pace Gallery, New York, 1981, cat. p. 11 (ill.)

Das Spätwerk: Themen 1964–1972, Kunstmuseum, Basel, 1981, cat. no. 67

Picasso: The Last Decade, The Solomon R. Guggenheim Museum, New York, 1983–84, cat. pp. 63–64, no. 93, fig. 119, pl. 50

This exceptionally bold example of Picasso's late painting style, in which the artist presents himself as old, grizzled, and nude, with a haunting masklike face, relates to a series of works from 1970 and 1971 on the theme of the family (see also Schiff, 1983, pls. 45, 46). Gert Schiff has offered a cogent analysis of it:

> Many of the last paintings deal with the subject of parenthood —mothers with small children, fathers with older ones, family groups, including one in which part of the subject got lost in a web of pentimenti: *Man and Woman*. Once more, the man's head is compounded with his yellow straw hat. Such is the radiance of his wide-eyed stare that he appears like a sun, as the woman beside him appears like a crescent moon. The man's body is easy to read: he squats with his left knee raised, his right hand forming a fist. The woman's body is divided into arbitrary "Cubist" segments and remains largely undecipherable. However, part of the jigsaw puzzle can be resolved if one focuses upon a lozenge-shaped form in front of her body, partly overlapping with a red wedge. This form has two fanlike extensions that can be read as the spread arms of a child; a navel and the schematic indication of the female sex can also be recog-

שד' שאול המלך 27-29.   ת.ד 33288   תל אביב 61332   טלפון 257361-03

27-29 shaul hamelech blvd.   p.o.b.33288   61332 tel aviv, israel   tel. 03-257361

the tel aviv museum   מוזיאון תל אביב

the tel aviv museum מוזיאון תל אביב

במידה והיצירה תשועתק, נא לציין באותו דף:

If reproduced the following credit must be given on the same or facing page

רמון דושאן-ויון

Artist אמן

סוס גדול, 1914

Title יצירה

פטסי ורעימונד נאשר

Collection אוסף

מאה שנות פיסול מודרני

Exhibition תערוכה

שד' שאול המלך 29-27. ת.ד 33288 תל אביב 61332 טלפון 03-257361

27-29 shaul hamelech blvd. p.o.b. 33288 61332 tel aviv, israel tel. 03-257361

אמן: קלאוס אולדנבורג
ויצ'וב: העתק של מכונת כתיבה, 1976
חומר: בד' ורישומה ...
תערוכה: ...

שד' שאול המלך 27-29. ת.ד 33288 תל אביב 61332 טלפון 03-257361
27-29 shaul hamelech blvd. p.o.b. 33288 61332 tel aviv, israel tel. 03-257361

מוזיאון תל אביב the tel aviv museum

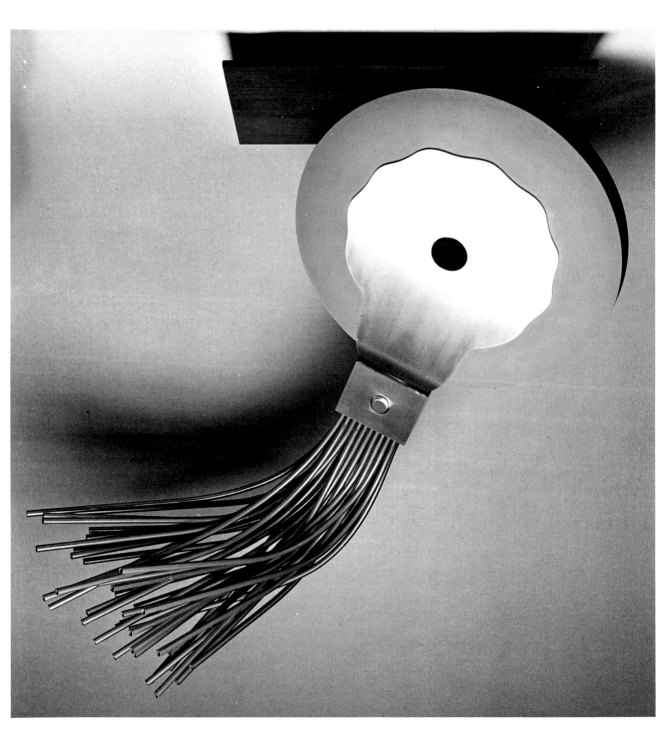

nized. One also notices the man's other hand, half wiped out, which was meant to hold the child on his knee. But the child's head and legs could not be fitted into the composition. Hence, Picasso dropped the idea and left part of his painting as a magma of undefined forms [Schiff, 1983, pp. 63–64].

In the rush of forms and ideas that drove Picasso's brush in his late work, the lack of resolution in a passage and the lack of "finish" held little concern for him. What counted was expressive impact. Jacqueline Picasso has related that this particular painting represents a premonition on Picasso's part of his own impending death (in conversation, Dallas, 1985).

Acknowledgments

Since many of the individual works selected for exhibition from the Nasher collection had not been thoroughly studied, the researching and writing of catalog entries was an exciting process of discovery. Much new information was uncovered and was then interwoven in the entries with critical and interpretive commentary. With a drastically abbreviated timeframe for accomplishing this extensive research, however, we had to rely for information on the kind cooperation of various individuals and institutions. First and foremost, I would like to thank Annette Schlagenhauff, McDermott Curatorial Intern, for the yeoman service she provided in researching the individual entries. The book could not have been accomplished without her dedication. Mr. and Mrs. Nasher endured countless inquiries, always with patience and an enthusiastic spirit of participation. Ellen Gordesky, Dee Penrod, and Andrea Nasher all assisted in various research tasks. In Jane Fluegel we had an ideal editor, both strict and sensitive. My assistant Janine Orzes worked diligently for many long hours on the manuscript, somehow managing to retain a sense of humor. Nan Rosenthal and Jeremy Strick at the National Gallery of Art supplied information for certain entries. Amy Schaffner, Librarian at the Dallas Museum of Art, and Elizabeth Simon, Curatorial Assistant, helped obtain research materials and assisted with editing.

To the following individuals, we owe special thanks for their generous assistance: Vivian Barnett, The Solomon R. Guggenheim Museum, New York; Richard Bellamy; Jessica Boissel, Centre Georges Pompidou, Paris; Ronnie Caran; Anne Carley; John Cavaliero; I. C. Deal; Diane Driessen, Milwaukee Art Museum; Mrs. Marcel Duchamp; Valerie Fletcher, Hirshhorn Museum and Sculpture Garden, Washington, D.C.; Noel Frackman; Sidney Geist; Wanda de Guébriant; David Fraser Jenkins, The Tate Gallery, London; Ellsworth Kelly; Linda Konheim, The Brooklyn Museum, New York; Cornelia Lauf; M. and Mme Claude Laurens; Christina Lodder, University of St. Andrews, Scotland; Luanne McKinnon; Jörn Merkert, Kunstsammlung Nordrhein-Westfalen, Düsseldorf; Stanley Moss; Annalee Newman; Brenda Richardson, Baltimore Museum of Art; Paterson Sims, Whitney Museum of American Art, New York; Jane Smith; Greta Stroeh, Fondation Arp, Rolandseck, West Germany; Georg Syamken, Hamburger Kunsthalle, Hamburg, West Germany; John Tancock, Sotheby's, New York; Dorothea Tanning; Alan Wilkinson, Art Gallery of Ontario, Toronto; Judith Zilczer, Hirshhorn Museum and Sculpture Garden, Washington, D.C.

Staff members at the following art galleries and companies also gave freely of their time and knowledge: Thomas Ammann Fine Art, Zürich; Galerie Beyeler, Basel; Louis Carré & Cie, Paris; Leo Castelli Gallery, New York; Paula Cooper Gallery, New York; Andre Emmerich Gallery, New York; Larry Gagosian Gallery, New York; Arnold Herstand and Co., New York; Sidney Janis Gallery, New York; M. Knoedler & Co., New York; Galerie Louise Leiris, Paris; Lippincott, Inc., North Haven, Connecticut; Lisson Gallery, London; Lords Gallery, Ltd., London; Galerie m, Bochum, West Germany; Galerie Adrien Maeght, Paris; Galerie Maeght Lelong, New York and Paris; Studio Marconi, Milan; Marlborough Gallery, New York; The Pace Gallery, New York; William Pall Gallery, New York; Max Protetch Gallery, New York; Galerie Rosengart, Lucerne; Editions Schellmann, New York; Waddington Galleries, Ltd., London.

STEVEN A. NASH

Photo Credits

LARRY BERCOW, New York: 43 top, 46 left, 59 left, 60 top, 61 left, 68 top left and right, 90–91, 102 top left, 107 top, 108 top, 129, 135, 149, 153, 169 top, 175 bottom, 176, 180, 187 bottom, 192, 202, 205. **E. I. BLOMSTRANN** © G + N Williams: 83 top. **GEOFFREY CLEMENTS**, courtesy André Emmerich Gallery, New York: 119 bottom, 141. **LEE CLOCKMAN**, Dallas Museum of Art: 24, 32, 38, 42, 43 bottom, 46 top and bottom, 47, 48, 49, 50, 51, 54, 55, 57, 58, 59 right, 61 top right, 62, 63 top, 64, 65, 68 bottom, 69, 72, 73, 76, 77, 80 left, 81, 82, 83 bottom, 86 bottom, 87, 88, 91 right, 94, 95, 96, 97 bottom, 98, 100 right, 102 top right and bottom, 103, 105, 106, 107 bottom, 110, 112 top, 113, 114–15 bottom, 116–17, 118, 119 top, 121, 123, 124, 130, 131, 134 top, 136, 137, 138, 139, 140, 143, 144, 145, 146, 148, 151 top, 155, 156, 157, 158, 159, 160, 161, 162 bottom, 163, 164 top, 165, 166, 167 top, 168, 169 bottom, 170, 171, 172, 173, 174, 175 top, 177 top, 179, 181, 182, 183, 184, 185, 186, 187 top, 188, 189, 190, 191, 193, 194, 196 bottom, 197, 198 top, 199, 200, 204 top. Courtesy **DALLAS MUSEUM OF ART**: 33. **JAMES DEE**, courtesy Larry Gagosian Gallery, New York: 97 top. **ED HERSHEY**, Los Angeles: 80 right, 100 left, 120 bottom, 121, 142. Copyright © **HICKEY-ROBERTSON**, Houston: 1, 2–3, 4–5, 6–7, 8, 14. Courtesy **M. KNOEDLER & CO.**, Inc., New York: 122, 198 bottom. Courtesy **LISSON GALLERY**, London: 112 bottom, 162 top. Courtesy **MR. AND MRS. RAYMOND NASHER**, Dallas: 15, 16 top, 16–17, 18, 19, 20, 23, 25. Courtesy **NATIONAL GALLERY OF ART**, Washington, D.C.: 30–31, 60 bottom. Courtesy **MAX PROTETCH GALLERY**, New York: 120 top left, 134 bottom. Courtesy **WADDINGTON GALLERIES, LTD.**, London: 104. **DAVID WHARTON**, Fort Worth: 63 bottom, 86 top, 108 bottom, 109, 114 top, 126, 127, 128, 164 bottom, 200 bottom, 201, 203, 204 bottom, 206 top.

Index

Page numbers in italics indicate illustrations.